Major Decisions

MAJOR DECISIONS

College, Career, and the Case for the Humanities

Laurie Grobman and E. Michele Ramsey

PENN

University of Pennsylvania Press
Philadelphia

Published by
University of Pennsylvania Press
Philadelphia, Pennsylvania 19104-4112
www.upenn.edu/pennpress

Printed in the United States of America on acid-free paper
10 9 8 7 6 5 4 3 2 1

Library of Congress Cataloging-in-Publication Data

Names: Grobman, Laurie, 1962– author. | Ramsey, E. Michele, author.
Title: Major decisions : college, career, and the case for the humanities /
    Laurie Grobman and E. Michele Ramsey.
Description: 1st edition. | Philadelphia : University of Pennsylvania Press,
    [2020] | Includes bibliographical references and index.
Identifiers: LCCN 2019031231 | ISBN 9780812251982 (hardcover)
Subjects: LCSH: Humanities—Study and teaching (Higher) |
    Humanities—Economic aspects. | Humanities—Social aspects. |
    Humanities—Philosophy. | Education, Higher—Aims and objectives.
Classification: LCC LC1011 .G75195 2020 | DDC 001.3071/1—dc23
LC record available at https://lccn.loc.gov/2019031231

To our students—past, present, and future

Contents

Preface

As humanities faculty (Laurie in English, Michele in communication arts and sciences), we've dealt with stated and unstated assumptions about the humanities—the mythical English major who can only get a job making coffee or the communication major who wasted their time just learning about talking. These encounters are consistent, year after year, and include students, parents, faculty, administrators, career services professionals, and potential employers across many sectors. And though the audiences shift, the discussions largely remain the same. We find ourselves constantly having to explain and defend the humanities. And we know we are not alone.

But we see change coming. Hundreds of articles in popular and academic presses and a handful of important books over the past two years demonstrate that a "movement" is stirring. The humanities matter in a global economy that is shifting dramatically, quickly, and in the direction of college graduates who think broadly, critically, and ethically. The fast-paced, high-tech, global economy—and the communities in which we live—need humanities thinkers to help guide decisions that understand the human benefits and human costs of the tech revolution now and to come.

We hope *Major Decisions* will be read by several audiences, including current and prospective students and their parents, faculty, administrators, prospective employers, and university administrators. Current students who have chosen a humanities degree will feel confident in their decision and have the words and evidence to support it by telling their humanities story when they seek that first post-graduation job. Students just starting to think about a college major can feel emboldened to choose a major that they love. We encourage current and prospective nonhumanities students to consider supplementing their degree with a humanities minor or several courses in the humanities. Parents who may be concerned or even confused about degree options can have faith in the humanities should your child choose that route.

The book provides our colleagues in the humanities who regularly face the same set of doubts, questions, and conversations concrete examples and justifications to share with students, parents, administrators, and career services. Together, we will turn the tide of negative assumptions about the humanities.

It's likewise critical for administrators to be more supportive of the humanities and promote these programs and faculty with the stakeholders you encounter. We encourage you to be leaders in programs and opportunities that marry disparate programs, such as STEM (science, technology, engineering, and mathematics) and the humanities, for example. And we hope that you'll begin to recognize that the academy is stronger when we stand together and support one another and weaker when we continue to give credence to rhetoric that trumpets some majors, vilifies others, and creates damaging divisions in the academy.

We know that career services professionals have few resources available for learning about and promoting humanities degrees, and we hope to provide ways for you to guide humanities students who seek your services in the same way that you're able to guide students engaged in programs that have a clearer path for students from the get-go, such as accounting or engineering.

Finally, throughout the book we cite numerous CEOs, entrepreneurs, and leaders in their fields who understand the value of the humanities and who are firmly committed to making sure that humanities graduates are "in the room," making important decisions in all areas of business. But we are concerned that the managers and supervisors who are charged with hiring people in entry- and mid-level positions are not as aware of what a humanities graduate can add to their workforce. We hope that this book makes clear the excellent investment that companies make when they hire a humanities graduate.

Introduction

Major Decisions: The Case for the Humanities

At the unveiling of Apple's iPad 2 in 2011, Apple founder Steve Jobs proclaimed, "It is in Apple's DNA that technology alone is not enough—it's technology married with liberal arts, married with the humanities, that yields us the results that make our heart sing."[1] His successor, Tim Cook, struck a similar theme at the 2017 Massachusetts Institute of Technology (MIT) commencement by stating, "If science is a search in the darkness, then the humanities are a candle that shows us where we have been, and the danger that lies ahead."[2] Both men stressed the interdependency of STEM (science, technology, engineering, and mathematics) and the humanities.

Like the titans of technology noted above, captains of industry in the world of business laud liberal arts and humanities majors. Billionaire investor and businessman Mark Cuban predicts that there's going to be a greater demand for liberal arts majors in the future of increasing automation because "when the data is all being spit out for you, options are being spit out for you, you need a different perspective in order to have a different view of the data," one that a "freer thinker" from the liberal arts can deliver.[3] Further, the healthcare industry, expected to drive economic growth through 2026,[4] needs plenty of graduates with core skills and knowledge. These workers need "adaptability, agility, comfort dealing with ambiguity and flexibility," according to healthcare consultant Jack Schlosser. He adds, "If someone is great at leading, strong in communication skills and able to deal with a diversity of challenges," he or she will "have great demand" in the healthcare industry.[5]

Study after study, article after article, report after report say the same thing: the humanities and liberal arts are vital to the current and future economy. Yet the myths and misconceptions about humanities degrees continue to escalate, encouraging students away from these majors. You've heard them:

- You'll end up in your parents' basement.
- You'll be underemployed in minimum-wage jobs that you could get without a college degree.
- Your major is impractical.
- The humanities are elitist.
- Humanities faculty and students live in books, not the real world.
- The humanities focus on nonsense like comic books or "outdated" works by Shakespeare.

Given these disparaging attitudes, the past several years have seen significant decreases in the numbers of students majoring in the humanities. A total of 212,512 humanities degrees were conferred in 2015, falling 9.5 percent from the 234,737 degrees conferred in 2012. The sharpest declines have occurred in such field staples as English, history, and philosophy. One exception is communication, which increased its share of all humanities degrees by 44 percent from 1987 to 2015.[6]

Currently, business, academic, and public realms are starting to recognize that humanities disciplines have been the tech revolution's *invisible partners* in our increasingly global economy. The modern economy's need for the core skills and knowledge developed through a humanities education opens up far more job and career opportunities than anyone talks about. The loudest voices have been urging (pressuring) students to major in STEM, business (e.g., accounting, marketing, risk management, management, and finance), and health sciences (e.g., nursing, physical therapy, and occupational therapy). These areas of study are great options, and students deserve to hear and understand the full picture.[7] For the time and money spent on a college degree, it's important for students to choose a major that they love but that also provides economic stability. For many students, that major is in the humanities.

We'd like to paint a more accurate picture of the global economy and the workplace landscape for humanities graduates. That includes a fuller picture of what the humanities are really about, including what we study and teach and why; concrete discussions of the core skills and knowledge areas promoted by humanities education and desired by employers across the economic landscape; and guidance to transition from a humanities degree to the workplace.

Why College?

The exploding cost of a college degree versus its value (literal and figurative) is a serious issue. From 2006 to 2016, college tuition and fees rose 63 percent.[8] Public and private college tuition and fees increased between 2.9 percent and 3.6 percent in 2017 (exceeding inflation, which was 2 percent).[9]

To make matters worse, student college debt is also at record highs. A 2017 study by global consumer credit reporting agency Experian indicates that college-loan balances in the United States are currently at an all-time high of $1.4 trillion, having increased in just the past ten years by more than $833 billion.[10] The average borrower owes $34,144, a 62 percent increase in the last ten years. In addition, a report by the Consumer Financial Protection Bureau indicates that the percentage of borrowers who owe $50,000 or more has tripled over the same time period.[11]

Compounding increases in both college tuition and college student debt are the remaining setbacks resulting from the Great Recession of the late 2000s and early 2010s. CNBC personal finance writer Jessica Dickler notes that while job prospects have improved in recent years, new graduates may be competing with job seekers with college degrees and years of experience who were underemployed after the recession. In addition, an oversupply of college graduates can mean a drop in wages.[12] Even so, most of the post–Great Recession jobs were secured by college graduates, and a larger proportion of workers in the postrecession economy are college graduates.[13] Moreover, the Center on Education and the Workforce at Georgetown reports that "the recession hit those with less schooling disproportionately hard—nearly four out of five jobs lost were held by those with no formal education beyond high school." In other words, college degrees have sheltered Americans during tough economic times.[14]

Generally speaking, college education in any discipline is worth the investment. According to the Economic Policy Institute,[15] college graduates earned 56 percent more than high school graduates in 2015. Moreover, college graduates earn about one million dollars more over their lifetimes than high school graduates.[16]

Certainly, the job market has changed. Georgetown researchers Anthony P. Carnevale, Tamara Jayasundera, and Artem Gulish report that more than 95 percent of jobs created during the recovery went to workers with at least some college education, while those with a high school diploma or less were the first fired and the last rehired.[17] At the same time, high school students and others should consider that while traditional blue-collar good jobs have declined, skilled-services good jobs—meaning those with a median yearly income of $55,000—are increasing.[18] These jobs are going to holders of associate's degrees.

Ultimately, the data does point to college degrees as being very important in the current economy. But students and their parents need to consider a host of factors, including the very different costs of higher education institutions, the costs of room and board, the amount of financial aid and scholarships, the amount of debt that will be incurred, and the career being sought. Students also need to begin thinking about their college major well before enrolling, keeping in mind that nearly one-third of bachelor degree seekers change their major at least once in their first two years of college.[19]

What Are the Humanities?

This book is focused on the humanities, not on the larger umbrella category of the liberal arts. The term "liberal arts" is used in many of the sources we cite in this book, and we were careful to assess each source to determine whether the use of the broader term applied to our use of "humanities." Further, there is no consensus about what the term "liberal arts" refers to at present.

Historically, the liberal arts referred to grammar, logic, rhetoric, arithmetic, geometry, music, and astronomy. Timothy Strode suggests that in the late twentieth to early twenty-first centuries, the disciplines of the liberal arts "divorced." As a result, the liberal arts became the humanities, and the sciences, including the social sciences, became STEM.[20] The Association of American Colleges and Universities acknowledges this separation of the humanities and STEM when they discuss the additional scrutiny currently placed on the so-called liberal arts, which they define as the humanities and social sciences.[21]

We focused this book on the humanities. Still, when people discuss the liberal arts in the true sense of the word instead of as a synonym for the humanities, those statements still support our claim that a more well-rounded education that includes the humanities is an excellent option for most students. At the same time, we carefully assessed each use of the term to determine whether it applies to the arguments we make about the humanities. In almost every case, it does.

The National Endowment for the Humanities (NEH) defines the areas within the humanities as follows:

> The term "humanities" includes, but is not limited to, the study and interpretation of the following: language, both modern and classical; linguistics; literature; history; jurisprudence; philosophy; archaeology; comparative religion; ethics; the history, criticism and theory of the arts; those aspects of social sciences which have humanistic content and employ humanistic methods; and the study and application of the humanities to the human environment with particular attention to reflecting our diverse heritage, traditions, and history and to the relevance of the humanities to the current conditions of national life.[22]

We consider the following additional areas to be within the purview of the humanities: American studies and area/region studies; human communication studies; ethnic, gender, women's, and cultural studies; and selected interdisciplinary studies (e.g., medieval and Renaissance studies, classical and ancient studies, and Holocaust studies). Some disciplines—such as human communication studies, political science, and anthropology—include both fields grounded in the humanities and those grounded in the social sciences.

Why Study the Humanities?

There are many reasons to study the humanities—getting a job and launching a career are certainly among them. But loving what you study is also important. Considering big questions like "what is the meaning of life?" or "how do I live a good life?" is crucial; liberating your mind and your spirit and learning how to be a participatory citizen in a democracy are vital parts of an excellent education.

As students decide on a college major, it's important to know what it's like to be a humanities student. Most prospective students and their parents haven't heard about the nitty-gritty of teaching and learning in the humanities. The iconic image of a student sitting alone under a tree and reading a book is such a tiny piece of a larger and far more exciting story. Students in humanities classes think, research, write, debate, speak, create, and produce like scholars. They read books, articles, essays, speeches, and works of literature, and they debate with classmates, faculty, and those traditionally deemed "great thinkers."

Humanities students produce exciting work of their own to help hone the core skills and knowledge that employers seek. A student might turn in an extensive comparative analysis of historical political events applying what we know from history to an important current political issue, or a class might work together to create an annual report for a local nonprofit organization and then present that report orally to the organization's marketing team. Students might create a short film or music video to be used at new student orientation, write and direct a play that is produced on campus, engage in performance art, exhibit a painting in the campus gallery, break important news for the campus newspaper, or launch an activist campaign.

One caveat before we continue: Not everything about studying the humanities is uplifting. We study love, but also hate. We study peace, but also war. We study equality, but also injustice. We study the best and the worst of humanity. Everything about this process is important to human life and the world we live in.

Choosing a major in the humanities is a great investment in a global economy that is shifting dramatically, quickly, and in the direction of college graduates who think broadly, critically, and ethically. Students settled on a nonhumanities major should consider the importance of general education courses in the humanities and/or think about a minor in one of the humanities. The fast-paced, high-tech, global economy—and the communities in which we live—need humanities thinkers to help guide decisions that understand the human benefits and human costs of the tech revolution now and to come.

Toward those ends, the book is divided into five parts.

Part I, "Invisible Partners: The Humanities and the Modern and Future Economies," demonstrates that students in the humanities get good jobs; that the skills and knowledge gained in a humanities major are precisely what are most desired by employers; that today's economic and workplace landscapes need humanities majors; and that the need for humanities majors will only grow in the future. Chapter 1 explains the economic landscape facing college graduates now and in the future and discusses the roles that the humanities play in our global economy. In particular, the knowledge, creative, and services sectors in the economy offer an abundance of jobs and careers for humanities graduates. Most importantly, the current and future economy needs humanities students. Chapter 2 explores the most popular categories of majors—business, STEM, and health—and why students interested in these areas should also consider the humanities, based on employment and earnings. Chapter 3 covers the array of jobs and career opportunities available to humanities graduates across all sectors of the economy. We include the long-standing staples of humanities employment—such as careers in government, social services, news media, culture, philanthropy, and education—but also cover those careers, according to author George Anders, that are *"indirectly catching the warmth of the tech revolution."*[23]

Part II, "Understanding the Humanities," expands popular understandings of the humanities with a more complete picture of what faculty and students study. We live in the "real world," not only in books, and how and what we study and learn is intellectually challenging, ethically significant, and critical to the human experience. Chapter 4 focuses on the value of the humanities for both individual enrichment and the contribution to the common good. In Chapter 5, we explain faculty research in the humanities. Chapter 6 exposes you to what goes on in humanities classrooms.

Part III, "Learning Core Skills and Knowledge in the Humanities," explains how eleven of the top skills and knowledge areas that employers seek from new college graduates are learned in humanities classes and programs. These include critical thinking; written communication; verbal communication; collaboration; problem-solving; creativity and innovation; technological competence and technological literacy; ethics; diversity, inclusivity, and equality; globalization, global understanding, and a global perspective; and leadership. While these important sets of skills and knowledge are often labeled "soft skills," we rename them here as what they really are: *core skills*. Given that these skills and knowledge domains are listed by employers again and again in study after study, there's nothing "soft" about skills that are the most in demand year after year in every sector of the economy.

Terms associated with core skills and knowledge are tossed around a lot, but rarely described or explained in concrete terms. We will explain each category of skills and knowledge areas in concrete terms and demonstrate how humanities courses help students develop them. Thus, each chapter will discuss what leaders in business and published studies say about each specific core skill or knowledge area, what we know about teaching it, and what everyone should know about it. In-depth assignments illustrate how students work to learn each skill and knowledge area in humanities courses.

Part IV, "Creating and Communicating Your Humanities Story," helps students plan, craft, and tell their humanities story to potential employers. They must learn to link their humanities curricular experiences and their cocurricular and extracurricular activities, work experience, and civic and community engagement experiences to core skills and knowledge.

The concluding chapter, "Higher Education, Democracy, and the Humanities," argues that for both the economy and the social fabric of the United States to survive and thrive, the narrative about the value of the humanities in higher education and in the workplace must change.

Part I

Invisible Partners: The Humanities and the
Modern and Future Economies

Chapter 1

The Humanities and the Modern and Future Economies

The information explosion has transformed the economic and workplace landscape. Data and information are developed faster than ever before, and that data must be assembled and analyzed to be meaningful. As a result, opportunities for humanities graduates abound in the current and future fast-paced, global, and technology-driven economy. The major technological changes that paradoxically led to the narratives claiming STEM (science, technology, engineering, and mathematics) disciplines as the only way to be successful in the current and future economies have likewise created many opportunities for humanities graduates.

Understanding why this is happening requires a basic knowledge of this fast-changing economic landscape. Certainly, we are scratching the surface of these vastly significant and complex topics.

The Economy in the Information Age

Economists typically classify economies into three sectors of activity: the primary sector is the extraction of raw materials, the secondary sector is manufacturing, and the tertiary or service sector consists of services. The primary sector includes agriculture, farming, forestry, fishing, mining, and gas and oil extraction. Businesses in the secondary sector refine, manufacture, or construct goods with materials produced in the primary sector. These businesses typically include manufacturers of steel, textiles, and automobiles, as well as construction.

In the United States, the services sector is the largest and includes a wide range of service and distribution businesses and industries, both private and public as well as for-profit and nonprofit. Among these many industries are transportation, electric, gas and sanitary services, wholesale and retail trade, finance, insurance, real estate, health care, and public administration. The growth of the tertiary/services sector has dramatically transformed the modern economy, opening up numerous job and career opportunities for students in all majors, including in the humanities.[1]

Most people have heard about the shift from the Industrial Age to the Information Age. The following passage from Thomas A. Stewart's *Intellectual Capital: The New Wealth of Organizations* explains it well:

> The economic world we are leaving was one whose main sources of wealth were physical. The things we bought and sold were, well, things; you could touch them, smell them, kick their tires, slam their doors and hear a satisfying thud. . . . In this new era, wealth is the product of knowledge. Knowledge and information—not just scientific knowledge, but news, advice, entertainment, communication, service—have become the economy's primary raw materials and its most important products. Knowledge is what we buy and sell. You can't smell it or touch it. . . . The capital assets that are needed to create wealth today are not land, not physical labor, not machine tools and factories: They are, instead, knowledge assets.[2]

In 2016 the tertiary sector constituted approximately 80 percent of the U.S. economy, a figure projected to increase to 81 percent by 2026, much of that attributable to the information explosion.[3] Two important terms are being used to describe these significant changes in the tertiary sector: the *knowledge economy* and the *creative economy*. Both realms offer many opportunities for humanities graduates.

The Knowledge Economy

The knowledge economy refers to the collection, processing, and distribution of information in a wide range of business and industry and other professions. Rather than producing material goods, the knowledge economy produces and distributes information. A knowledge-based economy relies primarily on ideas, not physical abilities. It relies on the application of technology, not the transformation of raw materials.[4] Knowledge is created, acquired, transmitted, and used to promote economic and social development. In short, the knowledge economy relies on intellectual capabilities more than on physical inputs or natural resources.[5]

The knowledge economy needs more college graduates now than when manufacturing flourished. Wealth is generated by workers who create ideas, solve problems, market and sell services highly dependent on knowledge, and by workers who make and sell products whose primary component is knowledge. Knowledge management is among the most important economic enterprise of individuals, businesses, and nations.[6] "Knowledge workers" include, for example, design engineers; research scientists; software analysts; lawyers; biotechnology researchers; financial, business, and tax consultants; and marketing specialists.

As Richard Florida puts it in his book *The Rise of the Creative Class*, knowledge workers "control the means of production because it is inside their heads; they *are* the means of production." The term "means of production" is well known in economics and refers to all of the physical elements, aside from human beings, that go into producing goods and services, including natural resources, machines, tools, offices, and computers. But as Florida stresses, that has changed. Human knowledge, rather than physicality, is among the most significant elements in the means of production.[7]

Knowledge-intensive industries are now at the core of growth in the U.S. economy. The impact, size, and significance of the knowledge economy are vast. According to a report by the Organisation for Economic Co-operation and Development (2001), there are three main knowledge-based industries: "the main producers of high-technology goods, high- and medium-high technology manufacturing and the main users of technology (namely knowledge-intensive services such as finance, insurance, business, communication and community, social and personal services)."[8] To get a sense of the wide array of knowledge sector jobs, note that the U.S. Department of Labor lists 127.1 million total knowledge workers in the following ten widely inclusive categories in 2010: architecture and engineering; arts, design, entertainment, sports, and media; business and financial operations; community and social services; computer and mathematical; education, training, and library; healthcare practitioner and technical; legal; life, physical, and social sciences; and management.[9] Moreover, knowledge work occupations have been adding about 1.9 million jobs per year since the 1980s, growing faster than any other job category.[10]

Furthermore, the knowledge economy is present in all sectors of the economy, even in manufacturing.[11] Strategic technology consultant Dale Neef notes how vital innovation and knowledge are to manufacturing, "where high-skill industries have doubled their share of manufacturing output to 25 percent since 1975." Neef offers the example of car manufacturing, in which value has been added mainly through "employee knowledge and skills—creativity and design proficiency, customer relationships and goodwill, innovative marketing and sales techniques."[12] Human, social, and knowledge factors are as important as the fabrication of the cars, if not more so.[13]

Today and in the future, economic growth is dependent on knowledge and innovation because, as Peter F. Drucker—who first coined the term "knowledge worker"—puts it, "It is only in respect to knowledge that a business can be distinct, can therefore produce something that has a value in the market place."[14] In other words, when thinking about what the global economy holds for you in the next four, ten, or twenty years, don't only think about who is going to create the fundamental elements of that economy—the programs, the logistics, or the tools. Think, rather, about who is going to make that new program the most popular among consumers via social media campaigns, who is going to sell that program to an industry in order to change the way they do business, and who is going to explain to the general public and consumers what amazing things these new tools can do.

The Creative Economy

Closely related to, and sometimes overlapping with, the knowledge economy is the creative economy—"the socio-economic potential of activities that trade with creativity, knowledge, and information."[15] The creative economy includes economic, social, and cultural aspects. There appear to be two primary ways to view the creative economy.

First is the influence of creativity and innovation across business and industry, and particularly in the knowledge economy. Author and professor Bruce Nussbaum explains how the creative economy drives economic growth in the knowledge economy, largely through innovation and imagination:

What was once central to corporations—price, quality, and much of the left-brain, digitized analytical work associated with knowledge—is fast being shipped off to lower-paid, highly trained Chinese and Indians, as well as Hungarians, Czechs, and Russians. Increasingly, the new core competence is creativity—the right-brain stuff that smart companies are now harnessing to generate top-line growth. The game is changing. It isn't just about math and science anymore. It's about creativity, imagination, and, above all, innovation.[16]

As CNN commentator Fareed Zakaria explains it, companies must be at "the cutting edge of design, marketing and social networking." For example, "You can make a sneaker equally well in many parts of the world. But you can't sell it for three hundred dollars unless you have built a story around it. . . . The value added is in the brand—how it is imagined, presented, sold, and sustained."[17] In other words, in business and industry that relies on ideas, not material goods, creativity is the route to the top.

In a column for Quartz, Silicon Valley engineer Tracy Chou describes how she first disliked her humanities courses but later realized how valuable they were to her success as a software engineer. Part of building great technology is making important decisions about defining what the technology should be, for whom it's being built, and what the team wants to incentivize between users. The first feature Chou designed as she was building Quora, a question-and-answer service, was the blocking function. She says that her team pondered philosophical questions about the nature of humans, freedom of speech, and the impact on the construction of knowledge if people were ranked as "high" or "low" quality users. She laments that she did not learn to think critically about the world or seriously consider "privilege, power structures, structural inequality, and injustice" as a student. She also laments that so many builders of technology are like her, people who haven't spent much time thinking about these issues in general or in terms of how they relate to technology.[18]

The discussions of broader thinking about technology and its impacts are also often linked directly to concerns about user experience, a key to engineering the next great technological wonder. In a blog post, Facebook product designer Geunbae Lee notes that user experience is about "satisfying the ease of use, usability, composition, connectivity, reliability, and the value within the product or service." He continues by defining a good product as one that makes people "feel worthwhile and joyful throughout their journeys." Crafting this kind of experience requires consideration of what users want, what they dislike, and what stimulates emotions. Engineers must combine "sensibility, cognition, experience, creativity, knowledge, norms, values, ideas and thinking [with] product planning"; thus, he argues, people with backgrounds in the humanities and social sciences can "contribute, ideate and work to solve the problems that users have."[19]

A second view of the creative economy includes "creative industries" that "lie at the crossroads of arts, culture, business, and technology—including advertising, architecture, arts and crafts, design, fashion, film, video, photography, music, performing arts, publishing, research & development, software, computer games, electronic publishing, and TV/radio."[20] Creativity is an input, and content or intellectual property is the output.

Also considered part of the creative economy are the *cultural industries* that include public cultural institutions such as cultural tourism and heritage, museums and libraries, hobbies, sports, and outdoor activities. These industries add social and cultural value to our lives and, like creative industries, are relatively stable even in lean economic times. Importantly, the creative industries provide relative economic stability.[21] Zakaria suggests that the most influential industry in the United States is the entertainment industry.[22]

What's Next: The Human Economy, the Fourth Industrial Revolution, and 5G

Learning how to learn and being flexible are as critical to the as-yet-unknown future jobs as they are to the jobs that exist today. We have identified three ways in which economists and others are describing the U.S. and global economic future: the "human economy," the "Fourth Industrial Revolution," and the "5G economy."

First, we are currently transitioning to the human economy. The industrial economy leveraged human brawn, the knowledge economy leveraged human brains, and the human economy will leverage the human heart.[23] The know-how and analytic skills that made workers indispensable in the knowledge economy will no longer give them an advantage over increasingly intelligent machines. But they will still bring to their work essential traits that can't be and won't be programmed into software, like creativity, passion, character, and collaborative spirit—in other words, their humanity.

The Fourth Industrial Revolution (the third being digital) is described in a 2016 report by the World Economic Forum, noting that the Fourth Industrial Revolution has already begun with developments in genetics, artificial intelligence, robotics, nanotechnology, 3D printing, biotechnology, and many others.[24] In this new internet of things, consumers want connectivity well beyond phones, laptops, and tablets. Within only a few years, 50 billion things will be connected to the internet, including items ranging from small home appliances to cranes on construction sites.[25]

Finally, digital coordinator Bianca DiSanto argues that "in the same way the Industrial Revolution dramatically altered the competitive environment of virtually every industry, the advent of 5G will completely reshape the way business is done in the not-so-distant future."[26] The fifth generation of the mobile network, 5G, will be much faster, and by networking even more items, will increase productivity. From convenience items like smart doorknobs, pet collars, home appliances, and medicines to smart cities and nearly total industry automation, the 5G economy will produce economic change on the scale of the Industrial Revolution. While noting that we are still several years away from widespread access to 5G technology, DiSanto stresses the need for today's graduates to be aware of the "disruptive" changes to come, upending the status quo like never before.

DiSanto's suggestion for the future economy is simply put: "Now is the time to learn how to learn." Workplace change of this magnitude will require adaptability and the ability to manage ambiguity. Liberal arts and humanities degrees offer what DiSanto identifies as demanded by the 5G economy: "the wide-ranging skillset necessary to thrive in this oncoming and unpredictable new age of tech development."[27]

The Main Characteristics of Today's (and Tomorrow's) Workplace Landscape

The dynamic workplace of today is influenced and defined by the following characteristics: the drive for innovation; technological advances and the consequences (good and bad) of automation; the rapid pace of change; globalization; and the changing demographics of the workforce. In scholar Deborah Brandt's words, when knowledge and creativity are key to economic growth, the "search for what is different, faster, smarter, and more effectively communicated and sold drives economic activity at an unprecedented pitch and introduces the potential for rapid and continuous change in the workplace."[28]

Of course, one consequence of technological advancement is automated machines replacing humans in the workforce. A Ball State University study shows that nearly nine in ten jobs that disappeared since 2000 were lost to automation in the transition from an industrial to information economy.[29] A 2017 study published by consulting firm PwC predicts that nearly 40 percent of U.S. jobs could be passed from humans to robots, most likely in industries related to transportation, manufacturing, and retail.[30] Automation of workplaces is more fast-paced than ever, wreaking havoc on many in the middle class, whose jobs are more easily automated.[31] And the software sector "constantly squeezes out its own older jobs almost as fast as it creates new ones."[32] This degree of job vulnerability is obviously disconcerting.

Citing a 2017 report, author Eboo Patel notes that several areas of business and industry are susceptible to automation that many had not thought about before, such as the financial sector. This goes for both entry-level jobs and positions paying more than $200,000. The report indicates that almost no occupation is entirely safe from automation because "about half of all the activities people are paid to do in the world's workforce could potentially be automated by adapting currently demonstrated technologies." Patel notes the report's findings that physical activities in highly structured and predictable environments, such as in manufacturing, accommodation and food service, and retail trade, as well as data collection and processing, across all wage levels, are especially at risk.[33]

But there is also good news about automation. New jobs are developing that require skills that computers cannot do, such as the ability to solve unpredictable problems and the ability to engage in "complex communications" with other humans.[34] Renowned MIT economist David Autor asserts that "tasks that have proved most vexing to automate are those demanding flexibility, judgment, and common sense—skills that we understand only tacitly."[35] In these tasks, computers are often less sophisticated than grade-school children. Robots will win some jobs, but college graduates will win those that demand complex and flexible thinking—the very skills acquired in humanities courses.

The *Washington Post*'s Steven Pearlstein suggests that these fast-paced environments need "employees who are nimble, curious and innovative. . . . The good jobs of the future will go to those who can collaborate widely, think broadly and challenge conventional wisdom—precisely the capacities that a liberal arts education is meant to develop."[36] Patel identifies work that involves managing and developing people, and work that emphasizes applying expertise to decision making, as two important areas where automation is not a risk. He also cites evidence that "jobs that rely on human interaction, creativity, and judgment"[37] are growing in certain sectors like health care, education, community development, and social services. The humanities are a good bet in this shifting economic landscape because the skills that emphasize human interaction—empathy, sociability, writing, communicating, analyzing, and reacting to people—are part and parcel of the humanities.

Jobs are also threatened by globalization, since many tasks are outsourced to countries where labor is cheaper, and because changing politics and economics overseas have enabled larger numbers of workers to qualify for these jobs.[38] Many of the jobs sent overseas are probably not coming back, and this means a tougher job market for college graduates. One means of protecting oneself from job loss is to be a worker who is creative and skilled in human interaction, as these are qualities that automated robots and workers in other countries have little chance of competing against.

Globalization also means that workers across the world are interconnected in business and industry. In *The Fuzzy and the Techie: Why the Liberal Arts Will Rule the Digital World*, Scott Hartley argues that deep thinking and cultural understanding are as vital as technological expertise in a world of big data and algorithms.[39] It is not enough to know a foreign language; employees must also be adept at verbal and written communication dealing with cross-cultural conflict management and problem solving, and have the ability to work in diverse teams using specific types of knowledge, sensitivity, and skills.[40]

In humanities classes, students learn in-depth information about cultures different from their own. They learn that doing business across the globe requires an understanding that American norms and values are not the norm elsewhere. Body language can make or break a deal. Not knowing how to behave in different contexts of formality and hierarchy can, too. And there may be different expectations for men and women. Further, individualism is a key American value that is often seen as arrogant in cultures that value collectivism. Americans who are accustomed to a frenetic pace need to slow down and not seem impatient when working in a culture with a slower pace.[41] Globalization is going to favor a college graduate who not only understands but also values the complexities of cross-cultural communication and work.

The "Human" in the Modern Economy

What does all of this information about the modern economy mean for prospective and current humanities students? Simply put, brain power of all kinds, not just the narrow technical expertise of computing or engineering, is needed throughout the economy. Writer after writer, economist after economist, and technologist after technologist say the same things about why humanities graduates are essential to the current and future economy—a potent combination of specific knowledge and specific skill sets. In the end, it's all about the *human* in the *humanities*.

We are not suggesting that a humanities degree is going to protect everyone from automation or overseas replacement. The humanities isn't the antidote for technological advancement, global capitalism, and the problems they cause for U.S. workers. What we *are* suggesting is that a degree in the humanities is an excellent option for those who want to find a place in the modern and future economy and be more competitive in those economies. Chapters 2 and 3 offer more detailed information about the kinds of jobs and careers across the economic and employment landscape that may await humanities graduates.

Chapter 2

Cheers, Jeers, and Fears: Understanding Choices Among College Majors

In his 2017 book *You Can Do Anything: The Surprising Power of a "Useless" Liberal Arts Education,* George Anders underscores the major changes in the economy discussed in Chapter 1 with this extraordinary claim: "Only once or twice a century, a wave of innovation changes not just an industry, but an entire way of life."[1] It happened in the first half of the twentieth century with the rise of the automobile industry. But it wasn't only the manufacturing of the automobiles that changed our economy and our way of life; it was all of the related needs and desires that came about from a motorized America, ranging from auto mechanics to motor insurance agents to mapmakers to personal injury lawyers. And now we are in another wave of innovation changing industry and how we live. Anders reveals the many ways the high-tech revolution opens up—rather than shuts down—jobs, work, industries, and careers for students in the liberal arts and humanities. As public anxiety about automation began to increase, the technology sector and others sought answers by training even more software engineers. But "here's the painful twist," according to Anders: "The software sector makes no attempt to shield its own workers from automation; instead, it constantly squeezes out its older jobs almost as fast as it creates new ones."[2] Of the 10.1 million net new jobs the United States has added since 2010, only 7 percent of them, 677,000, are in the computing sector. Those 9,423,000 jobs created since 2010 are in the fastest-growing fields that are "*indirectly* catching the warmth of the tech revolution."[3] The transformational changes in the United States and global economies, and in particular those related to advancing technologies, have brought many new opportunities to humanities students.

Numerous authors in some of the best-known national news and business publications as well as several recent books have discussed the important role for humanities majors in this new economy. These authors have begun a much-needed conversation about the importance of the humanities now and in the future. Students interested in the most popular categories of majors— business, STEM, and health—should also consider the humanities, based on employment, earnings opportunities in the future, and how they stack up to the more popular majors.

Majors and Careers—The Loudest Voices

Choosing a major is among the most important decisions facing college students. However, as we noted in the introduction, many students change majors; it is common and normal to do so. College enables you to explore your intellectual interests and to develop new passions and values, so changing a major is an expected outcome for many students. Importantly, many students select and reselect majors based on what we are calling "cheers, jeers, and fears"—the narratives about what the economy needs; what majors offer the greatest return on investment; what majors are "preprofessional," that is, provide a direct path from college to job and career; and what majors are impractical, useless, and a one-way ticket to residing in your parents' basement.

Unsurprisingly, the loudest voices encourage students to major in three areas: business, health, and STEM (science, technology, engineering, and mathematics). Students are filling these majors in droves. Here we provide an informed picture of these degree areas. It's worth repeating that our goal is not to send current or prospective students away from these majors based on hyperbole or our biases. Rather, we want to bring some semblance of fairness back into the "what major should you choose" question because we (and so many others, as this book will attest) believe that the humanities have been unfairly drowned out at precisely the time we need more such graduates. In reality, the humanities hold up well when compared to business, health, and STEM, both in terms of market demand and career opportunities. Thus, the jeers aimed at the humanities and the fears of underemployment with a humanities degree simply aren't justified.

A 2018 study from the American Academy of Arts and Sciences bears out these assertions. According to the report, 5 million workers with baccalaureate degrees in the humanities were employed in management and professional jobs in 2015. More than 1 million were employed as managers, 754,000 were employed in office and administrative support positions, and 696,000 were in sales. Moreover, humanities majors "account for more than 10% of the people employed in every occupational category except those that are specifically STEM-related."[4]

The report also shows that humanities graduates "engage in key work activities" at similar rates to other degree holders. Humanities majors were somewhat more likely to be engaged in teaching as well as sales and marketing work. The share of humanities majors engaged in STEM-related activities (basic and applied research, design, computer programming, and production) was below those for STEM majors, but close to the percentage for all graduates.[5]

The business degree is a highly popular choice, with 19.2 percent of all degrees conferred in 2015.[6] This includes both the general business degree and one of the degrees typically housed in colleges of business, such as finance, management, accounting, marketing, supply chain/logistics, and risk management. But as recruiter Bob LaBombard says about the humanities, "Go into any company, and you'll find that people with degrees in English are working in marketing, as financial analysts, and in any other kind of job you can think of."[7] He emphasizes that a student's major does not determine their career. And A. G. Lafely, former CEO of Proctor and Gamble, notes that while mastery of a discipline is important, an education that is too specialized limits graduates' workplace contributions. Because companies must constantly reinvent themselves with adaptability and agility, "Individuals must also continue to change and learn new capabilities and competencies to grow and adapt. Mental agility comes from a well-exercised mind."[8] His solution? Lafely encourages a liberal arts major that is broad in scope.

In other words, students majoring in the humanities get exceptional training that can prepare them well in a number of business positions. As we'll discuss later in the book, humanities students are well trained in the core skills and knowledge required for excellent careers in a variety of business fields, as well as elements of culture (e.g., history, politics, media, sociology) at home and abroad that will serve companies well in our increasingly global economy. In addition, humanities students meet a very specific need in this economy: they are agile and flexible thinkers and actors, rather than the specialized learners about whom Lafely cautions.

In 2015, 11.4 percent of total graduates majored in the health professions and related programs, often referred to as "health sciences."[9] Professions such as nursing, physical and occupational therapy, and other health careers require specific training in health sciences, of course. But there are many careers in the health industry open to humanities students. Jobs in administration, patient advocacy, education, health-care policy, public communication, development, outreach, human resources, and many others await humanities graduates with an interest in health care.

The health-care industry, expected to grow 18 percent by 2026, needs plenty of graduates with core skills and knowledge, according to health-care consultant Jack Schlosser. Further, the health-care industry needs workers who are adaptable, agile, comfortable dealing with ambiguity, and flexible. An individual with strong leadership, communication, and problem-solving skills will be in high demand in the health-care industry.[10]

As the health-care industry recognizes the importance of core skills and knowledge, new degrees have been created in areas such as health communication, public health, health-care administration, and professional communication. The need for health communication degrees is evidenced by the fact that communication failures were responsible for 30 percent of all malpractice claims from 2009 to 2013, costing $1.7 billion in malpractice expenditures.[11] More importantly, during this same period, 1,744 patients' lives were lost due to miscommunication.[12] For students interested in health-related fields who don't want to be practitioners, the humanities is a great place to hone the core skills and knowledge needed to succeed in the health-care industry. *US News and World Report* reporter Rebecca Koenig adds that in health care, "creative people who can turn data into attractive visualizations, compelling stories or persuasive social media posts are in demand."[13]

In recent years, the loudest voices, including politicians and many university administrators, are urging students to turn to majors in STEM. This makes some sense, given the major technological advances that continue to transform the economy. At the same time, alarm bells have gone off about what's referred to as the STEM "crisis"—the idea that there is a shortage of STEM-educated workers to meet the demands of the U.S. economy and that this shortage will cause the United States to suffer. For example, the most recent report by the President's Council of Advisers on Science and Technology (PCAST) estimates that U.S. industries face a shortage of 1 million STEM graduates over the next decade.[14] It's no wonder that many students are heeding the STEM call. In 2014–2015, 33.5 percent of all de-grees—635,673 out of a total 1,894,934 degrees—were in STEM.[15]

However, many media articles and reports also support the idea that students in STEM need to engage *more often* in humanities courses. For example, as noted in *Scientific American,* in addition to needing scientific knowledge to create new vaccines or fight climate change, STEM graduates also need to understand how to best *communicate* information about science to help confront dangerous campaigns against the vaccination of children or charges that climate change is "a hoax."[16] In fact, a number of colleges and universities now offer public speaking and communications training for their STEM faculty for this very reason.[17]

In addition, new technologies influence many facets of the workplace, including artistic decisions about layout and design in computer programs, knowledge of visual rhetoric in the construction of an app, and the grow-ing role of technology in those remaining manufacturing jobs—these are all places where the humanities can play a role.

We argue that the myths and misconceptions about humanities degrees have escalated in recent years, in part because a barrage of pro-STEM mes-sages undermines the humanities while propping up STEM. For example, in regard to the need to put more money into degree programs in science and technology, Florida governor Rick Scott said in 2011, "If I'm going to take money from a citizen to put into education then I'm going to take that money to create jobs. So I want that money to go to degrees where people can get jobs in this state. Is it a vital interest of the state to have more an-thropologists? I don't think so."[18] Similarly, Kentucky governor Matt Bevin proclaimed in 2016 that "all the people in the world that want to study French literature can do so, they are just not going to be subsidized by the taxpayer."[19] Both leaders unfairly demean students in the humanities and simultaneously threaten to cut public funding for students who choose these majors.

Claims like those are irresponsible and unsupported by evidence and detrimental to the overall health of the economy and the nation, as well as the world. Significantly, some research is calling into question the need for so many STEM majors. Labor and workforce analyst Michael S. Teitelbaum suggests that U.S. students' relatively poor showing on standardized test scores has been misunderstood. Yes, there is a need for higher-quality STEM education, especially in primary and secondary curricula. But Teitelbaum notes that we must be careful not to confuse the need for all students to be *more proficient* in science and math with the idea that we need *more and even primarily* STEM college graduates: "There is a big disconnect between this broad educational imperative and the numerically limited scope of the science and engineering workforce."[20] That is, curricular improvements in STEM across the educational system are needed; increasing numbers of STEM college graduates are not.

In his book *Falling Behind? Boom, Bust, and the Global Race for Scientific Talent,* Teitelbaum argues that nearly all available evidence contradicts concerns about widespread shortages or shortfalls in the numbers of U.S. scientists and engineers. Further, he argues that the whole idea of this crisis in STEM is the sixth round of "alarm/boom/bust" cycles surrounding the STEM disciplines and their relationship to the economy since the end of World War II. The most recent cycles were the "race to space" with the Soviet Union in the 1960s and 1970s and the dot-com bust of the 1990s.[21] Other researchers, such as Michael Anft, Daniel Costa, and Steven A. Camarota and Karen Zeigler, also challenge what they see as an exaggerated claim of a STEM shortage.[22]

Additional research studies both support and challenge these concerns. Researchers at the Bureau of Labor Statistics conducted a study on the "central question" of whether we have a "STEM crisis" or a "STEM surplus." As suggested by their article title, "STEM Crisis or STEM Surplus? Yes and Yes," the issue remains unresolved.[23]

One final indication that the needle is moving toward the humanities is the emergence of new acronyms that include STEM. For example, STEAM (science, technology, engineering, arts, and mathematics) adds the *arts* to STEM. STEAM increasingly is lauded by institutions, corporations, and education and technology professionals because STEM education and work involves art, such as in product design and visual display, and because the arts promote the creativity and innovation necessary for scientific and technology advances.

Additional acronyms have arisen: STREAM adds *reading* to STEAM, and STEMM adds *medical knowledge* to STEM.[24] The continuous modifications to STEM suggest an increasing awareness that STEM alone is not sufficient. As John M. Eger, director of the Creative Economy Initiative at San Diego State University, states, "At this point, the debate in America about art and science is coming to a conclusion: the disciplines very much need each other."[25] Our hope is that the embrace of the arts and reading as necessary partners of STEM is the next step to an explicit embrace of the humanities in the rhetoric of politicians, universities, and others, which appears to have already begun in business, health sciences, and STEM fields.

The modern and future economy will undoubtedly be strongly impacted by science and technology. But Steve Jobs's and Tim Cook's remarks noted in our introduction imply that new technologies become lifestyle choices in large part because of arts and the humanities, not because of the technology. Technology and science will continue to open the world up to businesses, but some businesses succeed at greater levels not because of engineers or chemists, but because of better ethical decision-making and because of their understanding of intercultural communication. Technology and science will continue to change our relationships to illness, and even death, but some organizations in health care will perform at higher levels than others because their employees are better trained in the importance of effective communication on health, wellness, and even the bottom line. The modern and future economy will need STEM, business, health sciences, *and* the humanities, arts, and social sciences.

Employment and Earnings: A More Accurate Picture

Put simply, good jobs are available to humanities majors. Of course, getting a job involves a lot more than simply choosing a major. And the word "good" is relative to the individual depending on interests, goals, and how much, if any, debt one will end up with. For most everyone, "good" includes salary, though what that salary should be is relative to the individual.

Here, we try to paint a fair picture of employment and earnings data for humanities graduates. We are confident in the studies we have chosen to discuss, but they are only some among many, many studies out there. It is difficult to draw definite conclusions from the research studies about employment and earnings because they frequently do not define their terms similarly. Finally, data is subject to different interpretation, and even the best economists interpret employment and earnings data differently.

Most important, we will provide evidence that the employment data and salaries for humanities majors are not as dim as the popular narrative implies. In addition, we think it's important to realize that it will take some time for employment and earnings data to reflect the increasing recognition of the value of the humanities in all areas of the economy. We are on the cusp.

A study by the Georgetown Center on Education and the Workforce finds that at the beginning of the recovery from the Great Recession (2011 and 2012), the unemployment rate for recent graduates in the humanities and the liberal arts was only 1.9 percent higher than engineering majors, only 1.4 percent higher than business majors, and even closer to recent graduates in majors such as computers, math, and biology. Today, with an improved economy, the numbers for all majors are almost certainly lower. The report also states that unemployment rates for experienced workers from most majors hovered between 5 and 6 percent at the beginning of the recovery from the Great Recession (2011 and 2012). Indeed, unemployment rates topped 5 percent among experienced workers with baccalaureate degrees in computers, statistics, and math.[26]

Further indications of a noncrisis in humanities employment are reported in *How Liberal Arts and Sciences Majors Fare in Employment: A Report on Earnings and Long-Term Career Paths* by Debra Humphreys and Patrick Kelly. Their data analysis of the American Community Survey demonstrates that the majority of humanities and social science majors find jobs after college and remain in a variety of professions over the long term.[27]

Washington Post columnist Steven Pearlstein also reports that claims of underemployment for humanities majors are exaggerated, citing research from the Federal Reserve Bank of New York. The researchers cited found that from 1990 to 2012, the percentage of recent college graduates in low-wage jobs only grew 5 percent. In addition, they found that, generally speaking, about one-third of recent graduates (from all majors) have always worked in jobs that don't require college degrees but pay decent wages nonetheless.[28] Thus, it's actually pretty normal for some recent college grads to land in jobs that do not make use of their formal education. Former CEO David Speed points to the "hard reality" of first employment immediately after college graduation, stating that it's common for graduates to begin an entry-level position not directly related to their degree right after college and that getting past that fact can get a new graduate started on a path to their eventual career.[29]

Additionally, let's talk frankly about salaries for humanities graduates. Humphreys and Kelly's findings are also cause for optimism. They evaluate earnings data based on four areas of undergraduate majors: humanities and social sciences; professional/preprofessional; physical sciences, natural sciences, and mathematics; and engineering. Table 1 shows the median annual earnings for these four areas for college graduates directly out of college (ages 21–25) and in peak earning years (ages 56–60).[30] The median annual earnings for college graduates with a baccalaureate degree directly out of college in a humanities or social science field are slightly higher than those with a physical or natural sciences or mathematics degree and only slightly lower than those with a baccalaureate degree in a professional or preprofessional field.

Table 1. Median Earnings for Undergraduate Majors Directly Out of College (Ages 21–25) and Peak Earnings (Ages 56–60)

Area of undergraduate major	Directly out of college (ages 21–25)	Peak earnings (ages 56–60)
Humanities and social sciences	$26,271	$66,185
Professional/ preprofessional	$31,183	$64,149
Physical sciences, natural sciences, and mathematics	$25,986	$86,550
Engineering	$41,577	$97,751

However, as earnings change over the course of an employee's career, the median annual earnings for those between the ages of 56 and 60 with a baccalaureate degree in humanities or social sciences is $2,000 higher per year than those in a professional or preprofessional field. As Humphreys and Kelly state, "Notably, and contrary to widespread assumptions, the earnings gap between those with a baccalaureate degree in a humanities or social science field and those with a baccalaureate degree in a professional or preprofessional field closes over time."[31]

The Economic Value of College Majors, another large study from the Georgetown Center on Education and the Workforce, classifies majors into seven "supergroups": (1) arts, humanities, and liberal arts; (2) business; (3) career-focused; (4) health; (5) social sciences; (6) STEM; and (7) teaching and serving. The study's researchers—Anthony P. Carnevale, Ban Cheah, and Andrew R. Hanson—also present earnings for fifteen major groups as well as two additional categories, "all majors" and "high school graduates."[32]

Median annual wages of college-educated workers (ages 21–24) are shown in Table 2. The study also looks at subgroups within these fifteen major groups. The breakdown for humanities and liberal arts, as well as three additional categories, "bachelor's degree holder, all majors," "all humanities and liberal arts majors," and "high school graduates," ages 25–59, are shown in Table 3.[33] Most recently, the results of the *Winter 2018 Salary Survey* by the National Association of Colleges and Employers (NACE),[34] based on annual salary projections for 2018 college graduates by a total of 196 NACE employer members, are shown in Table 4. Unsurprisingly, the highest salary projections are in STEM fields. But note that the humanities average is $56,688, which is nearly equal to business, at $56,720.

Importantly, salary data can be tricky. In addition to each study categorizing degrees differently, there are a lot of contextual issues to consider, too. For example, as noted above, age and experience make a difference in salaries. When median salaries of younger workers are compared to those of older workers, the difference between median salaries for humanities graduates

Table 2. Median Annual Wages of College-Educated Workers (Ages 21–24)

Major group	Annual wage	Major group	Annual wage
Architecture and engineering	$50,000	Humanities and liberal arts	$30,000
Computers, statistics, and mathematics	$43,000	Agricultural and natural resources	$30,000
Health	$41,000	Biology and life sciences	$29,000
Business	$37,000		
Social sciences	$33,000	Psychology and social work	$28,000
Physical sciences	$33,000	Arts	$28,000
Education	$32,000	Industrial arts, consumer services, and recreation	$27,000
Law and public policy	$31,000		
Communications and journalism	$31,000		
		All majors	$33,000
		High school graduates	$22,000

versus other graduates is reduced to only about 2 percent lower.[35] In addition, which professions are included in the data can change, too. In some cases, doctors may be listed as STEM majors and in others they may not, and some studies classify workers in industries such as air conditioner repair as STEM careers, even though those workers are not necessarily STEM degree holders. Moreover, as many as 50–75 percent of STEM majors aren't working in STEM fields, so we don't know the salaries of STEM majors who work in business careers in areas like inventory management and quality control.[36]

Regardless of the messy nature of the data, we see one significant trend dispelling the myth of the humanities graduate being unable to earn a good

Table 3. Median Annual Wages of College-Educated Workers (Ages 25–59) by Area of Study: Humanities and Liberal Arts; Bachelor's Degree Holders (All Majors); All Humanities and Liberal Arts Majors; and High School Graduates

Area of study	*Median annual wage*	*Area of study*	*Median annual wage*
History	$54,000	Linguistics and comparative language and literature	$50,000
Liberal arts	$53,000		
English language and literature	$53,000	Art history and criticism	$49,000
Intercultural and international studies	$52,000	Humanities	$49,000
French, German, Latin, and other common foreign language studies	$52,000	Composition and speech	$47,000
		Multi/interdisciplinary studies	$46,000
All humanities and liberal arts majors	$52,000	Theology and religious vocations	$43,000
Philosophy and religious studies	$51,000	Bachelor's degree holders, all majors	$61,000
Other foreign languages	$51,000	High school graduates	$36,000
Area ethnic and civilization studies	$51,000		

living. Humanities majors tend to start out earning less money than graduates in a number of other areas, but those numbers even out with time and/or with additional education. In fact, some of the most recognizable companies have CEOs or founders with a humanities background, including American Express, Overstock.com, Whole Foods, Campbell's Soup, Chipotle, FedEx, Goldman Sachs, Citigroup, Bank of America, and Merck.[37]

Moreover, the wage payoff for synthesis, critical, and related analytic skills has risen swiftly in recent years, while wage payoff linked to technical and creative skills has been less substantial.[38] In addition, from 1980 to 2012, jobs requiring social interaction increased by 12 percent, while at the same time jobs that required more math but fewer social skills, including a number of STEM jobs, shrank by 3.3 percentage points. Employment and wage growth were exceptionally strong in jobs requiring both high levels of math and social skills.[39]

These studies tell us that measuring opportunity by major doesn't always represent the whole picture. It's difficult to predict what future jobs will be, even five or ten years down the road.[40] Thus, propping up one set of majors while castigating another may be bad economic policy, not to mention a bad strategy for choosing a major. Second, these studies point to the need for the kinds of skills learned in the humanities, especially regarding communication, regardless of one's major/career goal.

Table 4. Winter 2018 Salary Survey by the National Association of Colleges and Employers

Area of undergraduate major	*Salary projection*
Engineering	$66,521
Computer science	$66,005
Math and sciences	$61,867
Business	$56,720
Social sciences	$56,689
Humanities	$56,688
Agriculture and natural resources	$53,565
Communications	$51,448

It is also important to note that graduates of the humanities and social sciences often head to careers in social services and education that pay less than other fields, such as engineering or business management, but that are necessary for healthy communities and for our national system of public education. Neither jobs nor people should be valued based on salary. While our society has chosen to provide lower compensation for fields such as public service, teaching, and social services, these professions are critical to the health and well-being of our society.[41] Without teachers, would we even have engineers?

Authors of a recent study from the American Academy of Arts and Sciences report that humanities majors have somewhat lower salaries and slightly higher unemployment relative to science and engineering majors. However, this study uses a broader range of measures to assess job satisfaction and demonstrates that humanities majors report similar findings regarding their perceptions of well-being. For example, 71.7 percent of humanities graduates expressed satisfaction with their salary, as compared to 76.2 percent among all college graduates. Indeed, results show that on every measure studied—for example, benefits, job security, and job location—"the share of humanities majors reporting satisfaction was within five percentage points." Humanities graduates scored high in responses to being "deeply interested in the work that I do" (72 percent) and that their job provided the "opportunity to do what I do best every day" (70 percent), even among those degree holders from education and the arts, the fields with the lowest median earnings. Importantly, almost 87 percent of all workers with a baccalaureate degree in the humanities reported that they were satisfied with their jobs in 2015.[42]

Factors beyond salary, like a passion for the employer's mission, can lead to job satisfaction. Economist Robert H. Frank states that the jobs that have more attractive working conditions, such as greater autonomy, better opportunities for continued learning, or greater workplace safety, tend to pay less. He also points out that studies show that developing expertise in whatever job you do leads to higher salaries: "those who become really good at what they do are capturing a much larger share of total income in almost every domain, leaving correspondingly smaller shares available for others."[43]

The good news for students majoring or interested in the humanities is that choosing a career that makes you happy, gives you a sense of purpose, and provides a livable salary are not mutually exclusive considerations.

Core Skills and Knowledge

The core skills and knowledge most desired by current employers, according to almost every published survey and study, are what makes us so confident that the humanities are, and will increasingly be, a good return on investment and necessary to the overall health of the economy.

Google is a good example. When you think about Google, you think about computer scientists, engineers, and mathematicians. It's all about technology. Except that it isn't—according to the results of a study the company launched in 2009.[44] Called Project Oxygen, this study is "the most thorough, data-intensive study that any company has undertaken to date to understand the qualities that lead to promotion and a successful career."[45] After studying substantial amounts of data and information from employee surveys, performance reviews, nomination materials for top Google awards, and more than ten thousand observations of top managers in action, Google researchers found the following qualities to be most important for corporate advancement:

1. Be a good coach.
2. Empower others (and don't micromanage).
3. Be interested in the well-being of your team.
4. Be bold and result-oriented.
5. Be a good communicator.
6. Help your employees with their own career development.
7. Have a clear vision and strategy.[46]

STEM knowledge/skills came in "dead last."[47] As reporter Valerie Strauss observes, these are traits more commonly associated with an English or theater major than a computer science graduate.[48] In other words, Google now recognizes that the company finds greater success with employees possessing the very core skills and knowledge that are integral to a humanities education.

Google's 2017 study of their inventive and productive teams, Project Aristotle, reaffirms the findings of Project Oxygen. Google analyzed data on what they label their "A-teams" (top scientists with specialized knowledge) and their "B-teams" (individuals who "don't always have to be the smartest people in the room"). Google researchers found that the company's "most important and productive new ideas come from B-teams," those stronger in terms of equality, generosity, curiosity toward the ideas of teammates, empathy, emotional intelligence, and, most importantly, emotional safety, which allows team members to be confident in speaking up, comfortable with making mistakes, and certain that they are being heard. Strauss drives the point home: "Google's studies concur with others trying to understand the secret of a great future employee."[49]

Thinking Differently About What to Cheer, Jeer, and Fear

As humanities professors typing on our computers and texting each other on our smartphones, we recognize and appreciate the importance of STEM innovation and all that it adds to our lives. As people who consume products just like everyone else, we recognize and appreciate the importance of business as well. And as humans who, like everyone else, face health concerns and challenges, we recognize and appreciate all that the health sciences add to our lives, in terms of both time on this planet and quality of life. We recognize that the world needs excellent leaders and workers in those areas of specialization and that we have benefited from what STEM, business, health sciences, and all other students bring to our humanities classrooms.

We also recognize that the time has come for students to make better-informed choices about their college majors as they look ahead to careers they will feel passionate about. Simply put, in spite of what the roaring crowds may be currently cheering, STEM, business, and health sciences degrees are not the only paths forward for college graduates to get a job and career that are meaningful and that will allow them to pay off college debt. And while STEM in particular is a great option for students, it is most certainly *not* the only option for a student who wants to succeed economically.

Students fascinated with computing may choose to be computer science majors or software engineers, but they can also consider product design and public relations in the computer industry. Students in love with science may choose to be a scientist in a lab, but they can also turn to health education or health-care policy. Students who are attracted to management may choose project management or marketing as a career, but they can also choose human resources or public relations. We want students who love science to be science majors, students who love literature to be English majors, and students who love using public and interpersonal communication to get the job done to be communication majors. Students have many great choices for majors, and they deserve to know about these choices. Steve Sadove, former chair and CEO of Saks Fifth Avenue, summarizes our position well when he calls it "foolish to underappreciate the value of liberal arts skills. It is bad for our country, bad for business and bad for those just starting in their careers."[50]

As we turn to Part III of the book, we make a bold statement: "soft" skills should no longer be called "soft," since they are anything but soft. Rather, as made clear by the Google studies and the information we've provided in the book thus far, these are clearly *core* skills. It's time to change this language in the academy and in the public. The designation of these as soft skills is in response to the designation of skills learned in STEM, health sciences, or business as "hard skills." But as humanities faculty and students know, language matters. Not only does language communicate information; language creates meaning and understanding. Therefore, we believe using the word "core" rather than "soft" is accurate and significant in changing attitudes about the skills so often tied to courses in the humanities.

The eleven chapters in Part III are based on our analysis of data from two major studies in multiple years: the National Association of Colleges and Employers (NACE; 2011, 2012, 2013, 2014, 2015, 2016, and 2017) and Hart Research Associates (2010, 2013, and 2015).[51] Part III includes the core skills of critical thinking, written communication, verbal communication, collaboration, problem-solving, creativity and innovation, and leadership. Part III also includes the core knowledge bases of diversity, inclusivity, and equality; global interests; technological competence and technological literacy; and understanding and applying ethics.

Chapter 3

Making the Invisible Visible: Careers and the Humanities

A number of the thirty-seven positions listed in Payscale's 2017–2018 report "Best Jobs for Humanities Majors by Salary Potential" are job titles typically considered to be for humanities majors.[1] In addition, newer positions such as "web content specialist" and "content writer" reveal the technological transformations in the economy.

The Bureau of Labor Statistics of the U.S. Department of Labor lists twenty-five "major occupation groups" ranging from entertainment and sports to media and communication to sales.[2] Most occupation groups have opportunities for humanities majors because in an economy in which "human interaction has proven decidedly difficult to computerize," "the labor market is placing increasing value on social and other non-technical skills."[3] There are many jobs and careers across the economic landscape for humanities majors. Writing, editing, public relations, communication, web content development, and so on are just a small part of the array, although they may be the best known.

One of the problems we've found in our roles as academic advisers to our students and as faculty is that most prospective college students and their parents—actually, most people—aren't aware of what knowledge and skill sets are most important in the majority of today's workplaces, and that there are jobs for humanities majors in many businesses and industries. This chapter identifies jobs and careers across the quickly changing economy available to humanities majors in four areas: the invisible partners of the high-tech and knowledge economies, the creative industries, the public service sector (government and nonprofit), and the medical humanities.[4] The categories overlap to some extent. For instance, all industries and sectors have been influenced by technology in varying ways and degrees. In addition, many creative industry jobs are in nonprofits. Yet we think this is a useful way to understand the broad employment landscape for humanities majors.

As a reminder, we note that the availability of jobs does not guarantee all humanities students a job in a career they love. But we do believe students should know what's out there so they can informatively balance the factors that lead to a rewarding profession, however that person defines "rewarding."

Technology Sector

In a column for *Fast Company*, Michael Litt, cofounder and CEO of the video marketing platform Vidyard, remarks that despite the emphasis on STEM, he's hiring more humanities majors than STEM graduates and doesn't see that trend changing in the near future. In fact, at his and many other tech companies, only 15–25 percent of the workforce is composed of developers, as many of the jobs require far more than coding ability or other technical expertise. Litt suggests that "the truly irreplaceable jobs—not just of the future but of the present—are the roles that intermingle arts and science." In his experience, employees that consistently show interest in learning new skills and experimenting with new ideas are those with backgrounds in the humanities.[5]

In *You Can Do Anything: The Surprising Power of a "Useless" Liberal Arts Education*, George Anders exposes the many ways the high-tech revolution opens up—rather than shuts down—jobs, work, industries, and careers for students in the liberal arts and humanities.[6] For example, we no longer need to know HTML to develop websites because programs like Wix, Weebly, SiteBuilder, GoDaddy, and Site123 have made it possible to create websites without programming knowledge. But it's the individual and/or team members who must make editorial decisions about elements like space, color, and audience analysis who cannot be replaced by a machine or computer program. Website-builder software cannot craft persuasive links to the site via social media, build audiences and followers, and encourage other businesses to link to that website and the services it offers. Those jobs can, will, and do go to graduates with other majors, including majors in the humanities.

These jobs are part of both the knowledge and creative economies.

Anders calls these jobs "tech-influenced" but not "tech-centered." They include compliance officers, entertainment producers, entertainment directors, event planners, fund-raisers, graphic designers, human relations specialists, management analysts, marketing managers, school administrators, medical administrators, technical writers, and training specialists. Together, these areas have created 716,000 new jobs since 2010, and most of these fields are growing at two or three times as fast as the pace of overall U.S. job growth. In addition, job growth in big "tech-influenced" categories, such as general management, finance, legal work, sales, and teaching, have added an additional 1.5 million jobs since 2010.[7]

The public, including prospective college students and their parents, may not know about this economic growth because, in Anders's words, "most of these new jobs have tiptoed into the U.S. economy with no fanfare whatsoever."[8] The overwhelming push for STEM and preprofessional majors has obscured all else.

Technology-influenced jobs, explains Anders, are those in which technology helps workers increase performance and productivity. We spend less time on routine chores, thereby becoming more productive. Many of these jobs require a minimum of technical literacy, requiring only a few months of concentrated effort, but not a computer science or engineering degree. They are in big sectors such as management, sales, teaching, and education—areas that employ nearly half of the 140 million working Americans, compared to the less than 3 percent employed in computer-related fields.[9] As Litt puts it, the actual creation of software is a minor part of any tech company. Sales and marketing teams and human resources teams are essential for any technology company to thrive.[10]

Along with technology, changing social dynamics and evolving public priorities lead to new kinds of jobs. All professions are influenced by fast-paced technological changes leading to new forms of data and information sharing, development of cultural products, and organizing workplaces and work tasks, all of which challenge older business models.[11]

Anders describes six sectors of the knowledge and creative economies with significant job growth (at least ten thousand jobs per year being added). The "booming demand" for fund-raisers, social media experts, recruiters, project managers, and designers are thriving opportunities for adaptable, innovative, and adventurous graduates—graduates with just the kinds of qualities developed in the humanities. For example, big data analytics and online polling have become big business. Tools like Qualtrics, SurveyMonkey, Clicktools, and Fluidsurveys were created by a relatively small number of engineers. But their impact is huge for market researchers and marketing specialists. Since 2010, the market researcher and marketing specialist industry has grown by 93 percent, with 245,000 new jobs added.[12]

In addition, from 2010 to 2015, 73,000 new jobs for human resources specialists were created in the United States. Full-time fund-raising positions, rare in 2010, jumped to 56,000 jobs by 2015. Project managers, once confined primarily to construction sites, have soared in companies and projects with a "high-tech twist." Further, approximately 67,000 web development and web design jobs open each year.[13] Some technical expertise is needed, Anders notes, but basic training in industry tools such as Adobe InDesign (and those that haven't been created yet) are relatively easy to pick up.

Furthermore, Anders notes that more than 400,000 openings a year are in positions requiring social media skills.[14] Humanities students are not only filling these positions, they are creating them. When Penn State Berks began offering a major in communication arts and sciences in 2007, the job title "social media director" scarcely existed, if at all. Fast forward a few years later and some of our first graduates were in positions such as digital manager, web content manager, digital marketer, and digital web analyst within a few years of graduation. We simply don't know all that we don't know about where these jobs are headed in the future. But we do know that, as Steve Burnett of the Burnett Group says, "Regardless of the changes in technology, the market for well-crafted messages will always have an audience."[15] Graduates in the humanities—perhaps especially those who major in disciplines such as communication studies and English, where attention is paid to rhetorical strategies and audience analysis—are in a prime position to ride the wave of technology, wherever it might go next.

At the same time, students can better prepare for these opportunities by making smart curricular choices while in college that will put them in a stronger position in the labor market after graduation and give them a better shot at higher pay. For example, an additional 900,000 jobs would be open to students in the liberal arts who add skills such as basic coding, social media, and web design to their skill sets on their own, via electives or via technical training.[16] Humanities students can get training in these areas through computing-related minors; the careful selection of electives and general education courses; engagement in student clubs related to technology; internships; and/or coding "bootcamps."

In fact, there are some who argue that far from being the center of importance in technology, coders are the "plug-ins" in the new age of technology. Software developer J. Bradford Hipps notes that it took him eighteen months to learn how to code proficiently. He characterizes those months as "long" and admits that he will never reach the heights of his "truly gifted peers," but he argues that to write code you only need a "few good books" and concentrated self-study.[17] Coding has also become easier with code and knowledge-sharing sites like GitHub and Stack Overflow.[18]

Creative Industries

The creative industries are positioned at the intersection of arts, culture, technology, and business. But as we have found, there is little agreement on which industries are considered creative. That's why it's hard to pin down data about jobs. What is clear, however, is that the creative industries offer many job and career opportunities, ranging from actors and fine artists to media equipment workers.[19]

Further, reports from the National Endowment for the Arts and the U.S. Bureau of Economic Analysis indicate that in 2013, arts and cultural production contributed $704.2 billion to the U.S. economy, or .23 percent of gross domestic product (GDP), increasing by 32.5 percent since 1998. Another key finding is that consumer spending on the performing arts grew 10 percent annually over the fifteen-year period. These industries surpassed the construction ($619 billion) and utilities ($270 billion) sectors.[20]

The Creative Industries: Business and Employment in the Arts, a report from Americans for the Arts, notes that nationally, 673,656 businesses are involved in the creation or distribution of the arts, and that they employ 3.48 million people, representing 4.01 percent of all U.S. businesses and 2.04 percent of all U.S. employees. This study also points out that the nonprofit arts and culture industry generated $166.3 billion of economic activity supporting 4.6 million jobs.[21]

Another powerhouse industry is entertainment. Fareed Zakaria calls it the "most influential" industry in the United States.[22] Chris Dodd, the chair of the Motion Picture Association of America, notes how significant the television and film industry alone is to the economy: it employs 1.9 million Americans every day, ranging from writers to makeup artists to public relations specialists and talent managers. The industry comprises 99,000 businesses across the United States, and, while often thought of as run by huge conglomerations, most of these are actually small businesses with fewer than ten employees.[23]

As in all areas of contemporary life, technology has highly influenced the creative industries. Technology spurred the fastest growth in arts and culture production between 1998 and 2013. Other information services—online publishing, broadcasting, and streaming services—increased by 12.3 percent, and arts-related computer systems design (including services for films and sound recordings) increased 7.7 percent. Job titles such as 3D modeler, digital archivist, and game developer have also been created.

Technology has likewise provided new opportunities for artists in terms of the promotion and distribution of their work.[24] In addition, cultural and creative products are fundamental to the digital economy primarily through digital sales—digital devices such as e-readers, tablets, smartphones, TVs—and digital content such as movies, music, books, and games.[25]

Finally, the book publishing industry is one example of a traditional go-to career for humanities majors that has been revolutionized by technology. The internet has transformed how literature is discovered, marketed, read, published, and distributed. *Publishers Weekly* headlined 2011 as "The Year of the E-Book,"[26] and since then, more and more readers are turning to online books. At the same time, sales in independent bookstores are increasing.[27] Newer, sleeker, and better e-readers, tablets, and smartphones continue to upend the industry.

Other changes include self-publishing and digital distribution. Self-publishing—through companies like Lulu or CreateSpace—opens up the world for more books, more writers, and more ways to produce and sell books. It has also led to an increased demand for freelance editors, with some editors leaving positions at major New York publishers.[28] Digital book distribution is offered by companies like Amazon, Apple, Google, and Barnes and Noble. In addition, big data enables publishers to rely less on hunches or gut instincts to determine whether there is an audience for a book.[29] Online marketing and social media are critical players in book sales and distribution.

Despite these many changes, however, some things remain the same. There remains a team of people who get a book from writer to reader. These positions include editors, copyeditors, literary agents, literary scouts, publicists, production editors, marketers and/or copywriters, and salespeople. In all ways, both for what is conventional and what is new, the publishing industry is a great fit for humanities graduates.

Public Service: Nonprofits and Government

Public service jobs include two main categories: public sector government jobs (city, county, municipal, state, federal, and international) and the nonprofit sector. According to the Bureau of Labor Statistics, nearly 22 million people were employed in the public sector in August 2016. Although there has been little job growth in federal, state, and local government in recent years, the public sector is an important option for all graduates. Data from 2016 shows that the approximately 2.7 million civilian (nonelected) employees in the federal government make it the largest employer in the nation, compared, for example, with Walmart's 2.2 million employees worldwide.[30] Jobs are available in many areas, including education, research, security, defense, law enforcement, health, infrastructure, utilities, transportation, community/economic development, trade, and finance.

Ironically, a 2012 study by Peter Rose identifies the millennial generation's high level of commitment to volunteerism, helping others, and having an impact on society, and yet surveys indicate that college students hold generally negative views about government employment.[31] Former secretary of agriculture Dan Glickman argues that it is important to attract young people to government jobs given the aging public sector population.[32] Good people are necessary for good government across the board. Public employees are commonly referred to as "public servants," indicating the critical role of government workers to the health of our nation, from the White House to local municipalities. Further, many government jobs provide more stability than private sector jobs.[33]

Qualified candidates have even more options in the nonprofit sector.[34] Nonprofit employment has been more stable than the private sector from 2007 through 2012, even during the 2007–2009 recession, when many organizations faced challenges due to lower monetary contributions. During this period, nonprofit employment increased 8.5 percent, from 10.5 million to 11.4 million jobs.[35]

Moreover, the nonprofit sector impacts the overall economy in positive ways. In 2013 nonprofits contributed approximately $906 billion to the U.S. economy, or 5.4 percent of the country's GDP. Between 2003 and 2013, the nonprofit sector grew by 2.8 percent, with approximately 1.41 million nonprofits registered with the Internal Revenue Service.[36]

Prospective humanities students should understand that many jobs in nonprofits overlap with jobs in private business and industry, including web design, accounting, research, management, communications, administrative work, information technology, and lobbying.

Heather Krasna identifies career fields that fit most or all nonprofits and government agencies. Management and support positions include executive positions; program and project managers; communications and outreach; human resource and volunteer coordination; fund-raising and development; contracting, grants management, and consulting; finance, accounting, and budgeting; administration; and information technology. Policy positions include policy analysis and research; advocacy and lobbying; federal, state, and local elected office; and legislative staff—campaign workers and researchers.[37]

Applicants interested in landing nonprofit jobs in the government sector in the next several years need design abilities, given the increasing research showing that design—for example, the layouts of physical spaces and neighborhoods—influences behaviors. In addition, nonprofit work environments tend to be diverse, so employees will need to be comfortable and effective working with people of all races, ethnicities, religions, cultures, and other differences in backgrounds and beliefs.[38]

The ability to tell stories both in narrative and in data is critical, regardless of which industry we're talking about. No industry exists that doesn't need good storytellers in its employ. But increasingly, nonprofits must rely on data to persuade donors and granting agencies in order to simply stay afloat. Thus, telling a compelling story in writing (in print and online, including social media) and orally are skills vital to a nonprofit's survival. Moreover, the ability to tell these stories in these different formats is perhaps most important for a nonprofit's social media presence, which has become vital to a nonprofit's work communication and advocacy work.[39] With courses in areas like "storytelling" and "creative nonfiction," the humanities is a perfect place to hone the storytelling skills that will be vital to the survival of organizations—corporate, nonprofit, or governmental.

The Medical Humanities

The health-care industry continues to expand as a result of the aging baby boomer population. The Bureau of Labor Statistics notes that occupations in health care are expected to grow 18 percent between 2016 and 2026, adding 2.4 million new jobs and growing faster than any other occupational group.[40]

In fact, the links between health care and the humanities have become so recognized that colleges and universities are offering programs that speak to these connections, such as health communication, public health, health-care administration, and professional communication. Baylor University, for example, offers a medical humanities degree program, defined as an "interdisciplinary field that has been described as the best of a liberal arts education with a medical focus. Disciplines such as history, literature, philosophy, religion, economics and the social sciences complement the basic sciences in a way that builds a bridge between the art and science of medicine."[41] Humanities students interested in health sciences are prepared to take on any number of jobs in the health-care industry in areas such as "health education, public education, community health and healthcare administration."[42]

In addition, disciplines such as communication studies offer pathways that speak to the important connections between health care and the humanities. These programs prepare students to work in health and health-related fields. They focus on topics like how delineations such as gender, geographical position, religion, race, ethnicity, and so on impact health and health-care decisions; how interpersonal, group, and organizational communication factor into health care and patient outcomes; the role of persuasion in encouraging specific health-care and prevention choices; and the role that social support plays in health-care outcomes.

Further, a quick perusal of job-hunting sites offers a great list of opportunities for humanities students interested in the health-care industry. Some of these positions include community organizing and development office positions in nonprofits linked to public health education; claims specialists in insurance companies; patient services representatives who help patients navigate complex hospital and insurance policies; coaches to train health-care staff in new programs for billing or in better interpersonal communication; volunteer and community development managers; and patient resource specialists.

Loving Your Major and Career

Anders points out that the kinds of first jobs for humanities majors generally pay less than first jobs with vocational degrees like nursing or computer science. This fact is especially true for first-generation college students and other students who don't have family connections or access to other kinds of networks. But as noted in the previous chapter, a recent study shows that in the long term, humanities majors make an average of $66,000 by the time they are 56 to 60 years old, considered peak earning years—$2,000 higher than those with professional and preprofessional degrees in their age bracket.[43]

Furthermore, it's worth repeating that all students should balance many factors in their pursuit of a major, job, and career. As English professor Robert Matz rightly claims, "If you love your major and are good at it, you're more likely to be successful than if you reluctantly undertake a major you're not passionate about because you think it will lead to a higher paying job."[44] This advice cannot be emphasized enough. Graduates should pick careers and jobs that they will love while making a living they will be satisfied with. Remember that making a good life isn't just about salary. It's also about doing things you are passionate about and believe in, as well as being comfortable with the work/life balance your chosen career may or may not offer you.

In a letter to the editor in the *New York Times*, Diane Goldstein Temkin makes this very point about her daughter, who graduated only a year earlier with a major in philosophy:

> At her liberal arts school, she volunteered at an organization in the community that offered disadvantaged people legal, emotional, vocational and educational support. After graduating, she got a full-time job with benefits helping disadvantaged middle-school students to better succeed in their educational careers and in life. She has moved out of our home and fully supports herself.
>
> Her education in philosophy and the humanities was far from

"irrelevant" and "self-indulgent." Rather, it taught her to care deeply about others and to help others as best she can. Such empathy is needed now more than ever in this rapidly changing and muddled world.[45]

As Martha Nell Smith, founding director of the Maryland Institute for Technology in the Humanities, puts it, "the Humanities are at the heart of knowing about the human condition; they are not a luxury."[46] We turn now to Part II to demonstrate that studying the humanities in college is incredibly fun, intellectually stimulating, and eminently worthwhile. There is tremendous value in the humanities beyond the workplace.

Part II

Understanding the Humanities

Chapter 4

Beyond Jobs and Careers:
The Enduring Value of the Humanities

Beyond employment and careers, perhaps the more important role that the humanities play in our world is teaching people how to understand their own lives as well as how to understand and operationalize the "common good," that is, the general welfare for all.[1] Even the U.S. Congress, which hasn't agreed about much of anything in the last decade, agrees about the importance of the humanities to our way of life. The 2013 report resulting from these concerns, "The Heart of the Matter: Humanities and Social Sciences for a Vibrant, Competitive, and Secure Nation," affirms the absolute need for the humanities given our desire for more civil public discourse, a more "adaptable and creative workforce," and even stronger national security.[2] The humanities emphasize critical thinking and imagination while helping us remember where we've been as well as visualize our future.

The humanities are vital to humans and human societies in multiple ways. We synthesize our primary arguments about the connections between the humanities, personal enrichment, and the common good into two main threads. First, we address the individual's life and its "big questions." How do you live a good life? What is the meaning of life? These questions are about personal enrichment, which is valuable in and of itself. Second, we attend to questions of the "common good." From upholding democratic values of equality and justice to making better decisions on urgent issues before us now and in the future via an understanding of historical, political, and economic contexts of the past and present, the humanities contribute to what is called "the common good."

Addressing the "Big Questions": The Individual and/in the Community

Matthew Arnold, one of the most highly regarded British poets and social and literary critics in the nineteenth century, captured the value of the humanities when he wrote about the importance of knowing "the best that has been thought and known in the world" in order to be able to challenge old ways of thinking.[3] By "the best that has been thought and said in the world," Arnold was referring to what are often called "the masterpieces"—those works of literature, philosophy, art, and religion that year after year, decade after decade, century after century, are considered the most insightful and beautifully written the world has ever seen. These are the texts that teach us how to live a meaningful life and how to be a good person and, therefore, what kinds of people it takes for a community or society to thrive.

For example, Plato's *Republic* in ancient Greece explores the interrelated concepts of justice and happiness.[4] Geoffrey Chaucer's *Canterbury Tales* narrates the stories of pilgrims from all walks of life on a journey from London to Canterbury in the fourteenth century, and the tales range from moralistic to reflective to gaudy.[5] *The Prince* by Niccolo Machiavelli is an influential rumination on political power. His assertion, for example, that a prudent ruler shouldn't keep his word if it places him at a disadvantage, and that a ruler "must know how to colour one's actions and be a great liar and deceiver" is as relevant today in the twenty-first-century United States as it was in the sixteenth-century European Renaissance.[6]

These and thousands of thinkers, writers, and artists explore what are considered enduring questions. What does it mean to be human? What is evil? What is worth dying for? What does it mean to be free? What is happiness? What is success? What does it mean to live a good life? Why are we here? What is truth? What is love? Can war be just? Does truth exist? What is justice? What are human rights? Do humans have free will? Are humans inherently good? There are many more enduring questions that engage our intellect, our sense of beauty and truth, and our morality. These questions are layered with other questions, foster deep thinking, require thoughtful and contemplative reflection, and resist easy answers.

To be clear, we do not suggest that anyone or everyone who studies the humanities becomes a good person as a result of their studies. As Geoffrey

Galt Harpham, former president and director of the National Humanities Center, argues, "No responsible scholar believes that humanistic study directly fosters private virtue and responsible citizenship."[7] Nor are we suggesting that any person who doesn't study the humanities will not be a good person. No doubt, the humanities puts us in conversation with some of the greatest minds throughout human history. We agree with *New York Times* columnist Nicholas Kristof's suggestion that the world would be poorer without "musicians to awaken our souls, writers to lead us into fictional lands, and philosophers to help us exercise our minds and engage the world."[8] But the humanities also engages us with some of the most evil minds in history.

Another productive challenge posed by Arnold's notion of "the best that has been thought and said" is what constitutes "the best," a "masterpiece," and "classic." Plato, Chaucer, and Machiavelli all noted above are all white men. There are thousands of brilliant and beautiful texts by women and writers of color and non-European backgrounds that we could have chosen. But still today, these white men are the mainstays. They are referred to as part of the "canon"—those writers and thinkers and artists whose works continue to be read, taught, and studied from generation to generation and place to place.

As we write, students at Reed College in Portland, Oregon, are protesting the curriculum of a humanities course required of all students. The course is a year-long study of classic texts and thinkers—the ancient Greeks, the *Epic of Gilgamesh,* the Bible, Apuleius's *Golden Ass,* and so on. Many students believe that the course is narrow in its scope, that is, overly Eurocentric, white, and male. These students want a more diverse curriculum that reflects not only who the students are but also great thinkers from all throughout the world, now and in history.[9]

This question of which writers and thinkers *should* or *must* be taught is among the most contentious and important debates across the humanities and other disciplines. As the number of important texts, writers, and thinkers expands, in part by the passage of time and in part by the addition of writers from previously oppressed groups, decisions must be made about what "counts" as great or a masterpiece or classic.

In our view, this debate itself is indicative of what is so important about the humanities. It invites and demands critical judgment informed by context, history, ethics, diversity, and difference, and an understanding of how power operates in society and for whose benefit. The debate is not merely or even primarily ideological, as some have claimed.[10] And the way we teach this—as many other faculty do—is to bring students into these multilayered debates that raise philosophical, ethical, intellectual, and aesthetic questions.

Simply put, we teach the canon because it's important to see where we've been, and much of the work is valuable. But we also add previously unknown or ignored writers to the canon, teaching works that challenge canonical thinkers and that help students become more critical thinkers, more sensitive to perspectives that might differ from theirs, and more aware of how generations speak to each other in venues like literature, popular culture, political shifts, and so on. We believe that teaching the canon and challenges to the canon encourages students to question, interrogate, evaluate, and judge through and within all of the complexities of history, power, ethics, justice, reason, facts, science, and more.

These issues are not simply "academic" questions with no significance beyond our campuses, publications, classrooms, or conferences. This work is a kind of *mind* training (as opposed to specific job training) that teaches us to look beyond what we know and sometimes beyond what we thought we could even imagine, and to make connections constantly between our past, present, and desired future. This mind training encourages students to do substantive, higher-order thinking, to understand the role of communication as employees and citizens, and to critically assess everything they see, hear, and read. Moreover, this mind training makes for much more talented and flexible employees.

Humanities students bring this higher-order thinking into their careers and communities, not only so that they can achieve at high levels as individuals, but also so that they can make their career and community environments more rich, just, equitable, sustainable, and healthy. The mind training that stems from the humanities is profoundly important in the world, not only because it makes for stronger employees or because it helps us grow as individuals, but because, as we discuss next, the humanities are of great value to the common good.

From the Individual to a Community: The Common Good

These intellectual, artistic, and moral pursuits by the individual have intrinsic value; that is, they are valuable in and of themselves. They enrich our lives and the lives of those around us. They open up new worlds and new ways of thinking to us, and they challenge our traditional, and sometimes even mindless or outdated, ways of thinking and acting. They are also vital to a functioning society that treats its citizens equally and justly.

Democracy requires wisdom, engagement, civic knowledge, and the ability to debate and dialogue. Arguably, great works of art, literature, rhetoric, and philosophy foster relationship building, empathy, the understanding and value of difference and diversity, democratic citizenship, and a well-functioning democracy. Martha Nell Smith, founding director of the Maryland Institute for Technology in the Humanities at the University of Maryland, College Park, writes that the arts and humanities "help us imagine other lands and cultures or . . . help us cultivate the compassion and empathy that are required for democracy, for practicing equality as a fundamental value."[11] The humanities stimulate our imaginations and provide new perspectives. Through areas such as literature, music, public address, political campaigns, film, media/film studies, performance studies, and other visual arts, we are exposed to people and cultures with whom we might never otherwise interact. This ability to imagine what others are thinking, feeling, and experiencing fosters a "propensity to act with kindness towards others, particularly those who are hurting or in need."[12] In other words, the humanities can foster empathy.

Democracy demands a lot from all of us, and the humanities help nurture these characteristics. The nonprofit Center for Civic Education presents an overview of the characteristics of citizens who "enable constitutional democracy to flourish."[13] The peoples' role in shared governance is paramount, and dependent on characteristics that include both civic knowledge (basic knowledge of history, political and legal ideas and systems, economics, foreign relations, and the critical assessment of information) and civic skills (thinking critically and objectively about public affairs, the ability to articulate positions, and the ability to collaboratively build community).

Francisco Cigarroa, chancellor of the University of Texas system, suggests that subjects like philosophy, literature, psychology, and political science "show us how we might reason together and reach common ground."[14] Indeed, dialogue and debate across cultures are at the heart of the humanities. Humanities study also fosters "oppositional thinking," necessary for a vibrant democracy.[15] The humanities promote free thinking, challenges to received wisdom, and the production of new—and hopefully better—ideas.

As Smith notes, some people have argued that "the systemic assault on the humanities is an effort to contain critical thinking" in order to transform colleges and universities into places where highly skilled but pacified workers are trained, instead of places where better citizens, capable of critical thinking, are fostered.[16] Along those same lines, Jason M. Kelly, director of the Indiana University–Purdue University Indianapolis Arts and Humanities Institute, argues that the critical application of the arts and humanities "disrupts groupthink" in that it cultivates thinkers with the capacity to be critical, evaluative, and judgmental of politics, economics, injustice, and ideologies.[17]

Each of these statements points to the immense importance of the humanities for the continued maintenance of our communities and democracy. The core skills and knowledge learned in the humanities encourage us to think beyond ourselves and our beliefs and to challenge our own communities and governments. This kind of thinking means learning about the current status of the world and how history has enabled particular futures, especially in the United States. In addition, this kind of thinking encourages us to think about what impacts (good and bad) our historical and current contexts have had on people around the globe. We have to try to make sense of the incredibly complex world we live in, and we have to understand how exceedingly connected we now are to others around the globe, thanks to advances in transportation and technology.

Mind training, as we refer to it, is fostered through the interconnectedness of humanities topics and texts. Students learn how a certain political philosophy encouraged a certain great speech, which inspired a particular political movement that was challenged by a specific genre of art, which motivated a new political philosopher to write the next great philosophical theory, which shifted the fundamental beliefs of a particular religion, which started a war, which encouraged another great speech, which was represented in a new genre of art, and so on and so on. These higher-order thinking, reasoning, and information synthesis skills are essential if we want to live in a world in which people make decisions that improve all peoples' quality of life.

Complicating this already complex kind of thinking is the fact that it is often difficult and uncomfortable to learn about humanity's history of inhumanity. We have to learn what humans in history have done to other humans in the name of political philosophy, religion, medicine, economics, and so on. Even more difficult is the fact that we have to learn about how our own mindless (as opposed to mindful) traditions and tendencies negatively affect people in our very own neighborhoods. For example, we have to learn about the impacts of racist and sexist language on women's experiences with sexism in the workplace, the implications of our "not in my backyard" tendencies on environmental racism, and how fundamental rights that many of us take for granted are not automatically granted, and are sometimes even purposefully denied, to many.

Those discussions are not easy, and they are not fun. They encourage guilt and anger and frustration in all of us. They are a process, not something completed in a day, a week, or even a month. In fact, they are often discussions that don't encourage "light bulb moments" for some students until years later. And these discussions encourage the disdain of politicians, unhappy about these challenges to the status quo, who disparage women's studies, gender studies, Latinx studies, African and Black American studies, Native American studies, environmental studies, and more as attacks on our country's traditions and "heritage." But these very difficult discussions are necessary. As the Rev. Dr. Martin Luther King, Jr., said, "The arc of the moral universe is long, but it bends towards justice."[18] We don't bend that arc toward justice without difficult conversations that change the way people think about and understand their world and their place in it. These issues are at the heart of a humanities education.

Finally, we want to bring attention to a new wave of commentary about the humanities in the contemporary global society. Humans have long faced the ethical questions of our new inventions and scientific discoveries: the atomic bomb; reproductive technologies, such as artificial insemination and in vitro fertilization; the transplantation of organs; and gunpowder, to name just a few. But there is increasing recognition that the current and future technological revolution needs the humanities as much as or even more so than in the past, even as they are being pushed to the back burner.

Some in the academy already recognize the error of this shift. For example, Dr. Melissa Nobles, dean of MIT's School for Humanities, Arts, and Social Sciences, recognizes that for humanity to survive and thrive in the global challenges of today, we need STEM *and* "an in-depth understanding of human complexities—the political, cultural, and economic realities that shape our existence—as well as fluency in the powerful forms of thinking and creativity cultivated by the humanities, arts, and social sciences."[19] To this end, the undergraduate curriculum at MIT requires all students to take at least 25 percent of their total classwork in the humanities, arts, and social sciences.

In addition, author Donald Drakeman, who has a Ph.D. in religion and a law degree, explains why the humanities "can help governmental decision-makers reach answers that best promote the common good."[20] Like Nobles, Drakeman argues that a modern high-tech economy that protects the rights of its citizens requires the "ongoing contributions" of the humanities in places such as biotechnology and pharmaceuticals, where costs like the development of new drugs requires "really difficult moral and political judgments" about which drugs are and are not funded by government, and to whose benefit and loss. Drakeman argues that "social value judgments" about health care are steeped in principles of justice.[21] This is where the humanities come in.

Venture capitalist Scott Hartley demonstrates why higher-order thinking and cultural understanding are as vital as technological expertise in a world of big data and algorithms. "Fuzzies," he argues, those with training in the humanities, lead some of the most successful technology companies because their products are designed "with deep empathy for and understanding how their innovations can help solve pressing human problems."[22] Technology influences our behavior in powerful and often invisible ways, for example, through apps that are intentionally developed to "addict" us to social media sites that may share private information without consent. Thus, Hartley argues that humanities perspectives—the intellectual playground of the Fuzzies—are needed to help steer technology to help us do what is valuable and good.

In a similar vein, Christian Madsbjerg argues in *Sensemaking: The Power of the Humanities in the Age of the Algorithm* that data and algorithms are only information, which shouldn't be confused with the *interpretation* of information. The book's philosophical grounding is in the work of German philosopher Martin Heidegger, supplemented with the author's experiences as the founder of strategic consultancy ReD Associates, who has worked with companies such as Coke, Ford, Adidas, and Chanel. Madsbjerg claims that data and science need to be interpreted by humans who understand history, art, and culture.[23]

Madsbjerg discusses the concept of "sensemaking" as a way to navigate the world by encouraging us to include *both* human *and* technical data in decision-making. Sensemaking, he says, is a "method of practical wisdom grounded in the humanities." To put it another way, while algorithmic thinking goes *wide*, sensemaking goes *deep*. Sensemaking helps decision-makers to be "sensitive to how others in our world do things, change things, and think about things."[24] It provides the cultural contexts and connections absent in algorithmic data.

Madsbjerg uses the Ford Motor Company as an example, noting that former CEO Mark Fields made multi-billion-dollar decisions based on information that had in some way or another been filtered through 199,000 people working at Ford.[25] How did he have access to all the data he needed once Ford's market expanded well beyond the United States? The need to understand other cultures is enormous. How would individuals in New Delhi respond to a driverless car given that employing a driver is a norm and a status symbol in that culture? What good is a technology meant to keep cars in between white lines in Chinese cities without clearly drawn lines? How does Ford's long history of American "middle-class values" resonate in other parts of the world? The answer to these above questions and more is, in large part, sensemaking; Madsbjerg makes it clear that it is important to be able to think both algorithmically and critically.

Part and parcel of our everyday lives is technology, and leaders in technology are beginning to recognize more and more how important the humanities are to the products that they create. In 2011, contrary to the opinion of his business rival, Apple cofounder Steve Jobs, Bill Gates told a group of governors that a traditional liberal arts education would put students behind in the modern economy.[26] Fast-forward seven years, and Microsoft has published a book called *The Future Computed: Artificial Intelligence and Its Role in Society*, which argues that as computers start to behave more like humans, the humanities and social sciences will become even more important. In fact, the authors note that courses in the humanities and social sciences will develop the kinds of thinking and skills that are necessary for the development and management of artificial intelligence (AI).[27]

AI may seem like science fiction to us, but we already engage in these technologies on a regular basis when we use products like navigation systems that reroute us in case of traffic, ridesharing apps that make sure we minimize time spent waiting and pay current market value for our rides, spam filters in our email, chatbots, and banking apps that let us deposit checks from home. In fact, anyone who interacts with Alexa, Cortana, Google Assistant, or Siri is engaging with AI on a regular basis.

As Microsoft now recognizes, humanities graduates have an important role in AI. For example, someone has to create and write the "personalities" of these machines. A person with a humanities background is an excellent addition to Alexa's personality team.[28] Tech reporter Madeline Buxton discusses changes in writing for Alexa within the context of the #MeToo movement aimed at recognizing and eliminating sexual harassment and assault.[29] Alexa's "personality team" is made up of people with a variety of backgrounds who are tasked with crafting her conversational interactions with customers. They must think about Alexa's character traits and how they inform her responses. And because her name and voice mark Alexa as female, assumptions about gender expectations become a primary consideration for Alexa's writers. Alexa's writers have started considering even more complex questions than something like "Alexa, are you a feminist?" Now, writers have to consider Alexa's responses to communication about being sexually abused, which is currently a mixture of an empathetic response ("I'm sorry that happened to you") with information about places to seek help.[30] Personality team senior manager Farah Houston says that one of their overarching tenets is that "Alexa doesn't upset her customers," and thus they work very hard to make sure that she doesn't.

Comparative literature major and current vice president of product and strategy at integrate.ai, a company working to integrate AI into businesses, argues that STEM may just lead to its own obsoleteness as AI software is now actually making its own AI software. She argues further that this shift means that the value of professionals trained in the humanities will increase as the AI industry requires "design methodologies" to do things like transform thought processes into statistical techniques, troubleshoot user issues in the creation of "intuitive features for non-technical users," and think about what data is needed to create a "friendly chat bot." She adds that, most importantly, the future of AI "lies in the empathy and problem-solving skills that will be the essence of professional work in the future."[31]

As these authors make clear, the "human" in the humanities has an important place in technological advances. As we attend to the unprecedented changes in technology now and in the future, understanding and best implementing these changes so that they do the most good and the least harm requires understanding the world in a way that the study of the humanities provides.

"Slowness" and the Mind's Pursuits

We must challenge the notion that the study of the humanities is frivolous or, worse, unnecessary, because there is not an immediate, tangible "product" that emerges from its study. Thinking long and hard about the questions the humanities pose is not a privilege; it is a requirement if we want to live the best lives that we can and participate in innovative economies. We must sometimes slow progress down in order to think seriously about the implications of progress for our lives, communities, and world.

Washington Post journalist Jeffrey Guo tells this story about himself: "I have a habit that horrifies most people. I watch television and films in fast forward . . . the time savings are enormous. Four episodes of *Unbreakable Kimmy Schmidt* fit into an hour. An entire season of *Game of Thrones* goes down on the bus ride from D.C. to New York." Guo uses new technologies that "speed up" videos. Just a few months later, he tells us, "live television began to seem excruciatingly slow."[32] Guo makes a case for what he calls a new era in the evolution of storytelling methods. But is that a good idea?

Sophie Gilbert, a staff writer at the *Atlantic*, believes that Guo's story "encapsulates how technology has allowed many people to accelerate the pace of their daily routines" and compares his story to the *slowness* of the humanities.[33] So without commenting on anyone else's desire to binge-watch television or view films in fast-forward, we do want to emphasize the notion of *slowness*.

We are drawn to this notion of slowness as a core method, value, and positive benefit of the humanities. We agree with Peter Burian, dean of the humanities at Duke University, when he writes that "humanities education offers the opportunity to slow down, to savor, to feast the mind at leisure."[34] The complexities of learning the humanities and the conversations they encourage serve an important function. They enrich us as individuals, and then we use this knowledge to enrich our local, national, and global communities. Watching the world's historical and current contexts in fast-forward, like Guo watches television, robs us of the ability to imagine worlds we have not yet experienced. Understanding what we pursue and why we pursue it is key to understanding the importance of the humanities. But it's not just the pursuit of these ideas that is misunderstood; how they are pursued—the vehicles, methods, or approaches we use—is also often misjudged. Chapter 5 delves into the humanistic method—the way we study what we study and the outcomes and importance of that research.

Chapter 5

Humanities Research: Investigating What Makes Us Human

Clearly, the humanities are vital to humans and human societies in multiple ways. It is through systematic research—in ways that both differ from and overlap with research in the sciences and social sciences—that humanities faculty substantiate and legitimize the questions we ask and the answers we provide regarding the myriad perspectives on the human experience. In addition, this intellectual work enriches our teaching and, increasingly, our communities.

In a nutshell, across the university and the disciplines, academic research is the discovery of new ways of understanding concepts, phenomena, and problems, and finding new solutions. In addition to teaching, many full-time college professors conduct research as part of their work responsibilities. Faculty across all disciplines conduct research and share their findings. In fact, "the production of new knowledge through discoveries that change our lives and the world" is one of higher education's core missions.[1]

When the term "research" comes up, many people picture scientists in laboratories working with beakers, petri dishes, and mice. Or research is thought to include data runs, spreadsheets, online surveys, and questionnaires. Fewer people think about investigating the meaning of literature or the persuasive strategies used in a presidential speech as research. But humanities research is valuable and necessary.

Jerome Kagan, a pioneer of developmental psychology, explains that there are three "cultures" of academic research: the physical and natural sciences, the humanities, and the social and behavioral sciences.[2] Each area, or culture, has specific practices, methods, assumptions, and guidelines for conducting research. Along with these differences, there is a basic similarity distinguishing academic research from other types of research: its emphasis on the systematic collection and analysis of data. In other words, humanities research, like research across all disciplines, is an important way of understanding and creating new knowledge, which is the primary function of academic research.

This chapter focuses on the specifics of humanities research—what we investigate, why we investigate, where the results of these investigations go, and the impacts of these findings. We have two primary reasons for sharing this information. First, we want you to understand the passion that most humanities faculty have for research and the significance of this work. Second, we want to convey that the ways humanities faculty conduct research are essential to student learning.

We don't come close in this chapter to the breadth or depth of what humanities research consists of, but we hope to give you a good sense of what humanities research is, why it's important, and how it impacts our students and communities. Changing perceptions of undergraduate education in the humanities includes understanding that humanities faculty conduct research that matters.

Humanities Research Tools and Methods

Humanists and social scientists like to quote Albert Einstein, who said, "Understanding physics is child's play compared to understanding child's play." As author Ziyad Marar notes, understanding phenomena like child's play, well-being, conflict resolution, social mobility, the causes of crime, political persuasion, racism, and war "is to grapple with 'wicked problems.'" By wicked problems, he means those complex problems that resist resolution, because as one aspect is understood, perhaps "solved," others crop up, much like a game of whack-a-mole. Human phenomena "don't often have right or wrong answers and don't tend to offer up easy scientific laws. But they can have better or worse answers and their study can cumulatively deepen our understanding over time, even if the impact is often relatively slow, diffuse and hard won."[3] Humanities researchers commit to finding the best answers to human phenomena.

English professor Christine Hult describes a primary difference between the sciences and the humanities as one of external (sciences) versus internal knowledge (humanities) of a phenomenon.[4] Scientists and medical research-ers discover treatments, even cures, for cancer. Social scientists might investi-gate the role of poverty in cancer prognosis or what nonmedical factors—for example, family support—might influence patient improvement. Humanities research can influence the ways in which doctors and other medical profes-sionals communicate with patients and their families and can show public health officials the most persuasive means of communicating important health information to the public.

The humanistic method is largely one of interpretation and critical evalu-ation requiring investigator participation. Subjectivity, not objectivity, rules. But subjectivity is an important value—it recognizes that we all go through our lives as subjects—humans—who must act in the world with critical judgment. Our inquiry involves the exercise of judgment; understanding that complex phenomena resist easy answers; logical, informed reasoning; an aes-thetic sensibility; various forms of primary evidence, especially the text itself; and secondary source research. Hult explains humanities research as offering no absolute proof for an interpretation or theory. Instead, humanities faculty make claims and support them with arguments and evidence that are crafted through hard work and rigorous study.[5] This demanding work leading to new knowledge includes multiple methods within the humanities researcher's toolbox, in part determined by discipline. Here, we provide a brief look at three of the many ways of investigating human phenomena through the per-spectives of the humanities.

Critical Analysis

Critical analysis is the study, evaluation, and interpretation of texts. A text can be a political speech, a film, an advertisement, an editorial cartoon, a fictional or nonfictional literary work, a national monument, or any other product of human activity. Scholars describe, interpret, analyze, and evaluate what is being communicated and make arguments about what that particular text may communicate to an individual, group, or society.

In literature, researchers attempt to understand the meaning (or mean-ings) of a poem, novel, short story, and so on. They use evidence in the work itself, but also through other approaches that account for context, culture, history, science, and more. We use the term "literary criticism" to designate a systematic approach to determining meaning in literary texts. This research involves formal, discipline-driven conversations among experts rather than informal conversations among a group of individuals or in a book club, for example. When students in our classes research literature, we ask them to become literary scholars while they are here.

For example, Charlotte Perkins Gilman's "Yellow Wallpaper" (1892) is a well-known and revered short story by a late nineteenth-century American writer. The first-person unnamed narrator is also the main character (protagonist) of the story. She is ill after giving birth to her first baby, or so she is told by her husband, a doctor. Bored and isolated, she begins to obsess over the wallpaper, ultimately attempting to "rescue" the woman she sees trapped inside.

Literary specialists explore meaning in this story in a variety of ways. For example, from the perspective of 2020, we can see the narrator may be suffering from postpartum depression, misunderstood in the late nineteenth century. Or we can approach meaning through gender relations—is the husband, John, attempting to control his wife or protect his wife, or both? What is suggested in the language and tone of the story, such as when the husband laughs at the narrator, and she writes, sardonically, "one expects that in marriage"?[6] The husband calls his wife "a blessed *little goose*"[7] and labels her desire to leave the house—where she has essentially been locked up for months—a "false and foolish fancy."[8]

We can look at the aesthetic qualities of the story, in particular the evolution of the wallpaper in the narrator's mind. And one of the main questions to consider is whether the narrator is mentally ill. One way to address these questions involves knowing something about accepted scientific knowledge regarding women's brains in the late nineteenth and early twentieth centuries. In 1905 Dr. Lapthorn Smith wrote that a woman's duties "do not require an extraordinary development of the brain." If the brain does develop, it creates a "decided barrier against the proper performance of these duties," since "the duties of motherhood are direct rivals of brain work."[9] From this perspective, it's not surprising that the husband would warn his wife not to give in to her "habit of story-making, which he considers a "nervous weakness."[10] A feminist perspective might view the narrator's increasing "mental illness" as actually the expression of a female artist's stifled imagination that could no longer be contained by the norms and expectations of women.

Ultimately, literary scholars search for meaning in a text while uncovering important knowledge about history and culture, gender roles, medicine and science, mental illness, socioeconomic status, the nature of creative expression, marriage, motherhood, mental health, and so much more. Literary research increases understanding of the work through multiple perspectives, expands and refines aesthetic sense and judgment, and contributes social and political commentary on important human issues.

Theory and Critical Theory

Theory is also significant to humanities research. College students often say they prefer "practice" classes to "theory" classes. Theory can be abstract; it's not easy to explain. And not everyone agrees on what theory means. In the sciences, a theory is a supposition or set of ideas to explain something, to base practice on, and to justify taking action. Theory operates in similar ways in the humanities. But it also has another function: theory asks critical questions to challenge assumptions and conventional wisdom.

Humanities scholars Jeffrey Nealon and Susan Searls Giroux explain theory by stating, "Everything comes from somewhere, exists, and functions in a particular context or set of contexts. . . . Nothing should be accepted at face value; everything is suspect." Theory helps us explain why something is the way it is, whether that something is a historical event, a well-known public speech, a poem, an archaeological finding, a religious document, and so on. Nealon and Giroux view theory as a set of tools that offer "opportunities to experiment."[11] Theory opens up conventional or received knowledge to new possibilities, perspectives, and ways of understanding, and this intellectual work can be both pleasing and/or uncomfortable, depending on the person and the idea.

One example to consider is when "history" is examined through theory. Most people think of history as a "self-evident concept"—"a record of things that have happened, an archive of the past's most pivotal events."[12] In this view, history is factual, neutral, and objective. Historians discover what happened; they don't surmise or guess what happened.

But as Nealon and Giroux demonstrate, questioning this conventional wisdom through critical theory reveals important new information and ways of understanding. History, they argue, is not neutral and objective, based on the following points:

- Historians interpret what they "find." The evidence does not speak for itself. Historians speak for the evidence.
- Historians assign order to evidence.
- Historians determine the significance of evidence they find and select what they document.
- History is always mediated through representations—words, images, symbols—whether from film, advertising, legal documents, oral history, or personal recollections. And there are layers of potential biases in these documents.
- Historians create a particular story about those facts. Historians who write about the same event have different versions of those events.
- A single history is a construction of the past, not a perfect reconstruction. Collectively, this forms the body of history.[13]

Whether the historian is a student using newspaper archives to write a ten-page paper about World War II or a professional historian writing a five-hundred-page book on the same topic, both historians intentionally and subjectively select, craft, narrate, and mediate what is ultimately read by others. They each decide what is most and least important about what they find. The professional historian will present more of that history in her five hundred pages, but it still is not complete or full. She made choices. Add to that a historian's conscious or unconscious biases. Most historians are ethical. But for a very long time, history that was documented and written down and shared in books was history about kings, and wars, and leaders. As Nealon and Giroux ask, what about the day-to-day lives of the soldiers?[14] Ultimately thinking theoretically about history both breaks down what we think we know and opens up new ways of knowing. These critical questions make it difficult to see "history" as the supposedly self-evident concept with which we began. Instead, we can distinguish *historical reality* (what happened in its entirety) from *historical knowledge* (what historians know and/or think they know).

But sometimes uncovering the distance between historical reality and historical knowledge is disturbing and difficult, exposing a different, and more accurate, view of what the dominant knowledge has circulated. Slavery is a powerful example. *How* does a nation deal with its "indigestible narratives," asks Edward T. Linenthal, referring in particular to "the enduring legacies of slavery, the Civil War, Reconstruction, Jim Crow, and . . . the modern civil rights era," that "stick like a fishbone in the nation's throat?"[15] With each new historical document or artifact, we learn something new about not only the horrors of slavery during the nineteenth century but also the strength of its continued legacies on Black Americans, race, and racism. For those who want to "put slavery behind us," so to speak, this kind of historical recovery creates feelings of shame, humiliation, guilt, and anger. Yet we must continue to understand and know our past in fuller detail. Theory opens up vital issues that complicate most of what we think we know—and we need to "re-know" it.

Newer Tools: The Digital Humanities

Humanities researchers are taking advantage of the tools offered by new technology, a method called "digital humanities." Situated at the intersection of computer science and the humanities, the digital humanities offer new research tools to explore the most important questions in the humanities—both those that have been asked throughout human history and those emerging from the contemporary world.

Two of these tools include visual mapping and computation.[16] At Stanford University, for example, humanities researchers are using creative spatial, textual, and digital analysis to investigate geographical history. One project, "Mapping U.S. Post Offices in the Nineteenth-Century West," is a visual, interactive map allowing the user to see an overall picture of 14,000 post offices dotting the landscape in the western part of the United States. In addition, the interactive nature of the map allows the user to hover over an individual post office (dot) to learn details about it, such as its location and the dates it opened and closed. The map also allows the user to look at the post offices in any periods of years, giving numerous pictures of the whole and how it changed over time.[17] Visual mapping and other digital tools enable humanities researchers to "better probe questions of how and why history unfolded the way it did and what makes us human."[18]

This sort of project allows historians, anthropologists, sociologists, and others to draw better conclusions about how the expansion of the West developed in a boom-and-bust cycle that, as historian Cameron Blevins says, was "as much about decline and collapse of communities as it was about growth." Not only does such a project mean that future historians won't have to transcribe "thousands of microfilmed handwritten ledgers from the time," but it gives scholars more specific information about how and why things changed in the West from 1840 to 1900.[19]

Humanities Research: Everything and Anything That Makes Us Human

As we've discussed methods of research in the humanities, we've also begun to identify a tiny portion of the nearly boundless subjects of humanities research. Humanities researchers investigate everything and anything that makes us human. This section barely scratches the surface but will hopefully convey the breadth and depth of what we study.

Humanities faculty research thoughts, ideas, and concepts. This list includes, for instance, human nature, how a society best functions, ethics, public memory, equality and justice, and the enduring questions discussed previously. We also study material things—texts, films, artwork, music, cultural practices, historical artifacts and documents, advertising, social media, ancient discourses, monuments, Facebook, and so much more. In addition, we study symbolic things—language, symbols, images, historical patterns, and milestone moments and events. Humanities researchers refer to the term "text" to capture a lot of these objects of study. By "text" we refer to something that has been deliberately crafted by an individual or individuals using words, language, symbols, and images and is open to interpretation.

Here's another way to understand the vast topics for research: It's not only about the quantity and range of topics, objects, texts, artifacts, symbols, and so on, but also the particular focus a researcher takes, from a general to very specific focus. For example, if we look at the broader topic of media and communication, we can break it down in so many ways, such as those shown in Table 5, among many others.

Each of these categories can be broken down even further and examined in multiple ways and for multiple purposes. As one example, many people think about major advances in communication technologies as the "digital revolution" occurring now. But these revolutions have occurred again and again throughout history. You may remember studying ancient Egyptian hieroglyphs—pictures of familiar objects that represent sounds—one of the oldest written communication systems in the world. Much later, other technologies—like the printing press, telegraph, radio, and cable—transformed communication capabilities and influence.

Today, much of the focus is on the newest tools, not only Facebook, Snapchat, LinkedIn, YouTube, and Instagram, but newer apps, like Peach, Slack, and Kik.[20] Looking ahead, we must prepare for augmented reality capabilities on Snapchat and Instagram, Instagram stories, and digital "hangout sites" like Houseparty, a video hangout platform.[21]

Each generation of communication technologies brings new questions and returns us to older questions: What social norms are emerging? How are writing abilities being impacted? Are there gender differences in the ways the tools are used? How are the tools reinforcing or transforming gender norms? Who benefits, and who loses, from these newest technologies?

As historian Gabrielle Spiegel asserts, humanities research paves the way for the "reassessment of social attitudes, values, aesthetics, and beliefs as a constant goal, a stance toward the world that is sufficiently flexible to enable us to adapt to shifting circumstances and agendas."[22] Objects themselves might be static, but how they are to be interpreted, and what meanings they hold, is always evolving as we gain new perspectives and understanding. We look through new lenses at texts that have been looked at before and at new texts through both traditional and newer lenses.

This discussion of texts and meaning and value changing over time raises other questions: How do we decide what is worthy of our time and research energy? What is or isn't valuable to study? This, too, is debatable and changes over time. Previously, we discussed various implications of Matthew Arnold's well-known reference to "the best that has been thought and said in the

Table 5. Humanities Faculty Research Within the Broader Topic of Media and Communication

Communication technologies	Film history	Media use among children and adolescents
	Gender and media	
Democracy and freedom of expression	Media and ethics	Political communication
		Popular culture
Digital journalism	Media effects	Social media
Digital media	Media history	

world" to characterize the humanities.[23] How is "best" determined, and by whom? Who and what is excluded from consideration, and why? And what happens when a new form enters the cultural and literary arena, for example, spoken word poetry?

These questions also pertain to what humanities researchers investigate. Many people inside and outside academia malign researchers who study graphic novels, for example, considered by detractors to be less valuable or meaningful than "the Great American Novel." But the humanities recognize that all forms of communication and human expression teach us something important about human beings. Does it mean graphic novels are masterpieces in the same way? Probably not for most literary specialists. But graphic novels provide other important insights, such as the technological tools used to create them, their impacts on other media, their impacts on literacy learning, and the impacts of the visual on readers'/viewers' meaning making.

This debate is especially relevant when it comes to the value and significance of studying popular culture in addition to "high culture." Some scholars think of graphic novels as nothing more than "expensive comic books"—as if comic books aren't worthy of study. And many people think that comics are not worthy of study. Surely, Arnold was not referring to comic books or graphic novels when he referred to "the best that has been thought and said in the world." Rather, he was referring to "high culture," which belongs to the elite. The "high" in high culture means status, acquired by expertise, money, prestige, intelligence, and "good" taste. High culture includes theater, classical music, opera, and the fine arts. Popular culture, the *culture of the people,* is generally looked down upon as far less sophisticated than high culture.[24] Consider classical music (high culture) and pop music (popular culture), for example.

Is anything and everything that is part of the human experience worth knowing about more fully and deeply? That's not a question we can answer. But we can say with confidence that meaning or value is not limited to high art. Arguably, what is consumed day to day by all kinds of people is more vital to understanding human experience and human nature, given its impact on our daily lives and ways of thinking. No matter what, for research in the humanities or any discipline to mean something beyond the researcher's understanding, research findings must be disseminated and shared.

Outcomes and Dissemination

Generally speaking, faculty research in the humanities is evaluated in the tenure and promotion process based on *peer-reviewed* articles and books published and papers presented at academic conferences. Perhaps you've heard the phrase "publish or perish" when referring to academics. It means that regarding the research component of one's workload, to obtain tenure and promotion, academics must publish their research. And not just publish anywhere. Peer review—evaluation of research by other established scholars in one's field—is a critical component of academic publishing. Peer reviewers are expected to be impartial judges of the quality of the research, checking for accepted research methods and practices and for accurate documentation and writing.

Across the disciplines, the primary aim of traditional academic research is to further disciplinary knowledge. Even when there are social implications, dissemination is usually internal, to other academic researchers, through peer-reviewed journals and presses.[25] Academic research pushes the boundaries of knowledge and is the foundation for social, economic, political, cultural, scientific, and environmental progress. Researchers build on and extend the work of the research that came before theirs. Sometimes, new research contradicts previous research, as discussed earlier, facilitating new ways of understanding older and newer phenomena and explanations.

The outcomes, or products, of humanities research are often intellectual, furthering knowledge and insights in that discipline and other disciplines. As a brief example, Laurie, a professor in writing studies and literary studies committed to multicultural education and one of the authors of this book, was stuck in an intellectual and ethical bind between what's called "foundationalism" and "relativism." She was concerned that the concepts of oppression, racism, sexism, liberty, compassion, and justice lose their ethical force if they are nothing more than a culture or community's contingent belief system. She felt stuck trying to reconcile multiculturalism's ethical aims and apparently relativistic implications.

She found help from anthropology professor Carolyn Fluehr-Lobban, who argues that while anthropology as a discipline has traditionally embraced relativism, many anthropologists have begun to challenge this view on the grounds that it promotes human rights abuses worldwide—especially abuses against women. After years of studying the practice of genital mutilation in the Sudan, and after reflecting on how she felt "trapped" by her simultaneous allegiances to cultural anthropology, the Sudanese culture, and feminism, Fluehr-Lobban concluded that we "need to be sensitive to cultural differences but not allow them to override widely recognized human rights."[26] By challenging her disciplinary norms and conventions, Fluehr-Lobban gave Laurie the tools to challenge her own by arguing that justice is the first principle of multiculturalism, thereby making egalitarianism and humanitarianism central to its work.

It's difficult to summarize this research here. In fact, it took Laurie several research publications that appeared in scholarly journals over a few years to work through these complex ideas and apply them to literary studies. Critics of humanities research tend to view this kind of internal communication as a major shortcoming—that humanities researchers talk only or primarily to ourselves in technical jargon about topics too obscure or abstract for anyone outside a small number of academic specialists to care. But we believe that this is a necessary part of the process before bringing research findings to the public. It was through these journal articles that the ideas were tested. Many other scholars who peer-reviewed article drafts provided feedback that helped Laurie rethink and improve her arguments. And this jury of her peers, along with journal editors, gave her ideas the credibility that enabled her to ethically bring them into her teaching.

Other practical, public uses of humanities research include cultural institutions such as museums and heritage sites, government agencies like the Centers for Disease Control and the Federal Bureau of Investigation, human and animal welfare organizations, political organizations, community decision-makers, and other groups and organizations. Drakeman points out that scholarly work by "professors of philosophy (both ancient and modern), law and jurisprudence, history, theology and religion, medical ethics, politics and social psychology" is often used in decision-making in such areas as health-care policy and Supreme Court cases.[27]

Nonetheless, there need to be more public uses of academic research. Increasingly, across the United States and the world, universities and colleges are gradually making efforts to bring academic research to the public in more intentional ways. Open-access, online scholarly journals are making research publicly available at no cost to the consumer. The digital, interactive map about the history of post offices in the western United States discussed earlier in this chapter is a publicly available study, published on the website of Stanford University's Center for Spatial and Textual Analysis. Digital technology is expanding the reach and accessibility of academic research.

The "public humanities" is a growing movement within the humanities to bring all facets of humanities research and creative activity like performance and art into public life. From larger programs and projects to individual faculty who carve out paths to reach into their communities, the public humanities are enriching communities and individuals across the nation.

For example, the public humanities programs funded through the National Endowment for the Humanities (NEH) "enable millions of Americans to explore significant humanities works, ideas, and events" and "offer new insights into familiar subjects and invite reflection upon important questions about human life."[28] As one among hundreds of examples, the NEH is partnering with the nonprofit organization Blue Star Families to expand its "Books on Bases" literacy program, which brings military and civilian families into dialogue through reading.[29] Most state humanities councils also promote and fund projects that benefit communities through humanities work. One primary example is the Pennsylvania Humanities Council (PHC) community stories projects that promote community development.[30] Imagining America: Artists and Scholars in Public Life has supported a wide range of projects, such as literacy programs in public schools, university community dialogues on a range of topics, theater performances to engender democratic participation, and much more.[31]

In our own careers, we are active in public humanities in different ways. Laurie is active in instructional projects that bring community partners and students together to produce and share local history and oral histories. For example, continuing a decade-long partnership through which our college and the Central Pennsylvania African American Museum (CPAAM) pursue the museum's mission to recover, uncover, document, preserve, and disseminate local Black history, undergraduate students interviewed twenty-two African Americans who lived in Reading during the Civil Rights Movement. From these rich personal stories, students, community members, and the professor researched, wrote, preserved, and shared *Through the Eyes of Local African Americans: Reflections on the Civil Rights Movement in Reading and Berks County, Pennsylvania.*[32]

Michele engages the public with her research through blogs, workshops, and panel presentations on popular and documentary films linked to her areas of research and teaching. For example, in conjunction with a local church and a local service organization, she's offered free "iParenting" and media literacy workshops to help parents understand what their children are seeing, hearing, reading, and engaging with in the media. In addition, she informs parents about the impacts of that engagement and how parents can help their children navigate the sometimes very problematic issues of mass and social media.

Finally, humanities research is shared beyond the faculty network of publications and presses through the thousands of students we teach. Our research informs our teaching, and bringing our latest research into our courses is among the most satisfying features of our research. A report by the Teagle Foundation finds that scholarship and teaching are "mutually sustaining endeavors." Student learning outcomes are stronger through "the interplay between teaching and scholarship. . . . Faculty are likely to have the greatest impact on students when their teaching is connected to their roles as expert scholars."[33] Put simply, humanities research as practiced by faculty is essential to student learning.

All of the students we reach as faculty circulate knowledge into realms outside academia, whether it's in the workplace, the coffee shop, their family's living room, or social media platforms. These are the many venues in which students share their sophisticated understandings of diversity and difference, of how a work of literature illuminates the tension between the collective good and individualism, or how advertising relentlessly promotes the objectification of women. Critical ideas are always debated in the public realm, and students and faculty contribute perspectives informed by research and sustained thinking and discussion, not just personal opinion or experience.

Humanities Research in the Classroom

Whether they are in physical or virtual classrooms, students benefit from the humanities and the principles, practices, and outcomes of its research. Debate and dialogue are central to both humanities research and to students' learning processes. One way to explain research—and students' reading of research in their classes—is that students join an academic conversation among texts and authors, including their faculty's texts.

As Chapter 6 will illuminate, faculty take these conversations to our students in classes, independent studies, and other programs and projects. We ask students to enter the conversation by reading what others have said, by analyzing and interpreting humanities topics and objects of study, and by contributing to that conversation through written work, dialogue and debate, performance, oral presentations, and so forth. It is that process of research and inquiry that we refer to as *meaning making*—looking at multiple perspectives in context and history; analyzing, interpreting, and synthesizing information; and analyzing and evaluating claims and evidence—that encourages the kind of mind training that leads students to acquire the core skills and knowledge sets most in demand by employers.

Chapter 6

Come into Our Classrooms: What to Expect in Humanities Classes

We have vivid memories of significant moments in our undergraduate humanities courses. Michele was a political science major, and Laurie was a sociology and juvenile justice major. For Michele, it was a professor who constantly challenged students in her rhetoric courses. An atheist, he even challenged their belief in God when students supported their claims with religious or moral arguments. Michele's peers were often frustrated, annoyed, and sometimes even angry. To Michele's knowledge, the professor never convinced a Christian to be an atheist, nor did any Christian student ever convince the professor to believe in God. However, Michele left these classes being able to effectively argue for her positions because she had been required to determine good reasons for her beliefs and good supporting arguments for those reasons.

Laurie remembers a philosophy course assignment that asked students to consider arguments about whether it is morally acceptable to prosecute former Nazis today for their actions that were legal under German law *at the time*, even though they are nearly universally accepted today as morally atrocious.[1] Laurie remembers feeling like she was in a whirlwind of competing ideas and beliefs that she had never encountered before in such a complex way, from universal morality to the complicity of cogs in the Nazi machine to the meaning of law.

Both of us recall that those conversations and assignments were not always comfortable, but they taught us to think through ambiguity and complexities. Our humanities moments described above taught us that humanity's most enduring and significant challenges have few easy answers because they are laden with multiple readings, histories, perspectives, possibilities, and, often, relationships to other "wicked" problems. We also learned that while multiple answers may exist, some answers are sound and logical and others are not.

This work is a kind of mind training (rather than specific job training) that teaches us to look beyond what we know and sometimes beyond what we thought we could even imagine and to constantly make connections between our past, present, and desired future. This mind training encourages students to do substantive, higher-order thinking, to understand the role communication plays in all realms of our lives, and to critically assess everything they see, hear, and read.

It's important to note that Laurie and Michele had these humanities moments several decades ago. So much in higher education teaching and instruction has changed over the past two decades across the disciplines, though in varying degrees and ways. New and exciting teaching methods and assignments, such as applied learning, internships, service learning, undergraduate research, and more, have made the humanities classroom an even more vibrant learning environment. In addition, what remains the same—and powerful—about teaching and learning in the humanities are intensive, rigorous reading of texts; engaging with complex theories; debate and dialogue; and the classic college research paper.

So, come into our classrooms where our students learn to think, write, debate, speak, and research like scholars. Students join their faculty and all who have come before us as together we address the individual's life and its "big questions" and attend to questions of the common good. The work that humanities students conduct can sometimes be frustrating, is often uncomfortable, but is almost always intellectually challenging and meaningful.

What's New in Humanities Teaching and Learning?

Teaching and learning in colleges and universities have gone through significant changes in the past two decades. The most overarching change has been far less reliance on lecture, known as "the sage on the stage" model of teaching. Lecture is often replaced or supplemented by what are called *active learning* strategies, defined as "any learning activity engaged in by students in a classroom other than listening passively to an instructor's lecture. . . . This includes everything from listening practices that help students absorb what they hear, to short writing exercises in which students react to lecture material, to complex group exercises in which students apply course material to 'real life' situations and/or new problems."[2] Sciences have long had labs—where students *do science*—to supplement lectures. This active learning model is now prevalent across higher education, including the humanities. In a history class, for example, students *do* history by examining and making sense of primary documents such as ads for runaway slaves and manumission (freedom) documents when learning about slavery.

Major changes have also taken place in cocurricular and out-of-class assignments. Collaborative projects, service learning and community-based learning, writing-intensive courses, internships, and other applied learning projects, identified by George Kuh as "high-impact" educational practices, are beneficial to students of all backgrounds in several ways.[3] Internships, once unheard of in the humanities, are more prevalent in humanities courses than ever before. The opportunities are numerous and range from social media internships with professional sports organizations to assisting curators in museums to editing technical documents in engineering firms.

Findings from a survey conducted by Hart Associates emphasize the extent to which employers value candidates' applied learning experiences in college. Large majorities say they are more likely to consider a job candidate who has participated in an internship, a senior project, a collaborative research project, a field-based project in a diverse community setting with people from different backgrounds, or a community-based project. In addition, 88 percent believe that colleges and universities should prepare students for applied learning projects, 73 percent believe such projects better prepare students for their careers, and 60 percent think that all students should be expected to complete a significant learning project before graduation.[4]

Both Laurie and Michele regularly use these and other "high-impact" practices in their courses. Laurie often implements community-based research in her courses in the form of oral histories, local histories, and storytelling. Laurie's students have produced twelve books and accompanying websites about this local historical work. Many of Laurie's students have published their humanities research in undergraduate research journals and presented at professional and student conferences. Laurie has also published three articles with a total of twelve undergraduate authors in professional journals.

Michele regularly includes cocurricular trips to places like Salem, Massachusetts, to study the witch trials and Washington, D.C., to study the intersections of politics, the press, and the First Amendment. She also includes course projects that ask students to apply what they've learned to the creation of public informative and persuasive events, such as college-wide recognition of World AIDS Day and a gender fair where students engage the campus community with their research on issues related to gender.[5]

These high-impact assignments are now an important part of many humanities classrooms. However, threaded through these newer teaching strategies in humanities courses are the main staples of humanities education: reading, understanding and applying complex theoretical concepts, the classic research paper, and discussion and dialogue. We turn to these teaching methods now.

The Staples of Humanities Teaching and Learning

Reading Difficult Texts

Learning in the humanities begins with serious, intense reading. Because work in the humanities is often not about *the answer* but helping us think through to *an answer*, students have to read multiple perspectives to get a sense of the issue's many layers. Sometimes, students in humanities courses have a standard undergraduate textbook where all of the important words are in bold, and boxes in the margins communicate key concepts. Often, though, faculty assign original works of literature or research, thereby challenging students to make meaning of the original words on the page rather than through a textbook author's perspective.

For example, in a communication studies course on First Amendment law that Michele teaches, students read the original court opinions as they were articulated by the Supreme Court justices who wrote them. Students wrestle not only with content but also with language from the 1890s that is very different from what we use now. The more elevated language of legal texts offers a challenge for the students, who also learn how to write in ways that are common in legal texts today. Court cases may be augmented with readings about the cultural and historical contexts of the cases from a textbook, illustrating to students how to consider and use cultural contexts in their own problem-solving.

Putting students in the position of reading difficult texts helps them succeed later. Students complain about the levels of reading comprehension these assignments require, and for good reason—they are certainly tougher than reading out of a basic course textbook. But as a former student of Michele's learned once she entered the workplace, these assignments serve students well. As part of her contemporary American political rhetoric course, this student read journal articles on topics such as gender and political communication, social movement rhetoric, wartime speeches, and other topics in political communication. These scholarly articles are written at a level typically seen in graduate school.

This former student noted that at her first job, an entry-level position at a national bank, she was put into a team of other entry-level employees who were all given organizational reports to read as individuals. She told Michele that while the others on her team struggled to read the complex, wordy reports and make sense of them, she understood them in terms of both content and structure. Reading journal essays that were often over twenty pages enabled her to participate in prolonged consideration of complicated ideas and to comprehend and follow their development throughout the paper. This kind of preparation for the work world is invaluable.

Wrestling with, Then Applying, Theory

Many of the essays this student read are theoretical pieces that applied theory to specific texts or contexts. For example, theories of visual communication were discussed in essays that focused on the visual rhetoric of the abortion debate and various social movements agitating for a stronger response to HIV/AIDS in the 1980s and 1990s and environmental groups trying to draw attention to their concerns about pollution. In other examples, theories about women's public address were applied to contemporary women who held political office, and theories about war rhetoric were applied to presidential speeches calling on Congress to declare war and the American people to support those wars. Tough theoretical concepts are often especially challenging for students—but in a good "make your brain work hard" way.

Faculty work to make theories understandable and relatable for students. For instance, Michele's curricula often include theories about constitutive rhetoric. Just the term itself, "constitutive rhetoric," intimidates students at first. But it is simply rhetoric—persuasive language and other modes of communication—that helps create and organize audience members into a collective identity, like "Americans," for the purposes of persuasion. Often, students study specific political speeches that work to build an audience through constitutive rhetoric. But Michele also tries to get students involved in the intellectual challenges of theory through less seemingly theoretical topics—like horror and science-fiction films. Michele's students study horror and science-fiction films released during the Red Scare period of the late 1940s and 1950s, like *Invasion of the Body Snatchers, Them!*, and *The Blob*, which scholars argue speak to fears of communism during this time.[6] Students probe the ways "good Americans," "bad Americans," and even all "Americans" are represented in the films. Students learn about how decisions regarding narratives and film techniques invite audience members to "root" for a particular version of American citizenship against the pods, giant ants, and blobs representing the Soviet Union.

Understanding constitutive rhetoric means that students understand strategies for crafting audiences amenable to their persuasion. To do so, they must learn about the function of language, symbols, and texts (including popular culture) that help construct our social realities. As Michele explains to her students, unless you've been to Italy and experienced it firsthand, what you know about this country called "Italy" is what you've read, heard, or watched about the country. These texts shape our beliefs about Italy and its tendencies. If someone only grows up watching mafia movies and hears little else about Italy, you can imagine what their assumptions about that country are. Similarly, we can look to U.S. films and discover how those texts attempt to shape perceptions of our country and its people. Thus, films can be a very useful tool for teaching students how language shapes and defines what we deem as "reality," as well as how those realities can be challenged using the same methods.

This knowledge comes in handy for marketers, professional writers, or anyone else who wants to persuade an audience in one direction or another. For example, if you're a marketer trying to think about ways to persuade women to buy a particular product, you first have to develop your idea of what you mean by "women" in your marketing rhetoric. Are they career women? Women who work at home? Young, middle-aged, or older women? You're trying to persuade them to "see themselves" in your advertising so that they'll consume your product, something you learned through studies of constitutive rhetoric.

Once students have engaged with all of these readings, ideas, and theories, we ask them to apply that knowledge through various assignments. Students participate in these scholarly discussions through various assignments helping them further understand the content and making these complex issues even more relevant to their education and lives. Students might be required to provide oral presentations in which they are asked to teach a specific concept to their classmates or debate two ideas about solving a problem related to crime with another student. They may be asked to create films or multimedia projects that communicate their understanding visually and verbally. They might be asked to create a performance piece illustrating a problem and their proposed solution. Or they might be asked to write a research paper that digs deeper into a specific object of study—it is this classic research paper assignment that we'll talk about next.

The Research Paper

A cornerstone of many humanities classes, the phrase "research paper" can strike fear in the hearts of students. Many students don't understand why they have to write research papers on a great work of literature, a film, or a contemporary world problem. "When will I ever need to know so much about *this?*" they ask us. However, research papers help students develop and refine a number of the skills they need to succeed during and after college.

Research papers, extended study of some topic, vary in what they require of students. Assignments may ask writers to compare and contrast ideas, to apply a particular theory or method to a text, to communicate the important general knowledge about a topic, or to make an argument. Whether it's a literary analysis, a report on the propaganda used during the Holocaust, or a film study, research papers teach students how to apply their research to problems or questions and to develop solutions from that work. The same skills one needs to determine the choice of one business or engineering proposal over another are, in large part, the same skills needed to develop a research paper.

Students writing research papers must also be able to locate, evaluate, and organize information from many sources so that they can cover a topic fully and/or craft the strongest arguments possible. Sources may include scholarly articles, books, popular press essays, trade journals, and other sources found via search engines and databases. With entire books and journal databases at their fingertips, students no longer have to comb the library stacks or microfiche reels for information. Abundant sources are right there on their phones. But the physical ability to get to that information and the intellectual ability *to use that information well* are two entirely different things.

Once a student has all of that data, they have to evaluate it by putting their critical thinking skills to use. A critical thinker looks at all available information and makes informed decisions about what research to use and what not to use if the research isn't strong, even if it's a perspective that suits a specific argument. They also have to synthesize the information they deem legitimate. This involves deciding what that information has in common and where it differs, turning fifty pages of research into much more succinct writing that they purposefully use throughout their paper to inform the argument.

Discussion and Dialogue

The three primary methods we have discussed thus far—reading, theory, and the research paper—are all critical foundations for discussion and dialogue, a central tenet of humanities teaching. Although dialogue and discussion are part of most everyone's everyday lives, the standards and expectations in the classroom are higher.

Humanities faculty teach students what it means to deliberate together in the constructive, respectful conversation required for democracy to thrive. As Angelo J. Letizia writes in *Democracy and Social Justice Education in the Information Age*, "Dialogue is one of the quintessential actions of life in a democracy. Students and citizens must come together and intelligently discuss their ideas, criticize their representatives and understand the issues facing them individually and as a society."[7] Civil discussion and dialogue are as important as ever, if not more so, in the highly polarized United States. Furthermore, the dialogue and discussion students practice and engage in again and again in their humanities curriculum prepares them for collaborative teamwork in the workplace.

It is through good dialogue that conflicts are solved and decisions acceptable to many people are made. In humanities classes, students talk a lot about uncomfortable topics like politics, religion, and racism. Sometimes these conversations are difficult and definitely not fun. They require a good deal of emotional and intellectual energy, and they can challenge some of our most fundamental beliefs about ourselves and our world. But they are necessary. These conversations are central to our humanity and to how we can better understand, and thus work and exist with, others.

But good dialogue isn't easy. Dialogue and discussion in humanities classes are not free-for-alls. Rather, they are carefully guided and facilitated based on a body of research of best practices and principles for class discussions. This includes, for example, recognizing who is typically silenced in public discussions and decision-making and to aim for more inclusive conversations. Scholar Rosa Eberly has called the classroom a "protopublic space," meaning students can practice civil and effective public discourse without the risks of actual public discussions.[8]

At the same time, dialogue and discussion in humanities classes are not and cannot be without risk. You are probably familiar with the commonplaces "Everyone is entitled to their own opinion" and "You need to respect everyone's opinions." Laurie begins almost all of her classes with a clarification about these common refrains, too often misunderstood. The First Amendment right to free expression means that the government does not have the right to forbid us or penalize anyone from saying what he or she wants to, with certain limitations, such as language that creates imminent danger. But students tend to think the First Amendment protects them from being judged based on anything and everything they say. It does not. Even though we are all entitled to hold any opinion, opinions are not all equally valid. Students' expressions of opinions in college will be evaluated on their soundness and reason. So, too, in the workplace, where your opinions and views will be aggressively assessed and evaluated by your peers and supervisors.

Humanities faculty engage students in difficult conversations in order to teach them *how* to think, not *what* to think, and how to express and argue for what they think in informed, civil ways. This is such a critical point. Several years ago, Michele addressed an audience of incoming students and their parents about the college's common reading for first-year students. In common reading programs, incoming students read a selected book over the summer to provide a common experience for all new students. In *Gaviotas*, a book about a community designed in Colombia that attempted to create a sustainable community, Alan Weisman challenges the very core of how most Americans live, including our consumption habits, our garbage production, and our contributions to pollution.[9] One parent in the audience publicly expressed his displeasure with *Gaviotas*, stating, "I'm not sending my son here to have him brainwashed into believing political positions that I don't believe."

Michele replied that the common reading was not an attempt to brainwash his son, but rather was part of a good education. As she explained to the audience, *Gaviotas* challenges the status quo and encourages the questioning of authority, two tasks necessary for progressing as a society. Being asked to consider a proposition, opinion, or even a fact that you don't agree with isn't brainwashing. It's part of the critical thinking process and a requirement for exceptional problem-solving. When students are challenged to think differently about a topic, they are learning to think *well*.

The parent in this story, like probably most everyone reading this book, had likely heard that "faculty members, on average, lean left."[10] However, as *Inside Higher Ed* editor Scott Jaschik reports, the research also shows that "conservative students and faculty members are not only surviving but thriving in academe—free of indoctrination if not the periodic frustrations."[11] Jaschik refers to research by Amy J. Binder and Kate Wood, which found that while conservative students may sometimes feel uncomfortable in their majority liberal colleges, "the students said that attending the colleges they did was a positive experience and helped shape their—conservative—political identities." The students said they wouldn't want to change institutions. Wood stated in an interview in 2012, "There was this sense that being in an environment they perceived to be overwhelmingly liberal did challenge them, but in ways that were positive and beneficial for them. It made them clarify values and ideas about different issues or about what being a conservative means."[12]

It is the job of humanities faculty to help students make the best arguments they can, whether we agree with them or not. For example, Michele does not believe in the death penalty. She has a moral objection to it, but she also believes that the available evidence points to the practice as counterproductive and cost inefficient. Still, she helps students craft arguments in favor of capital punishment in her public speaking class. Michele helps students understand that arguments for capital punishment as more cost effective than a life sentence are unsupported by evidence. And Michele helps her students make good arguments she disagrees with, such as a philosophical grounding of capital punishment being "an eye for an eye." Michele also teaches students how to identify the unstated assumptions inherent in the argument that the death penalty deters crime, for example, that a person committing a capital offense is thinking they'll get caught or even clearly thinking at all. And she teaches students about how to effectively present statistics on controversial issues such as gun control by checking source bias in data from the National Rifle Association (NRA) and the Brady Campaign to Prevent Gun Violence and assess these data against that of government agencies at the federal and state levels that deal with similar statistics, like the Federal Bureau of Investigation or state law enforcement agencies.

The Humanities Classroom, Real Conversations, and the Real World

It's too often suggested that humanities students aren't engaging in the "real world." But what could be more "real world" than engaging in the wicked problems that are part and parcel of humanity? For example, how can we best communicate across cultures in this increasingly connected world? What can early American history tell us about how to best deal with immigration? How does a poem by Langston Hughes give us insight into the philosophies and rhetoric of Black Lives Matter? What can the Triangle Shirtwaist Factory fire of 1911 tell us about labor relations today? What can the mistakes that were key to the ill-fated *Challenger* launch tell us about how communication in large organizations can function more effectively?

It's these "real world" questions that are often at the center of humanities course content. If students have taken their studies seriously, they are well prepared to confront a host of important issues, to solve problems, and to engage with members of local and global communities in ways that encourage civil dialogue and debate.

When discussing the humanities, Peter Burian writes, "Close reading, creative reflection, cogent response, spoken and written: these are skills the humanities foster and our students need, even if they do not recognize it yet." That last phrase seems the most important one for our purposes: "even if they do not recognize it yet."[13] Our students may not always realize it at the time, but they eventually discover that the skills and knowledge they've taken from their humanities courses have prepared them for what the real world entails.

Part III

Learning Core Skills and Knowledge in the
Humanities

Preface to Part III

Part III, "Learning Core Skills and Knowledge in the Humanities," explains how eleven of the top skills and knowledge areas employers seek from new college graduates are learned in humanities classes and programs. These include critical thinking; written communication; verbal communication; collaboration; problem-solving; creativity and innovation; technological competence and technological literacy; ethics; diversity, inclusivity, and equality; globalization, global understanding, and a global perspective; and leadership.

These chapters are based largely, but not exclusively, on studies done by the National Association of Colleges and Employers (NACE) (2011, 2012, 2013, 2014, 2015, 2016, 2017, and 2018)[1] and by Hart Research Associates (2010, 2013, and 2015) for the Association of American Colleges and Universities.[2] Each year, NACE surveys its employer members to rank particular core skills and knowledge areas. Employers are given a list of these core skills and knowledge categories and asked to rank them. In similar form, the Hart Research Associates' survey on behalf of the American Association of Colleges and Universities, sent to hundreds of executives in business and nonprofit organizations, asks respondents to rank certain core skills and knowledge.[3]

Each of the research reports measures some identical skill and knowledge sets. Both studies measure employer interest in written and oral communication skills, problem-solving skills, teamwork skills, and innovation and creativity. But they also measure different categories, too. For example, the NACE studies regularly ask about leadership, flexibility/adaptability, and organizational ability, while the Hart studies repeatedly ask about skills and knowledge linked to various diversity and global issues as well as civic knowledge, including knowledge about democratic institutions and values.

Because the reports don't measure the exact same skills or knowledge, it isn't possible to determine a precise list of top-ranked skills and knowledge areas most sought by employers. Muddying the waters even more, the Hart and NACE studies provide lists for employers to rank, which is different from asking open-ended questions about skills and knowledge preferences. In addition, the studies don't measure the same exact skills and knowledge every year. They tend to be mostly consistent, but some skills and knowledge can appear one year and not in the other. In addition, NACE runs its study every year, and Hart has published three studies since 2010. This set of circumstances makes creating the list of skill and knowledge sets we talk about in this part of the book both a subjective and an objective process.

We conceived the eleven chapters using both sets of studies, supplemented by extensive research. Objectively, we can compare the lists and see that written and oral communication skills, teamwork skills, and problem-solving skills are consistently ranked highly on both reports. Subjectively, we've looked at the places where the reports come close to asking about the same skills (e.g., Hart asks about the "ability to connect choices and actions with ethical decisions" and NACE measures "strong work ethic") and we've combined those ideas and others into one chapter on ethics. In another example, we've taken the categories in the Hart study that are focused on the "ability to understand the global context of situations and decisions," "the role of the United States in the world," "cultural diversity in America and other countries," "global issues and developments and their implications for the future," "awareness of and experience with" cultures and cultural diversity in the United States and globally, "staying current on global developments and trends," and proficiency in languages other than English and combined those concerns into the chapters on understanding and working with diversity and the global interests chapter. We include an additional chapter on critical thinking because it is fundamental to all skills and knowledge sets.

Therefore, we offer the chapters in Part III as the result of careful and thoughtful analysis about what skills and knowledge students are going to need in the workforce that can be learned, practiced, and refined in humanities courses.

Chapter 7

Critical Thinking

"This teacher really makes me think." For many faculty, this statement is the crème de la crème of student evaluations. Getting students to think deeply, reflectively, and complexly is the concept referred to as "critical thinking," a term bandied about a lot but also difficult to articulate and sometimes misunderstood.

One of the foremost researchers on critical thinking, Richard W. Paul, is often cited for articulating critical thinking as "thinking about your thinking while you're thinking in order to make your thinking better."[1] We love this sentence because it captures the critical mind in action, doing its best work. Critical thinking is intentional, multifaceted, and dynamic.

Terresa Carlgren argues that improving one's critical thinking is a never-ending process. "It must become a way of life," Carlgren suggests.[2] As we have shown in Part II of this book, critical thinking in the humanities is, indeed, "a way of life." Critical thinking cuts across all core skills and knowledge necessary for a deeper intellectual life, workplace success, and community and civic participation.

Critical Thinking in the Workplace

"Critical thinking moves individuals and organizations forward," writes Christian Fisher.[3] Workplace tasks like allocating resources, analyzing markets, analyzing and resolving personnel issues, assessing competition, hiring and promoting the right people, developing strategic plans and marketing campaigns, and resolving problems and challenges all necessitate effective critical thinking. "If you want to succeed in 21st Century business you need to become a critical thinker," states executive coach John Baldoni, adding that the global economy needs "sharp critical thinkers who can size up the situation, realize the potential where others may not, and seize opportunities through prompt decision making."[4] Ultimately, asserts Fareed Zakaria, critical thinking is "the only way to protect American jobs."[5]

Professor of management Christopher Neck conveys how important critical thinking skills are in the workplace.[6] Neck states, "The latest research shows businesses are *desperate* to attract employees with critical thinking skills, because organizations are undergoing such rapid change that they need employees to consistently introduce new, fresh ideas to stay ahead of the competition."[7] In a *Wall Street Journal* article, Melissa Korn cites a study by career-search site Indeed.com, reporting that job postings that include "critical thinking" in their descriptions have doubled since 2009.[8]

Brook Manville, writing in *Forbes*, also suggests that "leaders everywhere are seeking sharp critical thinkers," citing a 2016 Davos World Economic Forum report listing critical thinking as #2 in the top ten skills for the global economy in the year 2020.[9] Manville interviewed William Gormley, professor of public policy and government at Georgetown University, who stressed the need for critical thinking in a society that is interconnected and produces massive amounts of information. "And it's not just about assessing this or that argument," Gormley states. "We also need critical thinking to help set priorities and be adaptable to all the change coming at us."[10]

Based on their 2013 research study on the relationships between skills and salary, Yujia Liu and David B. Grusky claim that "the defining feature . . . of the last 30 years has been a precipitous increase in the wage payoff to jobs requiring synthesis, critical thinking, and deductive and inductive reasoning." They call it the "analytic revolution."[11] Critical thinking is directly correlated with higher earnings, indicating its significance in the current economy. Baldoni emphasizes "managing ambiguity" and "get[ting] comfortable with operating in an environment where change is constant and rapid decisions are required" as necessary components of critical thinking in the fast-paced economy of today.[12]

Critical Thinking, Higher Education, and the Humanities

Unfortunately, the findings of many studies on critical thinking in higher education merit concern. Scholars Phyllis R. Anderson and Joanne

R. Reid note that "there is ample evidence that this essential knowledge and skill set is not being taught or being acquired."[13] As Paul and Elder state, research shows that while faculty unanimously agree that teaching critical thinking is a central aim of undergraduate education, they are often unable to clearly define it or articulate how their instructional strategies promote these skills.[14]

Douglas Belkin reports that a *Wall Street Journal* analysis of a standardized measure of reasoning ability showed that many students' critical thinking skills do not improve over four years of college. The Collegiate Learning Assessment Plus, or CLA+, is taken by first-year students and seniors at about two hundred colleges across the United States. At more than half of schools, including some considered top tier, "at least a third of seniors were unable to make a cohesive argument, assess the quality of evidence in a document or interpret data in a table." Interestingly, the findings also suggest that "some of the biggest gains occur at smaller colleges where students are less accomplished at arrival but soak up a rigorous, interdisciplinary curriculum."[15] Moreover, Richard Arum and Josipa Roksa's 2011 book, *Academically Adrift: Limited Learning on College Campuses*, sent shockwaves throughout higher education, finding "no statistically significant gains in critical thinking, complex reasoning, and writing skills for at least 45 percent of the students in our study."[16]

However, *Academically Adrift* reports positive findings about the humanities. Students in humanities showed improvement in critical thinking, complex reasoning, and writing skills based on doing more reading and writing. The study relied on the Collegiate Learning Assessment (CLA) tool to measure critical thinking, analytic reasoning, problem-solving, and written communications. Arum and Roska note the "troubling differences" in curricular expectations and course requirements based on disciplinary concentration. For example, 68 percent of students concentrating in humanities and social sciences reported taking at least one course requiring more than twenty pages of writing during the previous semester. In addition, 88 percent concentrating in humanities and social sciences reported taking at least one course requiring more than forty pages of reading per week. Of students concentrating in humanities and social sciences, 64 percent reported both types of requirements, while only 8 percent experienced neither requirement.[17]

In contrast, students concentrating in business courses, education, social work, engineering, and computer sciences all reported relatively low likelihood of taking courses requiring more than twenty pages of writing or of experiencing both (reading and writing) requirements.[18] We shouldn't be surprised that humanities students showed improvement in critical thinking, complex reasoning, and writing skills, given that they write and read in their courses much more often than most other students.

In addition, critical reading of challenging texts like complex legal decisions and philosophical treatises is at the center of humanities courses. Critical reading means that students enter into dialogue with the sources they read and subject the reading's ideas and argument to the same questions about an author's premises, assumptions, biases, evidence, reasoning, and more.

Dialogue and discussion like those so common in humanities courses are also associated with critical thinking skill development. Abrami et al. studied more than six hundred published studies of critical thinking, concluding that involving students in dialogue and discussion in teacher-led, small student groups and in the class as a whole appears to advance critical thinking skills.[19] Dialogue allows for teaching students "how to think" rather than "what to think."[20] George Kuh, founding director of the National Institute for Learning Outcomes Assessment, has identified "high impact educational practices," such as collaborative projects, service learning and community-based learning, writing-intensive courses, internships, and others that study after study have shown to be beneficial to students of all backgrounds in several ways, including critical thinking.[21]

Similarly, learning activities that require students to apply their knowledge and skills to real-world problems and challenges also promote critical thinking.[22] Real-world application assignments benefit students through "practice drawing connections between the abstract concepts of critical thinking and the facts on the ground."[23] We turn now to one example of a real-world community-based learning project to illustrate how this happens.

Assignment: Critical Thinking Skills Applied

In 2015, undergraduate students in Laurie's upper-level rhetorical theory class partnered with a local museum to document the Civil Rights Movement (CRM) in the 1960s and 1970s in one northern city, Reading, Pennsylvania.[24] Students interviewed twenty-two African Americans who lived in Reading during the CRM to elicit these individuals' experiences. Topics ranged from the interview subjects' recollections of seeing and hearing about the major milestone events, such as the assassination of Dr. Martin Luther King, Jr. and the Rosa Parks–led bus boycott, to their participation in any civil rights activities on the national, state, and local levels. The eldest of the twenty-two interview subjects was 90, born in 1925, and the youngest was 62, born in 1943. The eldest was 43 in 1968 when Dr. King was assassinated; the youngest was 15.

From these rich personal stories, students, community members, and the professor researched, wrote, preserved, and shared a history of the CRM as experienced by African American members of the local community. This nearly 30,000-word manuscript, *Through the Eyes of Local African Americans: Reflections on the Civil Rights Movement in Reading and Berks County, Pennsylvania*, was drawn together primarily from the oral histories, also utilizing the limited documented historical information on the CRM in and experienced by residents of Reading. A total of 250 copies of the manuscript were printed and shared, and copies remain in the museum exhibit; moreover, the entire manuscript is published online.[25] For most students in the class, it was their first experience documenting and sharing history that was not already known or exposed. They knew their work would be read and preserved, and it would (and has) become a part of the historical record of the CRM.

They also knew from what they had read in the course that they were challenging the traditional story of the CRM as a successful effort to overturn racism and discrimination in the *South*. As they learned from historian Matthew Countryman, stories about the CRM in northern cities lead us "to see the problem of race in American society as a national rather than just a Southern issue."[26] They also learned from Harvard historian Leon F. Litwack of some of the "limits, significant limits, to the nation's commitment to racial justice" in the aftermath of the CRM and the relevance of those failures to see issues of race and racism in our nation today through new, more informed lenses.[27]

Within this overall framework that challenged most students' preconceptions and assumptions, how we got from the twenty-two individual interviews to write a larger story of the era in this community was an arduous, intellectually rigorous process that challenged students to put their critical thinking skills to work. It was a sizable amount of information that the students had to make sense of, both for the overall manuscript and each of their individually written sections. And they had to frame the book's content and organization around very complex issues that they read about, discussed, and learned throughout the semester. These topics included historical information about the CRM in northern cities, difficulties in writing African American history, the implications of missing evidence, and the necessity of oral history to a more accurate historical record. They also explored the limitations of oral history as historical evidence generally and pertaining to the CRM. These and other issues created layers of complexity that students had to juggle as they worked collaboratively with one another, community partners, and their professor. All the while, students were aware and conversing about the relevance of these issues from the CRM to the problems of race and racism that endure in our society today.

We turn to Paul and Elder's five capabilities of a "cultivated critical thinker" as a sound basis for explaining the connection between the assignment and the development of critical thinking skills.[28]

First, "*A cultivated critical thinker raises vital questions and problems, formulating them clearly and precisely*":[29]

Some of the pragmatic and conceptual critical questions and problems raised in this project resulted from the voluminous amount of information gathered in twenty-two interviews. Transcribed, the interviews averaged 6,000 words each, or a total of 132,000 words; that's equivalent to more than five hundred double-spaced pages of material. Some of the approaches that students considered included looking for patterns and overlaps as well as divergences, conflicts, or contradictions in the interviewees' responses. For example, what conclusions would students draw about the community's response to the sit-ins in the 1960s that began at a segregated Woolworth's lunch counter in Greensboro, North Carolina? Students had to make sense of very different experiences among the twenty-two interviewees. The students concluded that the shared sentiment in Reading was that the issues of segregation in restaurants such as Woolworth's did not apply to them in this northern city. One interviewee told a story about how he, then a teenager, and his friends walked into a Woolworth's location—which was not segregated—in Reading the following day with heads held high, almost daring the clerks not to serve them. This lighthearted story about teens contrasted with a far more serious one told by another individual of his cousin who was killed at the first sit-in in Greensboro after being run over and dragged by a police car. By raising "vital questions and answers" about the implications of keeping this outlier story out of the manuscript, students determined it must be included, or they would perpetuate the kinds of myths they knew their historical contribution needed to challenge.

At the same time, students were concerned about how these stories might perpetuate the myth that life for Blacks in the North was racism-free, when it was not. The students learned, first through Countryman and then through the interviews, of the term "Up South," an insider term used by Blacks acknowledging that "racial segregation was not enforced by laws but by the unspoken rules that told you not to walk on that side of the street or go to that swimming pool."[30] One of our narrators stated, "You're going north and you think you free to go anyplace and then they don't post signs but they'll come out and tell you that 'no blacks' . . . you think it's different in the North and it's not."[31] By including this quote along with the story of the relative killed in Greensboro, students did not reinscribe the myth of the CRM as an exclusively southern matter.

Next, "*A cultivated critical thinker gathers and assesses relevant information, using abstract ideas to interpret it effectively*":[32]

As noted above, students had a great deal of information to analyze, from the interview transcripts to the course readings. In addition, they read as many local newspaper articles about the CRM as they could find through an online searchable database. Students had to make decisions about evidentiary contradictions between the interview subjects' individual and collective memories that contrasted with newspaper accounts. They had been learning in this and other courses about research demonstrating stereotyping and racism in news coverage both historically, especially during the CRM, and in the present. For example, a 1969 local newspaper article reported "a series of disturbances involving more than 50 youths" on March 19, 1969, and "an estimated 100 youths, mostly Negroes, carrying baseball bats, chair legs, and rocks" on March 20, 1969. But the interview subjects who were old enough to remember that time described that two-day event differently, as in this passage:

> There was a day that a motorcycle gang was gonna burn us out. . . .
> I think it was the pagan motorcycle gang around here and that
> was a riot, nobody died, but there was a lot of fire and window
> smashing and things like that, because they had a night planned
> that they would come and drive all the niggers out of town. They
> came strong, maybe a hundred guys on bikes, and they pulled in

front of the place we were at and then a lot of conversation went
on and a lot of fights broke out.[33]

While coming face to face with racism's ugliness, students had to make
decisions about how to present this conflicting history in their joint project.
Racism as an action or attitude can be very concrete. It can be easy to see
in certain contexts. But "racism" is also quite abstract in important ways.
It includes a long history of chain reactions loaded with important political, economic, and social consequences, in addition to its moral component.
Students had to make their editing, storytelling, and organizational decisions
while considering the incredibly complex history of racism globally, nationally, and locally. They had to consider the impact of racism on the largest of
populations all the way down to the individuals sitting across the table from
them. In this case, students gained excellent experience interpreting information using the sometimes-abstract concept of racism.

Third, *"A cultivated critical thinker comes to well-reasoned conclusions and
solutions, testing them against relevant criteria and standards"*:[34]

For the overall manuscript, the students and community partners decided
on an introduction, conclusion, and five chapters, with two to eight sections
in each chapter. They came to this decision after testing out many other
organizational structures, from telling each oral history separately to focusing only on milestone moments. There were many subtopics to consider, and
students spent time grouping the subtopics in different ways before coming
to their final decision. For example, the students learned from historian Kim
Lacy Rogers that CRM oral histories often depict the individual's transition to becoming more politically engaged and aware.[35] They found similar
threads in the twenty-two interviews they conducted, and thus they chose to
include "political consciousness" as a subsection of a broader chapter titled
"The Politics of Racism as Experienced in Reading, PA."

At the same time, students decided they had to add an important component to the subsection, one that Rogers had not mentioned. Through their
analytical work, the students also concluded that together, the interviewees
told a story of a greater collective political activism than each individual alone
remembered. In so doing, they realized they were modifying Rogers's findings, confident in doing so because of the evidence in front of them.

Next, *"A cultivated critical thinker communicates effectively with others in
figuring out solutions to complex problems"*:[36]

The students did not work alone. Not only were they led by their instructor, but they also worked collaboratively with the community partners. These traditional-age, mostly white college students conversed and debated side by side with three African American participants who came to classes to help with decision-making. Generational, gender, racial, and educational differences meant students had to continually question their own thinking, evaluations, and judgments.

In one of many examples, the image on the cover of the book was created through a shared process of communication among the students, their professor, and community partners. The students came up with the idea to create a word cloud representing the range of the narrators' responses to the interview question asking them to characterize the CRM in one word (see Figure 1). When presented with this image, the community partners suggested different words for emphasis, so the students tried several configurations before settling on one. From all they'd read in the scholarly research and the twenty-two interview transcripts, the students were not confident that "freedom" was the best descriptor and leaned toward "unending," "illusionary," and "continuing." But by listening and learning, students yielded

Figure 1. Word cloud representing the range of the narrators' responses to the interview question asking them to characterize the Civil Rights Movement in one word.

to the desires of the interviewees, knowing it was really their story to tell.

Finally, "*A cultivated critical thinker thinks open mindedly within alternative systems of thought, recognizing and assessing, as need be, their assumptions, implications, and practical consequences*":[37]

As written above, the racial and other differences among the participants demanded that students interrogate their beliefs and perspectives as they interviewed, planned, and wrote. Students had to read between the lines of the newspaper accounts and the interview subjects' accounts. In one powerful example, one of the interview subjects described the present-day police killings of unarmed black men this way: "the young men who are being killed violently by policemen, I look at that and I think okay is this a new way to come through the back door?"[38] Most students did not at first understand that her reference to "coming through the back door" recalls egregious aspects of the Jim Crow South. Further, our students heard the phrase "Up South" for the first time, an insider reference to unwritten Jim Crow laws in the North. These accounts challenged many of the students to reconsider their misconceptions that racism and the CRM were then and now exclusive to the South.

Great Critical Thinkers

Gormley argues that "to be a great critical thinker you also have to be humble, and open-minded about your own views as much as those you are listening to. You have to be willing to admit you might be mistaken, and that what you believe might have to change—if the evidence warrants it."[39] The most important word in that sentence might be "evidence." Currently, proclamations of "fake news" abound in an environment in which too many people surround themselves with only the media, arguments, and facts that they want to see, hear, or read. Being able and willing to evaluate evidence that supports a claim is a crucial skill to have. The critical assessment of data underlies all of the processes linked to critical thinking.

Good critical thinkers are always open to other perspectives and arguments, but are also constantly assessing those perspectives and arguments, including their own, not only analyzing the supporting evidence used to make claims but also searching for the unstated assumptions and biases that may help prop up arguments. Excellent critical thinking requires courage. One must be willing to not only admit they are wrong but also challenge unstated assumptions, biases, incorrect data, conventional wisdom, and everything else that comes into play in decision-making. Thus, critical thinking isn't just an academic skill; it also says something about one's character when done effectively and fairly.

Employers in all facets of the economy and researchers in the academy make it clear that graduates with critical thinking skills are important to the success of any organization and are desperately needed. As the research of Arum and Roksa makes clear, higher education must do a better job of teaching critical thinking.[40] Faculty must be mindful of the processes linked to critical thinking and must ensure that assignments ask students to engage those processes. We also know that humanities students are well equipped as critical thinkers because of the work that they do in their courses.

Chapter 8

Written Communication

Writing is consistently at the top of two kinds of lists—the list of skills that employers say they want and the list of skills employers often complain that recent graduates don't have when they graduate. But what does writing look like in the workplace? In Table 6 we have listed fifty-four types (also called genres) of workplace writing, although there are certainly more. People look at this list and often wonder, how will a research paper on a comparison of historical periods of the Renaissance or a literary analysis of *Moby Dick* prepare anyone to write in workplace genres that they've never learned, practiced, or even heard of?

Table 6. Fifty-Four Types (Genres) of Workplace Writing

1. Activity reports	19. Health manuals	37. Product line brochures
2. Abstracts	20. Infographics	38. Proposals
3. Ad copy	21. Instructional books	39. Reports
4. Agreements	22. Instructions	40. Résumés
5. Annual reports	23. Labels	41. Signs
6. Articles	24. Legal briefs	42. Social media
7. Blogs	25. Letters	43. Software documentation
8. Brochures	26. Loan packages	44. Speeches
9. Business plans	27. Manuals	45. Style guides
10. Business rules	28. Marketing plans	46. Technical definitions
11. Business valuations	29. Memos	47. Technical descriptions
12. Contracts	30. Opinion pieces	48. Technical manuals
13. Direct mail writing	31. Pamphlets	49. Technical reports
14. Email	32. Personnel evaluations	50. Trial preparation notes
15. Employee agreements	33. Policies and procedures	51. Twitter
16. Facebook	34. Policy briefs	52. Web copy
17. Grant proposals	35. PowerPoint slides	53. Websites
18. Grant summaries	36. Press releases	54. White papers

With the exception of majors in professional or technical writing, most students do not learn or practice writing in more than a handful of these workplace genres. Yet, as the evidence suggests, humanities classes are critical for developing students' writing skills. One very simple reason is that in these classes, students write a lot. And employers recognize how important it is that students write in their college courses. The 2015 Hart study reports that "four out of five employers also say they would be more likely to consider an individual as a job candidate if he or she had completed multiple courses that require significant writing assignments."[1] But "more writing" is only one piece of a complex puzzle. In humanities courses, students learn *about* writing and the array of important decisions they must make every time they write.

Good writing goes far beyond the ability to write clear, succinct sentences and well-organized paragraphs—although these are vital elements. When you are tasked with writing anything, you are faced with numerous decisions, including some of these:

- How will I write for multiple audiences, each with a different expectation?
- How will I support my points?
- What kinds of sources should I cite?
- Should I take on a storytelling tone or a matter-of-fact tone, or both?
- Is traditional print text the best option, or should I use an infographic?
- What preexisting biases might I have, or might my supervisor have?
- Will my writing impact people's lives in any direct or indirect way?
- Will I be named as the author of this writing, and does this writing belong to me?

The point is that good writers should be able to write in any kind of genre as long as they have command of their skills and know what options they have and how and when to choose them.

As Max Nisen argues in *Business Insider*, "teaching writing isn't as mechanical as computer science. It comes with time studying the way other people think and write, writing a lot yourself, and a deep knowledge of culture and history."[2] Students experience this kind of writing instruction in their humanities courses, helping them prepare for postcollege writing in almost any career.

The Importance of Writing in the Workplace

The Burning Glass Technologies 2015 study reports that "clear communication, particularly writing, is at a premium in nearly every occupation," and writing skills are in short supply across the employment landscape. Further, job profiles often hide how important these skills are across the board, even in jobs that most don't consider as requiring writing expertise. For example, writing "is the second-most-requested baseline skill for Engineering and IT Occupations" and "even among 'low-skill' jobs (those paying less than a national living wage) it comes in fourth." The highest writing skills gap is in hospitality and food/tourism.[3]

But there are also large writing skills gaps across the economy, according to the report, and in jobs requiring various levels of writing ability. There are large gaps in jobs with clear writing demands, such as marketing and human resources, as well as in professions like information technology, where the role of writing is less obvious. The report makes it clear that "strong writing skills can set a job seeker apart when entering these fields."[4] George Anders quotes Liz Kirschner, head of talent acquisition at a Chicago investment research firm, who emphasizes the importance of already knowing how to write on graduation: "It's easier to hire people who can write—and teach them how to read financial statements—rather than hire accountants in hopes of teaching them to be strong writers."[5] That's also because workplace writing requires critical thinking.

According to Anthony P. Carnevale, from the Global Institute on Education and the Workforce at Georgetown University, "writing on the job often requires analysis, conceptualization, synthesis and distillation of information and clear articulation of points and proposals."[6] Jeff Bezos, founder and CEO of Amazon, is well known in business circles for beginning meetings with senior executives in an unusual way. Rather than viewing the more typical PowerPoint presentations and listening to the accompanying talk, Bezos's executives read six-page printed written memos—he calls them "narratives"—and make notes along the margins as they prepare for discussion. In an interview in *Fortune* magazine, Bezos explains, "There is no way to write a six-page, narratively structured memo and not have clear thinking."[7] Bezos, named *Fortune*'s Businessperson of the Year in 2012, identifies the close, intertwined relationship between good writing and clear thinking, implying that written communication is more complicated than often thought. Fareed Zakaria puts it this way: "No matter who you are—a politician, a businessperson, a lawyer, a historian, or a novelist—writing forces you to make choices and brings clarity and order to your ideas."[8]

Humanities graduates have that ability to navigate their way through workplace writing. Paul T. Corrigan reports on a survey he conducted in 2016 in which he received hundreds of replies from English major graduates who emphasized the significance of written communication to their array of careers. For example, John Orzechowski (Southeastern University, 2008), who works at a nonprofit, describes how his ability to write, communicate, and think has been important to his success as he's moved throughout the organization:

> I initially provided direct assistance to low income Tennesseans who need access to health care services or coverage. For that work, being able to clearly communicate was an asset. I drafted many letters, appeals, etc. on behalf of clients. We also use client stories to educate the public about needed policy changes, so being able to tell their stories in a compelling, straightforward way is essential. I now have a number of roles including writing and managing grants, handling the organization's financials, and preparing reports for boards and funders.[9]

Lydia Dishman relates the story of Kristin Peterson, speechwriter for the executive vice president of the AI and Research Division at Microsoft, who majored in French literature:

> As a speechwriter for the [executive vice president] of the AI [Artificial Intelligence] and Research Division at Microsoft, she needs to be well versed in the language of artificial intelligence (think: homomorphic encryption, GPU clusters, FPGAs, deep reinforcement learning, topological qubits, and the like.) To most of us, these are as foreign a language as any we don't understand, but it's Peterson's job to tell a story about their meaning and potential. . . . For her part, Peterson relies on metaphors to connect what exists today with the glimmers of potential that AI has in health care, education, and other industries.[10]

Many people, including the authors of this book, barely recognize or understand many of the words and concepts that Kristin writes about in her job. Yet her degree in French literature helped her become proficient with another kind of "foreign language." So how did graduates like John and Kristin develop their writing expertise and flexibility in their humanities courses? Verlyn Klingenborg, in a *New York Times* editorial, proclaims that "clear, direct, [and] humane [writing]—and the reading on which it is based are the very root of the humanities." These disciplines are "ultimately an attempt to examine and comprehend the cultural, social and historical activity of our species through the medium of language."[11] In other words, language in all its forms and media is at the heart of the humanities.

Writing, Higher Education, and the Humanities

The need for students to develop good writing skills is recognized throughout higher education. As noted by the Association of American Colleges and Universities, "Written communication abilities develop through iterative experiences across the curriculum."[12] The vast majority of college students take at least one first-year writing course, often referred to as "English composition." Many colleges and universities also have variations on Writing Across the Curriculum (WAC) and Writing in the Disciplines (WID) programs. George Kuh identities writing-intensive courses, such as those in WAC and WID, as one of the "high-impact" learning experiences for a wide range of students, as evidenced by research.[13] Both programs emphasize the importance of writing in courses across all disciplines and the understanding that in addition to "learning to write," students "write to learn." That is, writing fosters critical thinking and students' higher-order learning.[14]

Chapter 7 pointed to empirical evidence for the importance of writing and reading in the college curriculum in Richard Arum and Josipa Roksa's 2011 book, *Academically Adrift: Limited Learning on College Campuses*. Students in humanities showed improvement in critical thinking, complex reasoning, and writing skills based on doing more reading and writing.[15] Moreover, author Jeffrey J. Selingo affirms how important it is that students write, and write a lot—more than most students are doing based on the courses they're taking. Selingo asserts that "the 10,000 hours theory"—the idea "that it takes roughly that amount of practice to achieve mastery in any field"—is as relevant to writing as any other skill. Students who can become competent writers through college work will "also be able to compose anything on the job, from PowerPoint slides to reports."[16]

Overall, research tells us that the most important element of improving writing is to write a lot. Barbara Walvoord, one of higher education's leaders in college teaching, identifies the crux of the issue: *"In as many classes as possible,* students need to write frequently, receive feedback, and learn metacognition."[17] Nowhere is writing more prevalent and rigorous from course to course to course than in humanities majors. For example, students in a history course write analyses of President John F. Kennedy's executive orders to understand them in the larger context of his presidency.[18] Students in a philosophy course may present their research essay findings to the class by creating a poster presentation to visually showcase the findings.

Further, many faculty in the humanities have added digital writing assignments to their courses. "Writing no longer means merely words on the printed page," according to Writing, Information, and Digital Experience (WIDE) Research Collective at Michigan State University; it "means selecting among and scripting multiple media, including photographs, charts, video, images, audio, diagrams, hyperlinks, and more."[19] In addition, students compose blogs, websites, digital stories, and infographics. In a digital media course taught by professors Ingrid Sturgis and Hab Dugo, students study both the technical and conceptual foundations of digital media as well as relevant issues such as copyright and networking. They also develop digital media assignments such as an ePortfolio using WordPress.com; open and use accounts for Facebook, LinkedIn, Twitter, Google, Instagram, Socrative, and YouTube; and create media log spreadsheets.[20]

"Real-world" writing through applied projects—for example, writing reports about the campus art gallery—is increasingly common in the humanities. Laurie's students in a capstone course for the professional writing major worked with a local nonprofit and a city councilperson to research and write policy briefs to convince the local city council to adopt the recommended policies to enhance citizen participation and representation in local governance.[21]

As importantly, nowhere else are students taught consistently *about* writing—in addition to writing skills—than in humanities courses. Writers must be aware of how language works in the world and its influence on shaping attitudes and beliefs. Word choices such as "policemen" or "police officers," "projects" or "public housing," "riot" or "protest" have consequences in terms of shaping attitudes toward specific groups. In humanities classes, we teach students to analyze language choices in what they read, view, and listen to—analyses of everything from literature to film to music and Twitter—and in what they write. Surely, our nation is sensitive to the use of language, and many people are fired from their jobs for using language carelessly or recklessly. Humanities courses teach students to think about language in these deeper ways.

Finally, we suggest that it is in humanities classes where students learn that good writing requires awareness of and attention to numerous decisions as they research, write, organize, revise, and edit. We get it: Students often write a paper the night before it's due and give it barely a read-over. While we expect this will happen and understand there may be times it needs to happen, we do not recommend it as a general practice for any student. Put simply, the best way to transfer and adapt your skills and knowledge from humanities writing to workplace writing is to be very aware of options and decisions and to pay careful attention to every word. And it is in humanities classes where writing is both more frequently assigned and more frequently taught.

Assignment: Making Writing Complexities Visible

The assignment "Neighborhood Narratives" promotes the complex decision-making and problem-solving required in good writing and fostered in humanities courses. This assignment was developed by Laurie in a course about the role of narrative and storytelling in social change. The main text for the course was *Telling Stories to Change the World*, which includes more than twenty essays about various storytelling projects around the globe addressing an array of social justice needs.[22] Students read each essay with two primary considerations: understanding what the storytelling project was about and how it was shared publicly, and how the authors of each essay wrote the essay, considering such issues as point of view, writerly voice, and collaboration.

Then students turned their attention to social and economic conditions in Reading, Pennsylvania, to explore the way the local and national media have constructed dominant narratives of the city's poverty and people in contrast with its past thriving economy. Reading was a boomtown throughout much of the twentieth century, home of the Reading Railroad (the one on the Monopoly game board), and among the nation's leaders in coal, steel, textiles, and other business and industry. In 2011, however, Reading was ranked the poorest of cities in the United States with a population of 65,000 or above. Census data from 2013 indicate Reading's population to be 62 percent Hispanic/Latino, 9 percent African American, and 26 percent white.[23] Allan Mallach, senior fellow at the Center for Community Progress and the National Housing Institute, notes that Reading is much like other northeastern cities that helped transform the U.S. economy from agrarian to industrial and now struggle with a high unemployment rate.[24]

It's important to note that in this course and assignment, students had to learn and think about many topics in addition to those related to writing. The course brought together such subjects as media literacy, immigration and immigration history, cultural difference, community building, economics, postindustrialism, media literacy, theater and performance, and stereotyping and discrimination. Furthermore, these topics were interrelated and overlapping, another significant point about humanities teaching.

The assignment illuminates the depth and complexity of thinking in humanities writing assignments that foster strong skills and deep knowledge about writing. Students take these skills and knowledge into the workplace, able to tackle whatever writing situation they face. In part 1 of the assignment, working in pairs or small groups, students facilitated story circles (group interviews) with residents of Reading. From there, they coauthored a nonfiction narrative that closely related the stories the participants told in the story circles. Students had many choices to make as the narrator of other peoples' stories—form, voice, and arrangement, for example—but they were not to interpret meaning beyond those choices. The final written stories, approved by the story circle participants, were shared publicly through a printed book and a website.

In part 2, students wrote or cowrote analytical essays about part 1. The assignment description instructed them to analyze the neighborhood narratives project—as a whole or any of its "parts"—from any of the intellectually challenging concepts they'd read about and discussed in this class. Ultimately, their essay needed to accomplish two kinds of intellectual work: (1) provide insight into the neighborhood narratives project; and (2) provide insight/new perspectives on the concept(s) they were writing about, such as shared authorship and collaboration; authentic and nonauthentic voices, revised narratives of Reading, social justice and injustice, narration and narrative, and more.

In part 1, students paired up to lead story circles and cowrite the narratives. The class was composed of a diverse group of eleven students, including two African American students, an Asian American student, a Latinx student, and five white students. All groups being interviewed were African American and Latinx. Only two of the college students were from Reading; some lived in the suburbs of Reading, and others lived elsewhere in Pennsylvania or in another state. So right there, even the questions regarding "who is writing?" and "what are their beliefs and values?" are multilayered, since they wrote as pairs. The topic was fraught with challenges, given the racial, ethnic, and class divisions in the city and in the nation. The question of audience was also multilayered. Officially, the audience was the local community; the narratives were intended to inform the local public about these residents' lives and neighborhoods to perhaps provide alternative perspectives to the dominant narratives. But the students were also very aware of the story circle participants as another audience. How would they react to the way the students told their stories? Would they think their stories were told fairly and accurately? And of course, their professor was a third audience. What was she looking for in the students' writing?

The students' main purpose in part 2 was to satisfy the requirements of the analytical essay, which in itself was a bit tricky. The instructions for the essay stated: "Like the essays in *Telling Stories to Change the World*, your essays do not need to adhere to 'standard' academic essay form but can be creative as well as scholarly. However, your essay must advance a thesis and support that thesis with sound evidence—even if it does so by playing with style, narration, and form." In other words, students were encouraged to take risks in organization, format, style, and voice, much like the essays they'd read throughout the semester. At the same time, they were expected to provide insight on the neighborhood narratives project and to provide new perspectives on the concepts they were writing about.

The essays' purposes were anything but simple, and the context they were writing in also required that decisions be made. For example, one student who grew up in Reading positioned herself as someone whose mission it was to get the more authentic insider stories out to the public to break down stereotypes. Another student wrote about the challenges of collaborating across generations and ethnic borders.

Further, students had to adhere to elements of analysis and critical thinking expected of them in scholarly writing in an upper-division English course. They also made decisions regarding modes of reasoning, evidence, organization and format, sentence structure, and more. Students wrestled with the differing nature and extent of facts and evidence in parts 1 and 2. In part 1, all "facts" came directly from the story circle interviews. "Facts" is in quotes to stress that in this rhetorical situation, students did make some judgments about facts. Part of their job was interpretive: to present overarching themes based on the story circles as a whole. They also quoted specific dialogue from some participants and made decisions about what to include and exclude about dialogue.

In the analytical essays, students relied on the facts of the storytelling, for example, how many participants spoke and how many times, what the participants said, and what occurred when they met for the second time so that participants could read what the students wrote. They also used secondary sources, including the essays from the class text. Primarily, they used their own expertise as humanities students studying writing, voice, storytelling, and other matters, reflecting and analyzing the experiences and issues in writing these essays with what they'd learned in this and other classes.

Writing in Public

Another statement by Klingenborg strikes us as important and meaningful: "Writing well isn't merely a utilitarian skill," he says. "It is about developing a rational grace and energy in your conversation with the world around you."[25] Beyond the classroom and the workplace and into the world, a writer's "rational grace and energy" in public conversations are equally, if not more critical.

The world is a complex place, as we all know. We need dynamic, energetic, graceful writers and thinkers to lead, facilitate, and guide public conversations, from lobbying congress members to presenting proposals in a local city council meeting to writing the flyer for a local youth sports league. To argue persuasively about ideas, issues, and everything else that truly matters in people's lives, writers must be thoughtful, attentive, and ethical. Good writing matters in college, the workplace, and the world.

Chapter 9

Verbal Communication

When asked about the time it took him to write his speeches, Woodrow Wilson is said to have answered, "It depends. If I am to speak ten minutes, I need a week for preparation; if fifteen minutes, three days; if half an hour, two days; if an hour, I am ready now."[1] Similarly, a late mentor of Michele's, John Gossett, always noted that, usually, we don't need more communication; rather, we need *better* communication. Wilson and Gossett understood that it takes very little effort or skill to just talk, but that it takes exceptional planning, skill, and effort to communicate important information succinctly and effectively, both publicly and interpersonally.

Leaders across business and industry also understand the importance of good communication skills. Steve Burnett, founder of the Burnett Group, a New York marketing and communications firm, stresses that "regardless of the changes in technology, the market for well-crafted messages will always have an audience."[2] Google's Project Oxygen confirmed that communication skills are key to success, even in the technology industry. In fact, surveyed employees stated clearly that, most importantly, they wanted their bosses to be good communicators.[3]

The humanities discipline of communication studies includes a variety of different fields that focus on human communication, including but not limited to rhetorical studies, interpersonal communication, intercultural communication, group and organizational communication, health communication, and others addressing communication in specific contexts. All of these fields address problems associated with better communication in interpersonal, public, and work contexts that so many people, families, and organizations need.[4]

For most people familiar with college curricula, communication studies is most often connected to public speaking class—the class a majority of students dread. Public speaking classes teach students how to research and construct ideas and arguments and then present their speeches effectively to an audience. But being a good communicator is much more than just good public speaking.

In fact, oral communication ability is recognized as one of the skills (along with writing, customer service, supervision, and basic mathematics) with the largest gaps between employer demand and the supply of workers with those skills.[5] But in spite of employers' constant call for increased communication courses in college, less than half of all undergraduate institutions require oral communication training for all students.[6] Within this context, it is fortunate that students can also sharpen their communication skills in their humanities courses.

Effective Communication in the Workplace

Anthony P. Carnevale and Nicole Smith note that almost half of the top twelve skills "most valued in the economy are essentially communicative in nature," and the "ability to listen, interpret, follow instructions, and communicate these to other people both orally and written appear[s] time and time again in various jobs—even those with relatively lower levels of education required."[7]

The cost of ineffective communication for organizations and businesses is clear. Watson Wyatt reported that companies with highly effective communication practices had "47 percent total higher return to shareholders" over the five-year period between mid-2005 and mid-2009 when compared to companies with "less effective communication."[8] A study of four hundred companies around the United States and United Kingdom of 100,000+ employees each found that employee misunderstandings cost around $37 billion per year; the average per company was a staggering loss of $62.4 million per year.[9] In its own research, Best Buy found that for every 0.1 percent of increased employee engagement, stores saw more than a $100,000 increase in store annual operating income.[10]

In health-care contexts, communication failures led to 1,744 deaths and accounted for 30 percent of health-care malpractice claims and 1.7 billion in revenue lost to those claims from 2009 to 2013.[11] Further, Tina M. Marrelli states that nurses' communication skills are as important as clinical judgment. Nursing leaders listen, solve problems, and create excellent team environments.[12]

As Carnevale and Smith note, workers are communicating in some way throughout the majority of the workday, including messages about problems, procedures, and general information.[13] For example, effective communicators will be able to deal more successfully with people who have communication styles different from their own; they will be rhetorically sensitive, to use the language of communication scholars. They will understand styles, such as formality and informality, and strategies of communication, such as taking a firm stand or being flexible and collaborative. Excellent communicators will also have outstanding listening skills, which require paying attention to the speaker, listening with an attitude of wanting to understand, and being patient instead of trying to anticipate what someone is going to say.

Workplace communication—often referred to as "social skills"—is vital regardless of where one falls on the earnings scale. Moreover, jobs that require low levels of communication skills (including many in the STEM fields) have fared poorly and/or are those at the highest risk for automation because there is no technological replacement for a person who can foster interpersonal relationships and persuade people in the room.

Effective communicators are adept at forming and maintaining effective bonds with individuals on a one-on-one basis and in teams. They effectively advocate interpersonally and in public communication, building reasoned arguments designed to influence their specific audience. Conflict management skills are at a premium. Thus, successful communicators will effectively evaluate the different elements of the conflict and choose the right conflict style for each situation. Excellent communicators will also be able to decode nonverbal communication, for instance, the ways in which facial expressions and body posture can support or contradict verbal communication. People with strong communication skills will also fairly analyze their own communication style and others' responses to them to adjust their styles.

David J. Deming's research shows that while the share of tasks requiring social skills grew by 24 percent from 1980 to 2012, the market for math-intensive tasks grew only 11 percent, and other jobs "characterized by routine work" have continued to decline.[14] Measuring data from the 1979 National Longitudinal Survey of Youth, Deming also found a correlation between higher social skills and earning more money, even after controlling for education, standardized test scores, and job type. Hence, whether we're talking about one's role in the larger economy or one's role in an organization, department, or work team, effective public and interpersonal communication skills are key to success.

Communication Education in the Humanities

Graduating college as a competent communicator means being adept at message development and organization and recognizing context and what types of messages best suit each situation. This includes supporting arguments, managing relationships and conflict, enacting appropriate conversational and information exchange skills, communicating in groups, and effectively evaluating the communication of others.[15]

Humanities courses facilitate various kinds of verbal communication skills development. Students can speak to learn and learn to speak.[16] That is, as students prepare and practice presentations on specific topics, they are spending time thinking about the topic, and as a result, they come to know and understand that information better. Likewise, as they are planning and delivering those presentations on course content, their verbal communication skills increase.

In humanities courses, they do both. Students regularly give oral presentations in classes, giving them the chance to learn, understand, and organize information in ways that clearly communicate their messages. They also practice delivering those ideas to an audience with a conversational delivery using only notes, rather than reading or memorizing a presentation.

In a history course, "speaking to learn" is an excellent way to engage students with smaller sections of a long book, as well as the entirety of it. Students might be divided into small groups and asked to read a certain number of chapters and then report back to fellow students. In this case, students are "presenting to learn"—the assignment may require that students first summarize the section of the book read and talk individually about arguments or information in the book that interested them. Students are also "learning to present" as they get experience organizing a group and an individual presentation, thinking about audience analysis, and using visual aids while educating others on the chapters they read.

Students might also engage in structured and unstructured debates in a number of their humanities courses. For example, philosophy students might be asked to debate whether or not the death penalty should exist. In order to inform their arguments, students must research the topic, including arguments and support for those arguments that differ from the ones they are defending. In preparing for this assignment, they are "speaking to learn"—they're encouraged to look at more than just one side of the debate, to learn about perspectives that they initially even disagree with, and to make choices about which arguments are strong enough for presentation. As they debate their fellow student(s), they are learning to speak in a way that is structured, persuasive, and confident. In the unstructured debate category, students regularly engage in discussions about ideas and issues addressed in their humanities courses, giving them a chance to polish their discussion and social skills in civil, constructive conversations about important issues. Good public discussion skills are also a part of the skill set that these more unstructured discussions offer students the opportunity to develop.

Students in the humanities also get experience evaluating other people's communication—an excellent way to learn about better and worse communication styles and strategies. Students in political science may write an analysis of a presidential address and how it's tailored to a specific audience. Students in an anthropology class may observe and report on what happens when they violate the expectations of nonverbal communication, for example, by turning around and facing toward everyone in an elevator. Students in art history may discuss how a historical event was impacted by the visual messages of art before and after the event, and students in an organizational communication course may read and discuss a case study of how an organization's communication mismanagement affected its success. Regardless of the assignment, students in the humanities are constantly learning about and analyzing the successful and unsuccessful communication of leaders, individuals, small groups, and larger organizations. By studying the successes and failures of others, students leave the classroom able to avoid common communication errors and capable of crafting effective messages in interpersonal, group, and public contexts.

Each of these practices helps students develop communication skills they can use later in their careers and community work. For example, crafting arguments in favor of one policy over another prepares students to construct arguments about the benefits of one marketing plan over the other. Navigating a tough, informal discussion on the intersections of race and class in the United States prepares students to make their way through tough conversations about the ethics of one decision or another in the boardroom. Presenting speeches on course content prepares students to address a room ready to hear their business plan. And by working on group projects in which interpersonal, group, and conflict management skills are necessary to get the job done, students are ready to enter a workforce increasingly structured in work teams as opposed to individual work.

Assignment: Conflict Management Personal Inventory

The personal inventory assignment from Michele's conflict management class requires presentation skills, the use of data, and a thorough understanding of their personal inventory of social skills linked to conflict management.[17] In other words, students are learning how they communicate while honing their communication skills. The assignment uses the Thomas-Kilmann conflict mode instrument (TKCMI) to determine a student's general conflict style tendency. The instrument asks students to compare two statements at a time and choose which one most represents their tendencies. For example, students must choose between "I consistently seek others' help in working out a solution" and "I try to do what is necessary to avoid useless tensions."

Once they've completed all thirty sets of statements, they score themselves to determine to what extent they tend to use a particular conflict style (competing, collaborating, compromising, avoiding, or accommodating). Since there is no one "right" conflict style, only the style that's "right" for a specific context, there is no judgment placed on student findings regarding their conflict style tendencies. Next, students ask three people in their lives with whom they've had several conflicts to evaluate the student using the TKCMI. Generally, students give these evaluations to parents, siblings, significant others, roommates, close friends, and coworkers. Each person is asked to rate the student using the same criteria they used to rate themselves. The students score the three additional instruments to get a sense of how others perceive their conflict style tendencies.

Once all instruments are completed, the students analyze the quantitative data, comparing those scores separately and within the context of the relationship with the person doing the scoring and then comparing all of the scores with each other. What were the similarities and differences in scoring between all three people, and what accounts for those similarities and differences? Students must consider their scores in context, including their relationship to the other person, the situations they tend to be in with that person, and any other factors that differentiate one relationship from another. They must also think about the different conflict tactics—specific behaviors that, when patterned and consistent, become conflict styles—they tend to use with each person.

Most often, students receive analyses of their conflict tendencies that are very different from their own. Students get the chance to think about the different conflict styles they use and often talk with their respondents to get a better sense of why they scored them the way that they did, as well as discussing specific examples that explain those scores. Students may learn that they avoid conflict with a parent but are competitive with a best friend.

For most students, the differences make some sense after they think about things like how their interpersonal goals differ from those of their parents versus someone like their dating partner. However, for some students, these revelations are harder to accept. In these cases, students often dismiss the people who see them in ways they don't perceive themselves, for example, as competitive in conflict instead of avoidant. Students then try to justify the perception of themselves they don't like by saying that the respondents didn't understand the questions or just have things all wrong. In these instances, such an assignment may give students a wake-up call and encourage them to consider more carefully their interpersonal communication and conflict choices.

Students also consider what tactics succeed or fail in which contexts. For instance, they may consider what strategies for managing conflict might be effective at work versus at home or which strategies work when dealing with conflict in their family versus a work team. For example, they may realize that the competitive style that they use at work that places less importance on maintenance of the relationship is useful in a context when they don't have to have an interpersonal relationship with the people they work with, but is harmful to a relationship with someone who wishes to have long-term connections, such as with a sibling or significant other. Students must also consider what changes they could make to the way they manage conflict with these people and within specific contexts so that conflicts are better managed.

Students have a chance to apply what they've learned about conflict styles and tactics to their own lives and consider changes that promote healthy and effective conflict management. Students regularly comment that they'd never thought holistically about their conflict styles until this assignment. They also typically note that they learn a lot about how others perceive them. Perhaps most importantly, students comment on how much they learn regarding conflict, context, and the need to be rhetorically sensitive—that is, to be someone who understands how to best communicate in a given context while recognizing that in another context, their communication and conflict styles may need to be different.

The assignment also helps students improve writing and oral communication skills and teaches them the important differences between crafting messages in written versus verbal formats. Students also get practice in analyzing quantitative data and communicating that data in writing. They write a paper that presents their findings and include an introduction, a breakdown of their analysis of themselves, separate explorations of the three external analyses, a discussion section that explains the similarities and differences of the evaluations, and a conclusion. The assignment ends with a five-minute presentation to their classmates that requires students to effectively synthesize and edit their written work in order to package their report in a succinct and clear public presentation.

Verbal Communication and Marjory Stoneman Douglas High School Students

The need for effective messages has always been and will always be with us in public, interpersonal, team, or even social media communication. Humanities students leave college well equipped with the verbal communication skills that employers are demanding.

These communication skills are incredibly important for democracy, too. We need citizens who can craft persuasive arguments that are well supported and clearly communicated to the public. We need only look at the 2018 mass shooting tragedy at Marjory Stoneman Douglas High School in Parkland, Florida, to see the impact of communication education on the world. Agree with them or not, many of the students who survived that shooting immediately engaged the world in deft persuasive arguments in favor of gun control on the airwaves and social media. They worked together to craft a message, a strategy, and the national March for Our Lives on March 24, 2018. The world has been surprised and impressed by the eloquence, use of evidence, and effective arguments of these young public communicators.

Humanities faculty, however, were not as surprised once we learned about the Broward County Public Schools Debate Initiative that has twelve thousand students involved in debate programs in all high schools, all middle schools, and most elementary schools. The Broward County Public Schools get it right when they say, "Speech and debate students learn research, logic, organization of ideas, manipulation of language, assessment of audience, self-esteem and engagement in world events. These skills not only build better students, they build better college candidates, better employees and better citizens."[18] In an era when funding and support for debate programs is lessening in favor of funding for STEM, these students are shaking the world up using what they've learned in the humanities field of argumentation and debate.

Chapter 10

Collaboration

Sharing his thoughts on collaboration with the Duke University Fuqua School of Business, Apple CEO Tim Cook explains that the Apple "magic" happens when hardware, software, and services "come together." "It's unlikely that somebody that's focused on one of those in and of themselves can come up with magic," Cook continues. "And so you want people collaborating in such a way that you can produce these things that can't be produced otherwise." Cook speaks to the "why" of effective collaboration—it's just good business to pool the resources of a number of people who each have knowledge and skills that other people in the group may not have. We are often smarter and more innovative when we collaborate than when we work alone.[1]

The process of getting a team to a specific outcome involves excellent communication skills, effective methods of problem-solving, exceptional conflict management skills, and strong leadership. Good collaboration means the flexibility to work alone and in small groups while still engaging the larger organization in that collaboration. It necessitates ethical people putting the project above themselves and an understanding of, and adaptability to, team members' diverse cultures and backgrounds. In other words, the combined intellect of a team is one thing, but *working effectively as a team* of smart individuals is quite another.

There isn't one right way in which people work well together in teams. There are various types of discussion formats, decision-making techniques, and problem-solving agenda systems from which to choose, as well as a number of theories about how small groups learn and function. In just one popular undergraduate textbook alone, there are six different types of discussion formats, nine different decision-making techniques, and six different problem-solving agenda systems outlined.[2] Discussing the ins and outs of those processes is beyond the scope of this chapter and most humanities classes, other than courses on small group or organizational communication. Still, the humanities offer important opportunities to understand the dynamics of effective collaboration and hone teamwork skills.

Collaboration in the Workplace

Researchers Rob Cross, Reb Rebele, and Adam Grant note that time spent by both managers and employees in collaborative work increased 50 percent from 1996 to 2016. They also found that only 3–5 percent of employees contribute nearly one-third of a company's value-added collaborative work.[3] In other words, employers need to close this gap by hiring employees who have experience with collaboration, understand what effective collaboration involves, and will work as a good member of teams.

Not surprisingly, in a survey of ninety large, private Canadian companies, researchers found that 67 percent of respondents value teamwork as the most important skill for any new hire, and a World Economic Forum report lists "coordinating with others" as the fifth most important skill workers will need to have in 2020.[4] Additionally, the "Entry Level Applicant Job Survey" from the Society for Human Resource Management found that 83 percent of surveyed professionals rated teamwork as very important or important when assessing an applicant's qualifications.[5] And a recent study that surveyed 142 participants responsible for hiring scientists found that 60 percent of recruiters rank the "ability to work in a collaborative team" the most essential skill for new science graduates.[6]

The rise of the knowledge and creative economies means that groups are often working to create knowledge, enhance creativity, and innovate to add value to what already exists. For example, a tech company doesn't just need engineers to build software. It also needs marketers, salespeople, lawyers, and creative directors to keep the company thriving. Thus, building the latest app is going to require collaboration between a host of employees who may think and work differently, but who must work together to keep the business competitive. Robert Tabb, a salesperson for the app development company Phunware, notes, "It takes about ten meetings for us to get one of these deals put together. . . . And only two of those meetings are about the technology." The other meetings deal with guiding different stakeholders in the development process toward a fruitful collaboration.[7]

Companies who produce material goods have also begun collaborating to add value and innovation to their products. For example, skincare company Biotherm and car manufacturer Renault collaborated to create an electric car that maintained hydration in the car to protect skin, provided aromatherapy and ambient sound options for mood stimulation, filtered the air coming into the car, and improved the passengers' "sense of wellbeing" through a light therapy system.[8]

In addition, technology substantially impacts the nature and scope of collaboration. Technology has created the ability for people on five levels of a large office building or people on five continents involved in the same project to work together less expensively and more quickly than ever before. This means that along with understanding the basics of good teamwork and how to use new technologies, employees have to be aware of the impact of both U.S. diversity and intercultural communication and customs on group processes and communication. These topics will be covered in more detail in Chapters 15 and 16.

These advanced technologies mean that employees in both national and multinational companies must be able to collaborate virtually. The ability to use and adapt to multiple media technologies is critical. So are patience and flexibility, since the technologies often fail or glitch mid-meeting. Employees in the same or different buildings, states, or countries may meet virtually using more traditional means of technology-enhanced communication, such as video or audio technology, email, and Google Docs.

Relatively new to collaborative tools is web-based collaboration software, such as Slack, which was developed by a philosophy major. Slack offers teams the ability to create a cloud-based ecosystem for particular projects. Groups can organize projects using "channels" where information can be shared or stored on specific projects or even different elements of the same project, like "feedback" or regional work groups named something like "Boston" or "Midwest territory." Slack offers the ability to tap into thousands of other apps that focus on specific components of a project like communication, marketing, online security, productivity, and even travel. The app offers teams the ability to communicate and share information in a transparent, collaborative way.

The cost of a lack of teamwork in the workplace can be high. Porath and Pearson's study asked nine thousand employees how they were affected by coworkers who exhibited "incivility" in their groups, a range of behaviors including taking credit for others' efforts, checking email or texting during meetings, paying little attention or showing little interest in others' opinions, and making demeaning or derogatory remarks.[9] These researchers found that almost half of all employees facing incivility intentionally decreased work effort or decreased time at work. Among these employees, 66 percent said that their work quality declined, and 38 percent intentionally decreased work quality in response. Significant majorities of employees wasted time worrying about or avoiding the offender. Further, more than three-quarters of employees stated that their commitment to the organization declined, and 12 percent even left the organization in response to the incivility.[10]

It is clear that effective collaboration is important in most work environments and that globalization and technology are changing the way we think about teams and work in them. Understanding and valuing humanity are vital factors in successful collaboration, regardless of whether that work is done face to face or via any form of technology. Skills and knowledge learned in the humanities are fundamental to collaborative success in the workplace.

Collaboration, Higher Education, and the Humanities

When students hear "group project," the eye-rolling is palpable. After all, most people have experienced team members who make jobs more difficult. In some cases, that team member just doesn't care, drops the ball, or negatively impacts the group in other ways. But business and industry are demanding graduates with experience in collaboration, which is why students need to engage in group work across the curriculum and understand collaboration as a process that requires particular skills.

Collaboration in the classroom isn't new. However, it's often generally linked to business program case studies, engineering projects, or the lab sciences. But collaboration happens in the humanities, too, and for good reason. Elizabeth F. Barkley, Patricia K. Cross, and Claire Howell Major discuss a number of germinal studies about collaboration in the classroom and note that research on collaborative learning has found primarily positive outcomes, including greater academic achievement, improved higher-level reasoning, and increased innovative thinking.[11]

Collaborative learning also encourages "collective responsibility in a diverse world" and positively affects students' ability and motivation toward their personal development, understanding of science and technology, appreciation for art, analytical skills gain, and openness to diversity. Students learn to "break down stereotypes, . . . to work together in groups, develop listening skills, learn the art of compromising and negotiating, learn interpersonal skills, and are exposed to a variety of different people."[12] The humanities' emphasis on diversity, inclusivity, equality, and a global mindset positions these students to succeed and lead in group settings.

Working in teams also allows for metacognition—"thinking about thinking," which is linked to critical thinking skills and higher academic achievement.[13] Students get this practice and mind work in humanities classes. As one example, students begin in a history class studying the Great Depression by taking a test on course materials individually. This enables the students and instructor to ascertain where the students are in understanding the facts and dates and, more importantly, the relationship between that historical period and other periods or even disciplines. Next, students work in groups to take the test together, aiding them in comparing and contrasting the thought processes that led them to their answers. That is, the assignment encourages students to think about their own thinking, their group members' thinking, and the various ways these ideas relate to and build on each other and lead to better answers than simply working alone.[14]

As Jim Sibley suggests, once students have developed ideas in small groups, the groups benefit from interacting with one another. Together, the members of various groups talk through their solutions with other teams, comparing and contrasting, until the class agrees on the strongest answer to the problem.[15] For example, students in a legal studies class might prepare an opinion on a case study that includes issues of student speech rights, the "chilling effect" of a school's discipline of student speech, and time, place, and manner restrictions. Just as in true legal settings, different answers are possible. Thus, when students work in groups and apply precedent in addition to the specific contextual considerations of the case, different groups will likely "rule" differently on the case and use different legal precedents to justify their decision.

Students learn to effectively and civilly challenge the ideas of others, defend their own ideas, and consider how other teams rationalize their decisions. With proper guidance, students can focus their conversations on why they made a certain decision rather than concentrating on who is right and who is wrong.[16] These discussions in and between teams help students prepare for the "prospect of having their work changed or eliminated" for the good of the group and encourage students to help each other through "ego deflating moments" while learning that collaboration requires civil disagreement.[17] Group assignments help students understand that collaboration leads to better understanding of a problem as well as to better solutions than any person could come to on their own.[18]

In other types of assignments, students are assigned to teams that work together for the entire term. For example, in a history class, students can work together to create their own in-depth web-based units on historical events, issues, or social movements, adding depth to a survey course.[19] Students in women's studies can work together to create a "zine" addressing a specific issue linked to course materials, such as sexual consent or wage disparity, that can be distributed on campus as an informational tool.[20] Philosophy students can develop an end-of-semester campus event designed to link specific philosophers to popular culture to show the relevance of philosophy to everyday life. Political science students can plan debate watches with follow-up discussions or fact checks led by students to inform the public about political issues. Well-planned, long-term group work helps students practice collaborative processes that they will encounter in the workplace. They learn, for example, that when faculty create teams that are more balanced to encourage success, these are intentional decisions that mirror how collaboration operates in the workplace.

These long-term, collaborative humanities projects allow students to see the development of the kinds of relationship and group norms that can help groups complete tasks or doom them to failure.[21] Students can also experience a sense of belonging and connection, which is positively related to motivated behavior.[22] Further, these kinds of activities increase what Lev Vygotsky calls the "zone of proximal development," which is marked by the space in between what students can learn themselves and what they can learn with the help of others.[23]

Teaching students how to collaborate doesn't just happen when faculty require team projects. Helping students learn how to work as team members is about teaching students how to engage the *process of collaboration*, not just coming up with an answer. Humanities classes give students the opportunity to build the interpersonal, negotiation, critical thinking, metacognition, listening, and other skills vital to effective collaboration.

Assignment: Communication and Your Career Final Project

Michele's "Communication and Your Career" course helps prepare juniors and seniors to enter the job market after graduation. A semester-long team project culminates in a public event at the college to bring publicity to the communication arts and sciences (CAS) major, reinforcing a key goal of the course—to train students about how to talk about their major with prospective employers. The project involves three layers of collaboration as students work within small groups, these small groups work with the other small groups, and all students work together as a larger group to implement the event.

The project begins with a brainstorming process to determine an overall purpose and theme. The entire class works to first identify what problems need solving and what obstacles exist. In this stage, students participate in and experience a process in which a variety of perspectives, ideas, and perceptions are communicated, improved on, blended, challenged, and ultimately narrowed in a way that is civil and innovative. For example, classes have decided to focus on encouraging people to minor in CAS or changing the perception that CAS is only about the basic public speaking or small group communication courses.

Students then generate a number of possible solutions to the problem they've decided to tackle, necessitating that students tap into their creativity. No idea is stupid—they should shoot for the stars. What if resources were not a concern? Should this event be entertaining or serious? A carnival? A flash mob in the cafeteria? A tropical theme because spring has arrived? A panel discussion? Students get the opportunity to dream big while still linking those plans to an effective communication strategy. They add to each other's suggestions, taking the interactive, fun ideas from the student who lives on campus and is involved in the Campus Activity Board who knows what will get students' attention and meshing that with the experiences of the commuter student who knows that students who live off campus often don't identify with the campus as much as on-campus students do. In other words, each student adds ideas to the mix based on their knowledge and experience. One year, the students decided on the flash mob idea, supplementing that event with a week-long campaign of flyers across campus to reach students who may never go to the cafeteria.

Then, the whole group considers the market, how to best reach the largest percentage of that market, how different audiences in that market must be reached in different ways, and the cost of their solution. Students use specific criteria to measure possible solutions and determine as a team which one best fits the project's parameters. They also determine how their "big idea" will be delegated to smaller working groups.

Next, students are asked to rank their interest in being a member of the research, rhetoric, public relations, or project management teams. Each of the first three teams have deadlines for their work, and project managers make sure that the other three teams are working well together, work on getting the class the physical supplies they need for the project, and support the other teams when necessary.

Students in the research team look for information that the other groups can use. For example, they might research the general utility of humanities degrees, communication majors, and the desirability of the skills and knowledge garnered in the CAS degree that would persuade students to major or minor in CAS. They organize this research in the form of an annotated bibliography so that other students can follow the links between the research and the project goals.

Students on the rhetoric team use the work of the research team to create persuasive, succinct messages. They craft categories of messages and specific persuasive strategies and slogans that will make up the bulk of the project's public communication. They also consider how those messages are going to be communicated. In previous projects, students created posters with images of CAS alumni and their job titles and pretend dollar bills with information about CAS on them. Flyers noted courses in the major that might be attractive to students ignorant of what the major offers. Classes in topics like the rhetoric of American horror films, storytelling, organizational communication, health communication, and others were highlighted to communicate that CAS is "more than just public speaking"—the tagline at the top of all of these posters.

It's the job of the public relations team to use all of the project information to develop an overall public relations strategy for the event, including producing messages to advertise the event, a calendar for public release, and a social media plan. The class that decided on the flash mob idea used social media to tease the college community about what might happen. The class planned a flash mob to the popular Bruno Mars song "Uptown Funk." To arouse interest, the public relations group did a "countdown" to the event on social media that included clues about what might happen. They circulated an image of the CAS major logo with the fedora hat from the "Uptown Funk" music video hanging onto the edge of the logo, and later added the fedora to an image of the college mascot. The group built interest and excitement about what was going to happen and used a theme to link those messages to each other.

Once the primary pieces of the puzzle are ready, the whole class works together to put those pieces together and run a successful event. If one group has agreed to learn a dance for the flash mob, the other students create the persuasive messages for use at the event. If one group is creating flyers to post around campus, the other group is creating the "yellow brick road" map of the event that allows students to get stamps at each informational table that they can then trade in for a fun gift. The class moves (mostly) seamlessly between working in their small groups, working with other small groups, and working as a larger group to pull off the event.

Part of the final project grade for each student in the class is an analysis of their work as a team member. Students also evaluate their team members by answering questions about initiative, completion of independent work, input into group decision-making, and face-to-face and electronic communication. Student evaluations are aggregated for anonymity, and they get feedback from fellow students and Michele, based on observations about their strengths and weaknesses as a team member as well as suggestions for improvement. This part of the process helps ensure that students learn about more than just the successes and failures related to the overall project.

This assignment also has clearly defined processes for dealing with members of the group who aren't performing well. Team members who aren't pulling their weight are reported to Michele, giving her the opportunity to help the small group solve its own problems through small group discussion and, if things don't improve, through the process of "firing" the problematic group member. As a result, students receive guidance and practice in communication meant to *manage* conflict rather than exacerbate it. Students learn how to engage rather than avoid conflict in ways that are respectful, encourage stronger bonds between team members, and help ensure that smaller conflicts don't turn into larger conflicts that infect the whole class and its project.

The classroom isn't an exact replica of the workplace, of course. But projects such as this one mirror what students might encounter in the workplace and give them practice in some of the important skills associated with effective collaboration. They also feel immense pride and satisfaction when, in the end, all of the pieces and people come together to create something better as a group than they could ever create alone.

Juggling Multiple Perspectives in Teams

In global high-tech knowledge and creative economies, the best products result from technical specialists and creative, critical thinkers working together. The computer programmers and engineers building great products must consider the expertise of the humanities and arts graduates who know more about the impact of design on how humans engage with technology.

Whether we're talking about a multinational company like Apple or a hometown business with a staff of twenty, employees need effective collaboration skills. Humanities courses train students to compare, contrast, and engage with multiple ideas and contexts all linked to one larger issue. Practice in juggling the complexities of enduring human issues in the humanities classroom is excellent preparation for juggling multiple perspectives from multiple people or groups in a teamwork situation. With its focus on the processes that make that collaboration more or less successful, the humanities classroom is a great place to hone these essential teamwork skills.

Chapter 11

Problem-Solving

"In the dynamic environment of the technology sector, there is not typically one right answer when you make decisions. There are just different shades of how correct you might be," says CEO of web advertising platform MediaAlpha Steve Yi, who majored in interdisciplinary Asian studies. Danielle Sheer, a vice president at Carbonite, a cloud backup service, states that her academic background in philosophy sets her apart in her company. "I don't believe there is one answer for anything," she says. "That makes me a very unusual member of the team. I always consider a plethora of different options and outcomes in every situation." And Vince Broady, CEO of the content marketing platform This Moment, says that unlike his technology colleagues, who quickly move from one failed proposed solution to another, his educational background in religion forces him to look for long-term answers and lasting value.[1]

The stories of Yi, Sheer, and Broady highlight the problem-solving skills facilitated through the study of the humanities.[2] Too often, humanities faculty and students aren't seen as problem-solvers. The perception is that problems are concrete and pragmatic, and humanities faculty and students are thinkers, not doers. "Problems" come in all shapes and sizes, however, and, in most humanities courses, students aren't solving problems in the narrower sense of a problem—an unwanted situation that crops up and needs to be rectified before it hinders the organization you work for from reaching goals. These may be based on an angry customer, technology failure in a video conference with a potential client, lost files, and so on.

In humanities courses, students learn to problem-solve in the broader sense of "problem." Merriam-Webster defines "problem" as "a question raised for inquiry, consideration, or solution"; "an intricate unsettled question"; and "difficulty in understanding or accepting."[3] As noted earlier, humanities researchers often engage with complex problems that resist resolution because as one aspect is understood, perhaps "solved," others crop up. Humanities students do the same.

Humanities students spend a great deal of their time problem-solving, distinguished by the tools of our trade that foster the kinds of nuanced, multilayered thinking spoken about by Yi, Sheer, and Broady. In practical terms, Yi explains that studying Asian literature, politics, economics, history, and culture taught him to see all kinds of phenomena from multiple perspectives. He uses these same skills as the CEO of a technology company, "viewing our organization and our marketplace from different points of view, quickly shifting gears from sales to technology to marketing . . . to decide where we need to go as a company."[4]

The humanities promote the kinds of thinking that enable employees, leaders, and citizens to see, understand, and do things differently. This chapter explains the ways humanities education trains students' minds to address problems small and large, immediate and long-term, and concrete and abstract.

Problem-Solving in the Workplace

Put simply, problems are ubiquitous in the workplace, as Startup Professionals founder and CEO Martin Zwilling states: "In fact, every business is about solutions to customer problems—no problems, no business. Problems are an everyday part of every business and personal environment."[5] Whether that employer provides a service, manufactures a product, or trades in knowledge, ideas, or creativity, problems arise all the time.

Most employees will have to know how to effectively address problems, large or small. Some problems may be of your own making, while others occur for reasons having nothing to do with you. Perhaps a member of your team calls in sick an hour before the group is to present to your boss. Perhaps you have to learn a new software program and then teach it to your colleagues. Perhaps a customer has complained about how she was treated by one of your supervisees. Perhaps you have to decide how to best market your product to people in multiple countries. Whatever the problem, you must have the tools to solve it.

Unsurprisingly, the most recent NACE employer survey, *Job Outlook*

2018, lists problem-solving skills as the number one attribute employers seek on candidates' résumés.[6] But Kate Davidson points out in a *Wall Street Journal* article that companies across the United States report having trouble finding applicants who can problem-solve.[7] Clearly, students who graduate with strong problem-solving skills will be at an advantage.

Christopher "Topher" Speth, a 2012 graduate of Wheaton College with a major in philosophy and economics, is a great example of someone who has benefited from the cross-cutting need for problem-solving skills in nonroutine tasks. Speth raves about his philosophy education in connection with his success as a junior product manager at GlobalTranz, a transportation software firm. His position is all about problem-solving, from assessing and implementing changes to products to mediating communication on teams to agree to a solution. As Speth explains, "Philosophy also taught me to hone—and occasionally overhaul—my own theories by anticipating objections to my current line of thought. This is incredibly valuable in software development, where I am constantly on the lookout for what could go wrong as a result of the changes I'm making. Fixing issues during the conceptualization process is much less costly than in testing."[8]

While problems have always been abundant in the workplace, the nature of problems has become more complex, as has the workplace itself, in the fast-paced, global knowledge economy. Samuel Grieff et al. explain that the nature of work has shifted in the modern economy away from routine tasks mostly located within a specific area of expertise.[9] In their place are nonroutine tasks requiring skills that are broadly relevant across areas of expertise, like critical thinking, analytical reasoning, and problem-solving. David H. Autor, Frank Levy, and Richard J. Murnane label these nonroutine tasks as "abstract" and note their concentration in professional, technical, and managerial occupations.[10]

Jobs requiring nonroutine tasks "employ workers with high levels of education and analytical capability, and they place a premium on inductive reasoning, communication ability and expert mastery." Furthermore, employment in nonroutine occupations is increasing and will continue to do so; employment in most routine occupations, on the other hand, is diminishing.[11]

These nonroutine tasks are the most challenging of problems in the workplace today. In fact, respondents in a study by the World Economic Forum identify "complex problem-solving" as one of the core skills expected in 36 percent of all jobs across all industries in 2020.[12] Complex problem-solving expert Kate Isaacs claims that "complexity, unintended consequences and the unrelenting nature of many problems are now a growing part of every business leader's decision-making."[13] Brook Manville points out that problem-solving typically leverages critical and creative thinking to find a solution to a particular issue.[14] Given that humanities researchers and students have long addressed enduring, sometimes impenetrable problems and issues, humanities students graduate with the critical and creative problem-solving skills necessary for workplace success.

Analytical Thinking and Problem-Solving in the Humanities

George Polya put forth an early structured strategy for problem-solving that included understanding the problem, developing a plan, carrying out the plan, and looking back.[15] Since Polya's work, academics in disciplines such as psychology, mathematics, business, philosophy, and more have continued to theorize problem-solving. Generally, they include some or all of these steps, depending on the nature of the problem:

- Identify the problem.
- Identify the causes.
- Brainstorm, explore, and evaluate potential solutions.
- Select the solution.
- Plan and implement the solution.
- Check the impact of the solution.
- Reflect on the process.[16]

We do not aim here to provide a formulaic approach to problem-solving in the humanities. Rather, we argue that humanities education promotes the kind of complex problem-solving skills identified above, noting that a critical and creative thinker is always aware of the need for modifications based on the problem at hand and the many surrounding contextual issues. Further, problem-solving is recursive, not linear, meaning the problem-solver must circle back and forth between steps. Each step involves various other skills, such as information gathering and analysis.

Studying human experience is by its very nature complex and challenging because human nature is messy, unpredictable, and resistant to simple or easy solutions. So are real-world problems, rarely presented to us as neatly packaged. Therefore, in humanities classrooms and in the world beyond it, complex problem-solving requires negotiating multiple, interconnecting, and often competing perspectives. Problem-solving education in humanities curricula is what we'd call "purposeful floundering."[17] Students often want clear step-by-step instructions or guidance, and they want answers quickly. But it is this discomfort within the complexities that in our view is the best method for teaching complex problem-solving.

Assignment: The Policy Speech

One of Michele's regular assignments in her public speaking course is the policy speech, which combines practice in problem-solving with practice in effective persuasion and presentation skills. Students are asked to focus on topics that are of interest to them in terms of their major or another policy issue they find important. An agribusiness major might focus on genetically modified organisms or gun control. A criminal justice major may focus on privatizing prisons or on the issue of abortion. An engineering major might focus on our country's infrastructure or capital punishment. An art major might focus on increasing arts education in K-12 classrooms or paying college athletes. A science major might focus on climate change or drug policy. A history major may focus on national monuments valorizing the Confederacy or on standardized testing. The idea is for students to start thinking about a problem that they find important to their lives and to society. Depending on the topic, students select to advocate for or to oppose policy change.

Students advocating to change policy have to address three issues: significance, inherency, and solvency. They must try to persuade their classmates that the need to change is significant, that their plan allows for significant change, and that their plan provides significant advantages. As an example, students arguing to change U.S. drug policy would need to argue that the current system, referred to as the War on Drugs, isn't working. They must show why their plan is significantly different than the current plan, such as putting more money into rehabilitation, and they need to show why and how their plan has more advantages than current policy. Proving inherency means that they need to persuade us that disadvantages are inherent in the status quo. They might point to the dramatic rise in nonviolent drug offenders in prisons since the War on Drugs began and its costs to taxpayers and recidivism rates. Demonstrating solvency means that students must persuade their audience that the plan can work to solve specific needs, that it can produce claimed advantages, and that it is the best idea, which includes determining what group or agency would be responsible for carrying out this plan. This would likely mean talking about how the parts of their plans have worked well in other countries, providing evidence that the plan has worked elsewhere.

Students who decide to oppose change in the status quo must deal with significance, workability, and disadvantages. In order to argue against significance, they must persuade that the need to change isn't significant and doesn't justify costs involved with change and that any advantages are outweighed by disadvantages. A student arguing to maintain the War on Drugs as is would present evidence that the program is working and thus no changes are needed. The student would also need to compare costs (direct and indirect) and show that the new plan would cost too much to implement. Finally, they would need to point to the advantages of the program and argue that the advantages outweigh the disadvantages. The student must also argue against workability, attempting to prove that the planned change won't solve the problem. They might argue that moving money to rehabilitation isn't cost-effective and that the change they're arguing against can't provide claimed advantages by pointing to ways in which the plan might fail or make matters worse. The student will also focus on the disadvantages of the plan by comparing and contrasting the proposed plan's likely results and consequences with the existing situation. What might the end result of the new plan be? Are there unintended consequences or consequences not recognized by those arguing for change?

Students then develop a speech to effectively and succinctly communicate their ideas. They are not asked to "prove" that their argument is "true," but they do have to craft persuasive appeals that leave those in the audience thinking, "That's *probably* right." Students also have to consider those in the audience who are not open to their perspective and find ways to encourage them to open their minds, listen, and fairly consider their position.

This assignment provides students with excellent practice in problem-solving because it requires challenging intellectual tasks. If mastered, these skills will serve students incredibly well in their careers, as complex problem-solving skills are at a premium.

Messy Problem-Solving and Humanities Students

It's also vital to understand that problem-solving is impacted by several other "messy" factors discussed throughout this book. These include relationships, leadership, conflict management, ethics, democratic ideals, and verbal communication issues such as relating to each other interculturally, in small or large groups, in organizations, and in interpersonal contexts.

Accustomed to "purposeful floundering," humanities students help solve complex, multilayered problems. They do so while also considering important contextual factors that help groups see problems in a different light and perspectives of people they've never encountered and understand the problem and solution in relation to their histories. In other words, humanities students revel and excel in the complexity that defines problem-solving.

Chapter 12

Creativity and Innovation

A 2010 IBM survey found that more than 1,500 CEOs from sixty countries and thirty-three different industries worldwide believed that creativity was more important than rigor, management disciplines, integrity, or vision for "navigating an increasingly complex world." Because of fast and significant changes linked to globalization, technology, and big data, companies can no longer simply replicate what's worked in the past. Moreover, fewer than half of the same executives believed that their companies were prepared to handle the quickly changing and complex market.[1]

Research by the World Economic Forum in 2016 supported this earlier finding by noting that while creativity ranked as the tenth most important skill in 2015, it will be the third most in-demand skill by 2020.[2] One need only think about how fast we shifted from film-based cameras to digital cameras, from making mixtapes to setting up playlists on Spotify, or from being tied to a home landline to having a computer in our pocket that we sometimes even use as a phone, to see how important innovation is to our lives. But it's also important to our country's economic future and to an understanding of what skills careers will require for the foreseeable future. For example, jobs requiring creative thinking are less prone to automation.[3]

Too often, "creativity" is thought to apply exclusively to the arts rather than industry. Indeed, art has revitalized entire communities in the United States, and communities that embrace the arts tend to do better economically than those that do not, giving powerful credence to the notion that creativity matters.[4] But creativity isn't only applied in the arts.

Creativity is often used interchangeably with innovation, but they are distinct, circular concepts. Creativity is about producing the ideas that lead to innovation. Then, once an organization starts to work on an innovative product or idea, creativity is likely required to rescue that innovation from problems that emerge during its implementation.[5] Creative thinking and problem-solving have become so important to staying relevant in the economy that some corporations even craft specific places, processes, and procedures to bolster the kind of creative thinking that leads to innovation.[6]

Birut Irena Zemits argues that creative thinkers take approaches "outside established conventions to express a view or an idea that is not predictable," and that creative thinking forms and approaches questions in ways that are different from the norm.[7] As Dan Berrett notes, "Creative tasks are, by their nature, ambiguous, with no clear right or wrong answer. Such tasks require taking intellectual risks, trying, evaluating, and discarding ideas, and making connections."[8] These are some of the bedrock tenets of a humanities education. Creativity is a way of thinking that can be applied in any role in any industry. And in these days, when brand identity and the latest gadget or app rule the day, the need for creative thinking in our ever-changing economy cannot be overstated.

Creativity and Innovation in the Workplace

As Harvard business professors Teresa M. Amabile and Mukti Khaire note, creativity is essential not only to companies that want to continue growing but also to entrepreneurship, the foundation of new businesses. But because creativity has been considered unmanageable, difficult to pinpoint, and not linked to immediate payoffs, managers have not focused attention on this very important skill.[9] That habit must change if the U.S. economy is going to expand.

Creativity is a type of problem-solving—the ability to "redefine the problems and opportunities you face, come up with new, innovative responses and solutions, and then take action."[10] There are often any number of ways to solve problems, but the more *creative* ideas and solutions may be those that give a team or organization an advantage over the competition.

In a knowledge economy, economic performance will be linked to new ways of thinking and designing, to patents, and to new products that are developed with today's evolving challenges in mind. The most effective managers in the future will recognize that all members of a team should work to think creatively and to innovate. As executive Diego Rodriguez notes, the "lone inventor myth" will soon disappear, since it is generally the case that innovation is rarely the work of one person.[11]

Scott Cook, cofounder and director of Intuit, argues that increasingly, managers are not the sources of new ideas. Rather, managers more often prioritize and assign people to projects. In fact, Google's founders realized a higher success rate among those ideas that stemmed from employee initiative than those they had backed. Similarly, Phillip Rosedale, founder of the company that manages the online virtual world Second Life, notes that the best ideas in his organization come from workers' own initiatives, and he offers workers enormous autonomy to foster innovation.[12]

Furthermore, Nobel Prize–winning economist Edmund S. Phelps notes that ignoring the humanities and focusing solely on hiring technical workers belies the way that economic development actually occurs. Before any new machine or medical device is built, there is a desire and capacity to innovate, which typically emerges from the ability to imagine creative solutions, to communicate those ideas, and to work with teams to develop them more fully. These latter core skills, he argues, are imperative to the development of "creative solutions to complex challenges."[13]

Creativity and innovation also make an organization more adaptable to what Phelps refers to as "changing circumstances and new constraints."[14] A focus on the way "we've always done things" is deadly to an organization. We need only look to Eastman Kodak for an example of how a lack of innovation can harm an industry giant. Kodak focused its efforts on engineering ways to make traditional ways of taking pictures more efficient rather than on digital innovation and filed for bankruptcy in 2012.[15]

Managers who want to encourage creativity and innovation appreciate creative workers, recognize that each person probably performs better at some points in the creative process than others, and are tolerant of the subversive.[16] Moreover, managers who appreciate and encourage expressions of diversity can foster creativity and innovation. Research on identity integration by Chi-Yi Cheng, Jeffrey Sanchez-Burks, and Fiona Lee demonstrates that people who integrate various elements of their identity (for example, being female, a scientist, and Black) tend to display higher levels of creativity when they draw on their different realms of knowledge to solve a problem because they can look at issues and problems through multiple lenses.[17]

Creativity and innovation are going to be the lifeblood of robust organizations moving forward. Organizations and managers that embrace, recognize, and foster creativity and innovation will likely have a better chance of navigating the quickly changing global economy than those who don't. In addition, those that understand creativity as a way of thinking throughout all realms, rather than as exclusive to the arts, are poised to lead us into the future.

Creativity and Innovation, Higher Education, and the Humanities

Tracy Carlson is a Wharton MBA and an "unrepentant Yale humanities geek." She's also a leading consultant and author on branding and marketing who doubled the market share of Wisk detergent and restored the brand's profitability. Carlson understands why business needs more humanities graduates like her who are "comfortable with complexity and ambiguity." She writes, "A linear, instrumental mentality such as knowing protocols to solve specific problems isn't especially helpful when the problems are big, floppy, interconnected, and changing fast." Organizations need people who bring a healthy skepticism to projects as a means of finding "fresh ways to explore and reframe the issues, illuminate hypotheses, and challenge assumptions"; she notes that humanities students are well prepared to perform in this way.[18]

Physicist Mark Mills and Julio M. Ottino, dean of the Robert R. Mc-Cormick School of Engineering and Applied Science, argue that curricula from kindergarten through graduate school should support "whole brain" education because innovation requires "the attributes of the humanities found in right brain thinking[:] creativity, artistry, intuition, symbology, fantasy, emotions."[19] The humanities give students ample opportunities to hone their right brain—creative thinking skills that can lead to innovative ideas. Thinking that challenges students to consider, reconsider, and even reconsider again a problem from different angles happens in the humanities classroom on a daily basis. This kind of thinking leads students to new and unique solutions about all facets of their lives, including in the workplace and in the world.

Innovation, as French professor Dan Edelstein notes, is unlike other skills in that it is difficult to communicate. There are simply no rules to the practice, no steps to follow, and no means of copying the successful work of others. He notes that if fifty students provide the same correct answers on a calculus test, all will likely earn an A for the exam. If you hand fifty humanities students in a history course the same thesis to develop, however, all who hand in the same basic regurgitation of that thesis will probably not earn an A, because "original thinking is one of the criteria used to evaluate a student's understanding and assimilation of material." Thus, he argues, "the humanities demand originality from day one."[20]

CEO Tony Golsby-Smith echoes Edelstein in his essay, "Want Innovative Thinking? Hire from the Humanities." He explains that while business schools train students to "control, predict, verify, guarantee, and test data," they don't typically teach students to "navigate 'What if?' questions and unknown futures." He also points out that "any great work of art—whether literary, philosophical, psychological or visual—challenges the humanist to be curious, to ask open-ended questions, and to see the big picture. This kind of thinking is just what you need if you are facing a murky future or dealing with tricky, incipient problems." Humanists, he argues, are not only trained to be creative but are also "uniquely adapted to lead creative teams."[21]

For example, Gherardo Giradi leads economics students to think about their choice of profession by showing the film *Death of a Salesman*, and to consider whether money can buy happiness by screening *Wall Street*.[22] Dave Griffiths explains how discussions and activities about creating music and harmonies, conducting orchestras, and understanding jazz improvisation can help students understand ways of thinking about leadership as performance.[23] Clare Hopkinson discusses how lessons in poetry helps nurses be more empathetic with their clients, better understand the nursing experience, and more effectively handle the challenges, contradictions, and tensions at work.[24]

Assignment: Political Communication and World AIDS Day

In some semesters of Michele's contemporary American political rhetoric course, students studied the rhetoric of social movements, including the various social movements formed in the midst of the AIDS crisis in the 1980s and 1990s. The course's final group project focused on students informing the college community about HIV and AIDS on December 1, World AIDS Day. Students used skills in areas such as communication, problem-solving, research, collaboration, and persuasion to craft a unique campaign directed to a specific audience and focused on a particular context of AIDS. The assignment encouraged students to be creative and develop innovative messages and communication strategies to educate the campus community.

Course readings, writing, and discussion centered on the rhetoric of nonviolent groups like Queer Nation and ACT UP (AIDS Coalition to Unleash Power) that gained notoriety in the 1980s and 1990s with their direct, inspired, and creative challenges to government inaction regarding the AIDS epidemic.[25] Students also learned about the Names Project, the organization that began the AIDS Memorial Quilt, a quilt composed of sections made by the loved ones of those struck down by AIDS. The contributions to the quilt communicate about the people being memorialized and point to the extensive impact of AIDS in the United States.

Within these contexts, students chose what information they wanted to communicate and communication strategies that would be most effective in addressing their specific audience. This generation of students had generally been reared with access to information on HIV and AIDS throughout the course of their lives, so students knew that they had to construct campaigns that broke through the information boredom or overload many have on these topics.

As an example of this assignment, one semester's class focused on HIV/AIDS in Africa and in the African American and Black populations of the United States. Students identified two primary roadblocks: a feeling of disconnect from people so far away in Africa and the lack of information about HIV/AIDS in African American and Black communities.

The students knew that they needed an innovative way to grab their audience's attention while making the case personal to foster students' feelings about and engagement in the issues. As a result, they decided to create a week-long campaign that changed with each day, building on the last day with increasing levels of creativity and intensity. By creating a campaign that continually morphed and became more and more attention-getting with each day, the students crafted a memorable and persuasive campaign that had the campus talking.

On Monday, the first day of the campaign, to invite audience members to remember that not everyone "lives with AIDS," students scattered gravestones made of painted Styrofoam across the lawns and placed body outlines in hallways using brightly colored tape, as you might see in a crime scene investigation. On Tuesday, the students added names to the gravestones and taped body markers, including a body marker of a baby, to remind the community that HIV and AIDS affect everyone. On Wednesday, they added pictures of people's faces, followed by Thursday's birth and death information for each person, to communicate that the person had died from AIDS and how the virus was contracted. The students believed that it was important to communicate how the disease had been contracted in order to counter the still-prevailing myth that AIDS is a "gay disease."

These choices reminded the community that the HIV virus could be contracted in many ways, such as sharing needles, blood transfusions, and both heterosexual and homosexual sex. As this campaign transformed throughout the week, the campus community had access to exhibits in some of the library's glass cases that offered visual representations of the magnitude of the crisis. Both the United States and Africa were represented, with pushpins placed into colorful designs of both places to point to statistics about the prevalence of HIV and AIDS in the two regions.

Students also chose to display sections of the AIDS Memorial Quilt in the college's art gallery. These quilts represented a creative and artistic means of communicating about the vast impact of the AIDS epidemic and added a message of hope and love to the week's events, meant to juxtapose the emotions invited by the visual campaign of death throughout the week. Taken together, the intentional ratcheting up of the message had a purposefully jarring impact on the campus population, intensified by the more permanent reminders in the library and art gallery. On that Friday, World AIDS Day, students arranged for friends, faculty, and staff to wear red AIDS ribbons.

The week ended with a campus-wide gathering. Using masks and other costume elements, students dressed as current and former national politicians, the Grim Reaper, and pharmaceutical workers in bloodstained lab coats. Decisions about what masks to buy focused on what images would gain the most attention and be the most recognizable. Students agitated for more attention and funding for the HIV/AIDS epidemic in general and for their communities of focus more specifically by marching, chanting short poems created for the event, holding signs, and speaking out through a bullhorn.

The students thought carefully about how to frame arguments about HIV and AIDS depending on what character was holding which sign. The political leaders carried signs pointing to the privilege of being able to ignore the impact of the disease or slow down funding for HIV and AIDS. For example, one student dressed as Vice President Dick Cheney held a sign that said, "What Cheney doesn't know about AIDS won't kill him, but it will kill you! Fight ignorance about AIDS!" The Grim Reapers created messages that were personal, such as "I died of AIDS in 2004. So did 15,798 people in the United States" and "Don't know your HIV status? Neither did some of the 600 people who died from AIDS today." Students dressed in lab coats stained with blood held signs such as "Pills cost pennies. Greed costs lives," "No more generic drugs = death," and "Black lives for dollars."

Crafting this project was a creative endeavor for students, who used art, science, rhetoric, and research to create a memorable and persuasive campaign. Their right brains and left brains worked in concert as abstract statistics were made more concrete via the visual communication of maps, and research about the scientific protocols and funding related to drugs designed to combat HIV and AIDS was encapsulated into succinct data-based slogans designed to astonish. Further, the cultural and religious traditions of Africa and complex international AIDS policies were simplified in messages challenging the community to care about people far away from their own realities.

Michele recalls people commenting on the in-your-face visual strategies that stopped them in their tracks and encouraged them to reflect on AIDS and its impact on our communities. Communication from the college community made it clear that the students' work made the campus come alive, and students today still reflect on that experience using social media on each World AIDS Day.

"Think Different"

At age sixteen, Albert Einstein imagined what it would be like to ride alongside a beam of light.[26] That fantasy began his intellectual journey to the discovery of the theory of relativity. Einstein's intellectual prowess in physics more directly helped him make his case. But that magnificent innovation in thinking started with the willingness to think creatively and to imagine.

The United States and its organizations need people who can think *and* imagine. We need computer engineers to build machines and CEOs like Steve Jobs who are willing to study calligraphy to create an exceptional font for his Macs. We need doctors who can heal the sick and who can understand the power of narratives to hear what patients might not directly say. We need researchers who can offer scientific breakthroughs and explain to a general audience why their innovation should receive additional research funding or become an accepted new practice that can save lives.

The willingness to think more broadly about creativity should be fostered at all grade levels and in all aspects of life. The humanities offer students the opportunity to research and think, but to also imagine and create. Comfortable with thinking about old issues in new ways, challenging "the way things have always been," and muddling through ambiguity, humanities students are well trained in the kinds of creative thinking that spur innovation. Humanities graduates already demonstrate the courage to, borrowing a famous slogan from Apple, "Think different"—precisely what the burgeoning global economy needs.[27]

Chapter 13

Technological Competence and Technological Literacy

As we've argued throughout the book, the humanities prepare students well to engage in a number of careers, including those that Anders argues are "*indirectly* catching the warmth of the tech revolution."[1] Moreover, humanities students frequently bring a valuable voice to the table because technology is fraught with the kinds of important, fundamental, and complex questions that are typical in the humanities. The humanities can help the thinkers and doers of technology do their jobs better. They are also key to the promotion and explanation of technology to the public and business leaders who might make use of a specific technology.

This chapter addresses technology in the workplace at the nuts-and-bolts level in companies across the economic sectors—what entry-level employees need to know and do as they go about their daily work. Humanities students graduate with basic to intermediate levels of technological competence and strong skills in technological literacy. Technological competence is the ability to use a particular technology such as PowerPoint or a social media site. Technological literacy augments these skills by fostering critical thinking about a tool's use.[2] Humanities students come to the workplace prepared with both.

Technology in the Workplace

Generally, newer technologies benefit business and industry. Databases and analytics make companies more agile, telecommuting allows access to a larger pool of employees, file sharing and communication technologies increase work speed, clouds and paperless sharing make the internal sharing of information quicker and easier, mobile devices allow for work travel that remains connected to the workplace, and automation can make work more efficient and less expensive.[3]

But there are barriers to the effective adoption of technology in the workplace. Sometimes employers don't communicate the reasons for the change to employees.[4] New technologies can be intimidating, shift job responsibilities, add to an employee's workload, and require supplementary training and additional personnel. Adopting new technologies can bring fear and feelings of uncertainty for employees, who may not be comfortable with change or who feel their job responsibilities are shifting.[5]

Given the positives and negatives of adopting new technologies in the workplace, companies need employees who are flexible and adaptable. Humanities students are comfortable with new ideas and, as a result, are prepared to adapt to the new challenges of learning and thinking about new technologies as they emerge.

Basic technological competence in entry-level jobs across most economic sectors requires that candidates be proficient typists and have online etiquette skills for effective workplace and social media communication. They should know software suites like Microsoft Office and Google Drive and be able to produce effective documents, spreadsheets, and presentations. All college graduates should understand how to do research online properly, comprehend how to keep information on their computers safe, and know what information should and shouldn't be put into the public sphere.[6]

Graduates at a more intermediate level of technological competence are going to be in higher demand. For example, stronger applicants are going to be able to go beyond basic functions of Microsoft Word and run mail merges, create macro scripts, format documents, and effectively use smart art and graphics. In addition, graduates who can create the complex macros that organize data in programs like Excel are in "particularly high demand." Graduates with the ability to use Microsoft Access, graphics programs like Adobe Photoshop, and employment engagement software like Peoplesoft are even stronger candidates.[7] Humanities students are more than capable of learning higher levels of technology and, increasingly, get some intermediate-level training in the humanities classroom.

Beyond technological competence, technological literacies "are not solely about technical proficiency but about the issues, norms, and habits of mind surrounding technologies used for a particular purpose," as educational researcher Doug Belshaw argues.[8] Maha Bali explains, "Digital skills focus on what and how. Digital literacy focuses on why, when, who, and for whom."[9] Technological literacy is the ability to understand how to use these tools more effectively and with an understanding of their potential impact on society. These include, for example, understanding visual communication or copyright when thinking about images for a PowerPoint presentation and considering issues of privacy and audience when posting on social media.[10] Humanities students, with courses grounded in rhetoric, art, or visual communication, can create dynamic presentations that effectively use space, text, and images to maintain attention and to persuade.

Other examples of how technological literacy supplements technological competence are technologies linked to Web 2.0 that enable content creation and interaction with other content creators. Web 2.0 technologies have opened up new worlds for businesses, and therefore, graduates with exceptional web-related skills are in high demand. Anyone can post on a social media platform or write a blog, but graduates who can show employers that they can "leverage social media to convey messages about their organization" are highly valued.[11] Humanities students, with their training in excellent communication skills, are certainly in a good position to succeed using these technologies. But more than just getting the right words down, humanities graduates also understand the impact of those words and images, in terms of historical, present-day, and possible future impact. Their training in critical thinking and history helps them make better decisions about that communication.

Technological literacy is closely related to information literacy—the ability to distinguish the best information from that which is less credible. While researching via Google and other internet search engines may be sufficient for some tasks, more sophisticated research in the workplace involves more sophisticated skills in internet research, such as databases, online reference materials, and sites like Google Scholar that help make sure the information gathered is credible. The critical evaluation of digital source material is key, when web sources can contain content created by both humans and bots, hyperlinks and nonlinear text without "traditional signals of credibility," and sponsored text.[12] Critical assessment of information and data is crucial to effectively using these tools in the workplace. Humanities education, like the research paper, prepares students to effectively research, evaluate, and synthesize information in the workplace.

Finally, because communication technologies have fundamentally shifted the workplace, graduates need a firm grasp of effectively communicating via technology. According to a World Economic Forum global survey, 44 percent of human resources decision makers declared that technologies enabling remote working, coworking spaces, and teleconferencing are the key agents of change in the workplace.[13] For new graduates, it's not enough to know how to use communication technology; they must also understand the various writing expectations associated with different communication technologies (for example, texting versus email), the self-discipline to work from home, and the ability to effectively navigate other means of computer-mediated communication (such as conference calls and video conferences). Because computer-mediated communication lacks many nonverbal cues, graduates will need to learn to succinctly and effectively communicate their ideas in a context that is faster and less personal than face-to-face communication. Humanities graduates with skills in communication, collaboration, and leadership are poised to perform these tasks efficiently and effectively.

As more and more elements of the workplace adopt technological innovations, college graduates must be prepared to learn, use, and adapt to changes in technology. The flexibility and adaptability of humanities students make them excellent employees in the technology-infused workplace.

Technology, Higher Education, and the Humanities

As faculty, we both have adapted to new technologies in our workplace during our careers, and we continue to do so every year. Neither of us majored in anything related to technology, nor did we use these tools as college students since they did not exist. Some of the technologies we use include online testing; video lectures; presentation software like PowerPoint, Keynote, and Prezi; app-based quiz games for test reviews; and online discussion forums. And just like any other workplace, tools such as email, course management systems, and academic advising systems change in the academy, too. Thus, like our students, humanities faculty regularly adapt to new instructional and workplace technologies.

Because much of the college experience is infused with technology, most college graduates leave with both technological competence and technological literacy, to varying degrees, preparing them for the many ways in which multiple technologies are used in the workplace. For example, students engage in online presentations and discussion boards, deal with social media, take tests online, and navigate online schedule builders, registration, and academic advising tools. Many students also take online courses, in which they practice clear and concise online communication and hone the skills of self-discipline. In hybrid classes that meet both face to face and online, students also get valuable practice in navigating shifting contexts for learning—online and face to face. In these classes, students engage with classmates online one day and learn better strategies for face-to-face discussions at the next class meeting.

As a result of the variety of technologies they use, students learn the strengths and limitations of technologies, especially when it comes to written and verbal communication. They learn how to move seamlessly between different programs with different purposes and how to pay attention to expectations about which technology to use and how it's used most effectively.

Increasingly, humanities students often also get more advanced practice with a variety of technologies in the classroom. For example, English majors might develop an interactive visual presentation about a novel from the 1800s and its applicability to current politics or engage in fan fiction websites. Some communication studies students write and produce promotional videos for a local nonprofit or a social media strategy for a campus event. Students in history use transcription software for oral history projects, and art history students might create a multimedia presentation on a particular artist. Ideally, students learning the "what and how" of these various technologies are likewise paying close attention to the "why, when, who, and for whom."

In addition, some faculty and students in the humanities are engaged in the growing area of digital humanities. Definitions of the digital humanities abound, but broadly speaking, this field, in the words of Brandon T. Locke, "seeks to apply a liberal arts rationale for the development of critical analysis and development of web interaction and writing, multimodal projects, data analysis and visualization, and large scale analysis." Locke, a digital humanities expert, notes that digital humanities skills generally parallel the staples of liberal arts classrooms, "such as strong writing, critical reading, and research and information analysis."[14] At the intersections of the humanities and technology, students of the digital humanities can learn to program, encode, and edit text, as well as perform tasks related to electronic publishing, interface design, and the construction of archives. In addition, they learn about issues related to intellectual property, privacy, public access to information, and methods of text preservation.[15]

For example, in Ryan Cordell's course "Mapping Boston," students used Neatline, a suite of tools that allows the user to tell stories using tools like maps and timelines and build "deep maps" of specific neighborhoods or landmarks in a city. Students layered "historical photographs, maps, geospatial data, literary texts, and other elements to build arguments about their city."[16] By adding technologies to both create and disseminate their research, students used technological skills and creativity to "map" Boston history, allowing them to recognize the similarities and differences of a place, its moments, and its debates throughout history.

Students may learn to program for an open source like Wikipedia and add their research to this public knowledge base. At the same time, they learn about the importance of excellent research and the implied or earned credibility of a source. That same research could be developed into an interactive website that maps themes in a literary work or lines of thinking about a particular topic. Technologies such as these offer students the ability to learn course content and then develop arguments through language or visual communication that create interactive entertainment or lessons for visitors of the project's web page. Students become responsible for the knowledge they create because they have readers and users beyond their professor and peers.

Importantly, humanities students are asked to think about *why* they should choose one technology over the other, as well as what impact their use of technology can have on their lives and their community. The stories throughout this book about humanities students in the technology industry point to the utility of having a humanities person in the room for just this reason. Humanities students think about the links between technology and humanity, the environment, ethics, privacy rights, and persuasion—they think and interact with technology in meaningful ways that speak to its impact on our world.

For example, students in Michele's course on the rhetoric of American horror film think and talk a good deal about how changes in technology impact our world and how technology can provoke fear and change our relationships to others. Students watch 1931's *Frankenstein* and 1932's *Freaks* paired with readings and discussions to think about the films as they related to the public's changing views on science, on issues such as the eugenics movement, and the fear of disabilities often linked to both eugenics and religious beliefs. In watching *Invasion of the Body Snatchers* (1956), students learn about the interplay of influence between politics, science and technology, war, and the public's fear of nuclear war and takeover by communists during the Red Scare and the Atomic Age.

Other courses in the humanities challenge students in the same way. Classes in anything from gothic literature to science fiction will also address these complex technological and cultural issues. Anthropology, religious studies, and history classes employ their own disciplinary lenses to teach about technology's various impacts on societies around the world. Michele's communication and information technology course focuses on the philosophical and practical debates of issues like freedom of expression, privacy, piracy, and hacking as they relate to technology and society. Laurie's storytelling classes enable students to choose the technology of their choice to share their information, making these decisions on factors such as the audience they hope to reach, privacy issues, and the impact of text, audio, and/or video based on the topic. The unique ways in which humanities students use and think about technology encourage the very technological literacy that students need for workplace success.

Assignment: Digital Storytelling in a Women's Studies Class

Rachel Alpha Johnston Hurst uses digital storytelling and service learning to enhance her upper-level feminist theory course.[17] Digital storytelling blurs boundaries between the academic and nonacademic world, exposing students to multiple methods of knowledge production by using oral, visual, digital, and other forms. Hurst suggests that digital storytelling creates an opportunity for students to "find their voice," leaving them better equipped to "situate themselves" in relation to other voices. At the same time, the technology facilitates deeper understandings of the humans behind the stories.[18] By using video, students learn strategies for analyzing the relationship between video production and how reality is structured; as a result, they develop a "critical eye," more attuned to how their work and that of others extends distorted and unequal representational practices that uphold inequities and perpetuate stereotypes.[19]

Student projects center on many issues, including transgender, language, being a settler ally to Indigenous people, power, social construction, sexual harassment, and sexual violence. Through active engagement with their chosen organizations and course readings, students develop definitions of the concepts they are focused on to begin to brainstorm ways to represent those definitions with their work. Students write a script and plan for their project videos that develop a distinct perspective that is neither autobiographical nor documentary in nature. Forbidden from borrowing images from the internet, students rely on their own creativity.

Next, students learn how to use iMovie9, beginning with the basic functions of the software, such as creating a new project; importing audio, video, and still images; adding sound; editing photos and video clips; and saving their work to an external drive. They build on their technological competence with technological literacy, including how to create credits, titles, and other text to supplement their visual message. They add transitions between different sections of the video, make decisions about precise timing of video elements, and experiment with ways to combine image, video, and sound to enhance the film's emotional and intellectual impact.[20] Students share the projects with organizations for use in their work on campus and in the community. They write a reflection paper on the creative project as it related to the course and its readings as a whole.

One student video about issues of colonization and aboriginal populations in Nova Scotia considered the issues of decolonization through her eyes as a settler in the area. This student assisted the Aboriginal Student Advising Office in planning an annual gathering on campus, from which she also acquired material for her video. She had to remove her privileged self from the center of the conversations, deal with the discomfort of being a settler, and learn to understand decolonization from her personal standpoint and, more importantly, from the perspectives of those who lived through colonization.

Unsurprisingly, students did note anxiety and frustration with learning how to use iMovie. Although they initially were resistant to learning and utilizing a new technology, students reported that overcoming those anxieties made them very proud of their videos. Indeed, Hurst notes that a majority of students commented that making a video was a "tangible skill they acquired" and were "very proud of," one "that could be carried forward into the 'real world' or 'real life.'"[21] This assignment demonstrates the power and utility of the intersections of technology and the humanities.

Even Digital Natives Need Tech Literacy

Younger members of the Millennial generation and all members of Generation Z are often deemed "digital natives" because they've only known a world with the internet, cell phones, apps, and social media.[22] However, that students use various technologies does not necessarily mean that they are using them effectively or with intention and awareness. Many students come to college without understanding the differences between printed and digital journals, the different uses for and expectations of texts versus emails, the impacts of technology on human beings and the world, and the difference between an everyday Facebook post and a persuasion-savvy Facebook post.[23]

The humanities help bridge the gap between using technology uncritically and using it with a deeper understanding of technology's roles, implications, and impacts. And in a world quickly moving to immerse more and more technology into our society and home lives, these interrogations are vitally important to business and the common good.

Chapter 14

Ethics

Two interrelated, important changes in the corporate world have accompanied advancements in the knowledge and high-tech economy. First, there is a greater sense of corporate social responsibility among many small and large businesses, recognizing business and industry's responsibility to "mak[e] the world a better place" even as they pursue a profit-driven mission.[1] Socially responsible practices include reducing a company's negative environmental impact, philanthropy and community engagement, ethical labor practices, and more.

Second, as we've discussed already, changes in the economy and technology are generating considerably complex ethical challenges. For example, the World Economic Forum calls artificial intelligence (AI) "just as much a new frontier for ethics and risk assessment as it is for emerging technology."[2] Some of the critical ethical issues associated with AI include the already widening wealth gap, job loss (and gain), the ways in which robots and technology act on human cognition, and bias. Big data is another example. Arguing for the role of the liberal arts in data analytics, Adam Weinberg asserts that "we need a generation of people shaping the field who see, acknowledge, and grapple with ethical concerns, especially as they relate to issues of privacy and civil liberties."[3]

Advances in digital media also raise serious ethical dilemmas. On the one hand, social media enables information to be more accessible to larger numbers of people and provides opportunities for lay citizens to publicly voice their opinions and beliefs. On the other hand, what are social network sites' ethical responsibility to truth and to civil society? Should racist and other hateful language be prohibited?

Significant ethical challenges like these are vitally important for current and prospective college students. Linda K. Trevino and Katherine A. Nelson define ethics as "the principles, norms, and standards of conduct governing an individual or group."[4] Ethical behavior in business is "behavior that is consistent with the principles, norms, and standards of business practice that have been agreed upon by society."[5] Though there isn't complete consensus on these issues, Trevino and Nelson argue that there is more agreement than disagreement—some of it codified in law, some of it in codes of conduct in many businesses and industries.[6]

Trevino and Nelson's approach to business ethics recognizes that individual ethical decision making in organizations is "influenced by characteristics of both individuals and organizations," and that organizations "operate within a broad and complex global business context."[7] Countering the claim that a few bad apples inside an organization are responsible for unethical behavior, they argue that often "something rotten inside the organization is spoiling the apples."[8] Given the humanities' focus on both living a life with individual meaning and contributing to the common good, it is unsurprising that a humanities education helps students navigate ethics complexities in the workplace and come to understand humans' ethical responsibilities to one another.

Workplace Ethics

In 2015 the German company Volkswagen (VW) admitted to installing "defeat device" software in 11 million diesel-engine automobiles that could detect when they were being tested and deceive emissions-testing procedures—in fact, the engines emitted nitrogen oxide pollutants up to forty times above what is allowed in the United States. The U.S. Department of Justice indicted seven VW employees for wrongdoing and stated that forty or more staff helped destroy related documents.[9] The scandal has led to scrutiny of VW's management culture, described as "confident, cutthroat and insular." Among the most significant questions is the extent to which the organizational culture at VW enabled, even encouraged, these illegal and unethical practices.[10]

The VW scandal is one of the most egregious cases of corporate ethical and legal misconduct in recent years. Misuse of technology, harm to the environment, deception, and so much more, these ethical breaches also raise larger issues of how important "ethical cultures" are to ethical behavior. In an "ideal workplace," according to ethics professor Steven Olson, "structures and relationships will work together around core values that transcend self-interest. Core values will inspire value-creating efforts as employees feel inspired to do what is right, even when the right thing is hard to do."[11]

Fortunately, the majority of businesses "do business the right way"— ethically.[12] The "right way," according to the Ethisphere Institute, means committed action to "advance the human condition."[13] In more good news, overall, workplace misconduct has declined in the past several years, according to a recent study conducted by the nonpartisan, nonprofit Ethics Resource Center. Among private-sector workers, 41 percent said they had observed misconduct on the job in 2013, a third straight year of decline. Also, only 9 percent of employees felt pressure to compromise standards.[14]

However, workplace misconduct remains a significant problem. Managers from supervisory to top levels commit a "relatively high percentage of misconduct." Employees say that more than a quarter (26 percent) of observed misconduct represents an ongoing pattern of behavior. Another 41 percent said the behavior has been repeated at least a second time. Only one-third (33 percent) of rule breaking represents a one-time incident. Among those who observed misconduct in 2013, 63 percent reported what they saw, compared to 65 percent in 2011 and 63 percent in 2009. However, in 2013, 21 percent of reporters said that they faced some form of retribution, largely unchanged from a record high of 22 percent in 2011.[15]

When companies value ethical performance, misconduct is substantially lower, according to the *National Business Ethics Survey of the U.S. Workforce* from the nonprofit Ethics Resource Center. In 2013, only 20 percent of workers reported seeing misconduct in companies where ethical cultures are "strong," compared with 88 percent who witnessed wrongdoing in companies with the weakest cultures. The report's authors conclude that while there is reason to be optimistic, "Building strong ethics cultures remains a constant work in progress."[16]

Businesses with strong ethical cultures value employees who make ethical decisions and act ethically. Investment company CEO Rodney Martin expressed this sentiment in a *Forbes* magazine article in 2017: "Ethics is a reflection of our commitment to doing business the right way. We emphasize trust and transparency—and we reward our people based on not only *what* is achieved, but *how* it is achieved."[17] That is, good outcomes must be achieved ethically.

Though they don't typically make the evening news like major corporate ethics violations, it's important to realize that individual unethical behaviors are common. The five most common types of unethical behaviors are misuse of company time, abusive behavior, employee theft, lying to employees, and violating company internet policies. In an article in *Philadelphia Business Review*, Arthur J. Schwartz notes that "cyberslackers" and "cyberloafers," people "who surf the Web when they should be working," are a huge, multi-billion-dollar problem for companies.[18] Misuse of company time and resources is not a new problem, but cyberslackers and cyberloafers illustrate how ethics need to evolve as the workplace changes.

The VW debacle is an example of unethical decision making, as are probably many of the examples linked to the statistics about workplace misconduct mentioned above. Similarly, spending time surfing the internet instead of working is not only a theft of company time and money, it's also a work ethic issue affecting many organizations. In another issue related to work ethic, companies are saying that they need employees with a willingness to work hard, efficiently, and successfully. Employers need to be able to count on their workers to be responsible with deadlines, to be accurate, to be considerate of coworkers, and to maintain a positive attitude, even when facing intellectual and practical challenges.

Ethical decision-making and work ethic are clearly concerns in the workplace, as they should be. But at the heart of questions about ethical decision-making and work ethic is the fundamental notion of ethics in the more general sense. It is these deeper and more universal questions of ethics that are central to study in the humanities, and we believe that these deeper ethical considerations help graduates make better ethical decisions in the workplace.

Ethics, Higher Education, and the Humanities

Though the study of ethics has been part of humanities disciplines like philosophy for centuries, business ethics is probably the most generally recognized field of ethics in the academy. As an academic field, business ethics emerged in the 1970s as ethical theory and philosophy were applied to several corporate issues already being discussed in business fields.[19] As business has evolved, so has business ethics. The 1980s brought a new focus on international business, and recent decades have turned toward issues related to information and new technologies. Numerous topics are studied by researchers, including leadership, managerial styles, ethical cultures, ethical decision-making, child labor, minimum wage, equal pay, misleading advertising, distribution of earnings, and many more.

According to researchers at Ethical Systems, a business ethics research group housed in New York University's Stern Business and Society Program, there's been a greater focus on business ethics in MBA programs than in undergraduate business programs, leaving undergraduate students at a disadvantage.[20] These scholars also note that they don't believe that the teaching of one ethics course in isolation is going to have much of an impact on students and that undergraduate business programs would be more successful at teaching business ethics if ethics were integrated throughout the curriculum.

Students in science, technology, health, journalism, education, engineering, history, and all other programs and majors must grapple with ethical questions. Richard Paul and Linda Elder suggest that sound ethical reasoning "often requires us to enter empathically into points of view other than our own, gather facts from alternative perspectives, question our assumptions, and consider alternative ways to put the question at issue."[21] We believe there's a strong argument to be made that students in humanities courses and curricula leave college with a deeper understanding of ethics that may be applied to all areas of life, including the workplace. Across the humanities in course after course, students wrestle with meaningful ethical dilemmas. In anthropology, students may consider ethical issues relating to the preservation and use of ancient sites and artifacts. In environmental history, students may debate a state's efforts to place a landfill in one neighborhood over another. Students in an art history class may grapple with the ethics of whether art created by Nazis is worthy of study.

Michele's various communication classes address ethics and ethical decision-making in several ways. Students in public speaking, for example, contend with the ethics of emotional appeals in communication. In a First Amendment class, students have to think about how to balance a student's right to free expression on their college campus with the need for a teaching environment free from disruption. As another example: Are the ethical concerns with allowing a hate group to march in the streets more or less important than protecting the speech of people with whom we may disagree?

Laurie's community-based undergraduate research projects in oral and local histories raise ethical issues each and every time. For instance, when a student realized her late grandfather was being accused of racist behavior, it was a profound learning moment for her as she considered her various ethical commitments. She had to consider her late grandfather, who could no longer speak for himself; her family members who might be hurt by the information; the narrator, who, in his seventies, had experienced a lifetime of racism; and principles and best practices in oral history. Ethical issues also exist in other classes that Laurie teaches, such as literature. We turn now to one of the assignments she has used for ethical learning in Toni Morrison's novel *Beloved*.

Assignment: Ethical Complexities in the Novel *Beloved*

Ronald F. Duska, one of the leading scholars and consultants in the field of business ethics, tells us that "literature, good literature," helps readers "in dealing with ethical matters in general and ethical matters in business in particular."[22] Duska is not suggesting a one-to-one correspondence with an ethical dilemma that someone might face in the workplace. Rather, literature raises broader questions of ethical reasoning and seeing others' points of view, understanding the factors that push people into ethically poor choices and the complexities involved.[23]

Toni Morrison's novel *Beloved* immerses its readers in many complex ethical quandaries. At times poetic, serene, and hopeful, the novel is a brutal, graphic depiction of the horrors of the American slave system and its aftermath.

At its core, *Beloved* tells the tragic story of Sethe, a former slave, who killed her two-year-old daughter rather than have her captured and enslaved.[24] The infanticide haunts Sethe, her family, her community, the novel, and its readers and raises multilayered ethical issues.

Beloved opens in the year 1873 in Cincinnati, Ohio, where Sethe has been living as a runaway slave for eighteen years after fleeing Sweet Home Plantation in Kentucky. Sethe, her husband Halle, and their three children were slaves at Sweet Home, first with "benevolent" slave owners, if such a thing can even exist (another deeply complex ethical issue), and later with the wretched, hateful master they called "Schoolteacher." Sethe's harrowing escape north and across the Ohio River in 1855 reunited her with her two sons and young daughter, who is unnamed, and mother-in-law, Baby Suggs. She arrives with a baby, Denver, to whom she gave birth during her escape, helped by a white girl named Amy Denver.

After twenty-eight days of unslaved life, living with her four children in Cincinnati, Sethe sees Schoolteacher walking into the yard, obviously there to capture his runaway slave and her children. As Schoolteacher nears, Sethe grabs her children, runs into the woodshed, kills the unnamed daughter, and tries to kill the others. Morrison fictionalizes a true account of the slave woman Margaret Garner, a runaway slave who in 1856 escaped with her husband and four children from a plantation in Kentucky and murdered her children at the moment she and they were to be recaptured.

In the present tense of the novel, Sethe lives with eighteen-year-old Denver. Her sons have run away, and Baby Suggs has died. Sethe and Denver are socially isolated, abandoned by the community who turned away from Sethe after the killing of her daughter. Sethe's quest for psychic and spiritual wholeness in the aftermath of the infanticide lies at the center of *Beloved*.

In an assignment Laurie has used often and in varying ways, students explore the ethical complexities of the infanticide. We usually begin with a whole class discussion about the matter. Students tend to view Sethe's behavior as immoral, although they are aware of the extenuating circumstances— Sethe states, "it worked," since none of her children were returned to slavery (165). But students often point to other facets of the novel to justify their ethical position, such as the Black community's ostracism of Sethe and her family. They also point to Sethe's own sense of guilt and desperate need for self-forgiveness as well as the profound consequences of her actions: the loss of her baby girl and her reincarnation as the ghost haunting 124 Bluestone; the loss of her two sons, who run away from home; and the lonely life she leads with her only remaining child, Denver.

However, these judgments are complicated by the next part of the assignment, in which groups of students closely analyze, discuss, and then present their findings on sections of the novel where the author presents the thoughts and perspectives of different characters regarding the infanticide. In many ways, the assignment fulfills Donna Keinzler's framework for teaching ethical interrogation and decision-making by including four main aspects: students must identify and question assumptions, seek a multiplicity of voices and alternatives on a subject, make connections, and be actively involved in the learning process.[25]

For the sake of brevity, we focus here on Schoolteacher's and Sethe's perspectives. The assignment asks students to carefully consider the perspective offered by the characters based on several elements, including language, images, symbols, the narrator's tone, the emotions evoked, and other information from the novel.

The first of these interior descriptions of the event is from inside the mind of the slave catcher. The language, as students note, is stark: "Inside, two boys bled in the sawdust and dirt at the feet of a [n-word] woman holding a blood-soaked child to her chest with one hand and an infant by the heels in the other" (149). The students point to the slave catcher's dehumanizing language calling Sethe—a human being he is there to capture and return to slavery—the n-word. They note that Sethe held her "blood-soaked child to her chest." The violence of the act is juxtaposed with maternal instinct. When students report on Sethe's account of the moment, they often notice that her maternal instinct to protect her children is amplified: "When she saw them coming and recognized schoolteacher's hat, she heard wings. Little hummingbirds stuck their needle beaks right through her headcloth into her hair and beat their wings. If she thought anything, it was No. No. Nono. Nonono. Simple. She just flew" (163). Students connect the notion of maternal instinct in these passages with other parts of the book, as well as historical information about the slave system's capricious tearing away of children from mothers and fathers at will, valuing money over human life, and regarding slaves as nonhuman. Students also consider that Sethe had a mother she never got to know, and that her mother had thrown all her children but Sethe overboard on a slave ship. Students question what is ethical in a state-sanctioned horror imposed on our fellow human beings, even whether ethics has any meaning in such a circumstance. They also discuss whether white society is ultimately responsible for the murder.

The students then contrast an image of a hummingbird with Schoolteacher's callous comparisons of Sethe to hounds and horses. Having just witnessed Sethe murder her daughter, he thinks, "She'd gone wild, due to the mishandling of the nephew who'd overbeat her and made her cut and run. Schoolteacher had chastised that nephew, telling him to think—just think—what would his own horse do if you beat it beyond the point of education. Or Chipper, or Samson. Suppose you beat the hounds past that point thataway" (149). Students are sickened by schoolteacher's dehumanizing language as well as his total lack of compassion for the murdered child.

Moreover, students point to what they consider to be Schoolteacher's selfish thoughts—he laments that "the whole lot was lost now" (150), meaning he has to return home without the five slaves he intended to bring with him. In contrast, they focus on Sethe's selfless and loving thoughts as she does what she must to protect her children: "Collected every bit of life she had made, all the parts of her that were precious and fine and beautiful, and carried, pushed, dragged them through the veil, out, away, over there where no one could hurt them. Over there. Outside this place, where they would be safe" (163). Throughout the novel, readers learn more and more about the inhumane treatment Sethe received as a slave, for example, when Schoolteacher's nephews stole the milk from her breasts.

Ultimately, conversations and presentations about this human tragedy are deeply moving, ambiguous ethical experiences for students. Literature, like many other kinds of texts and experiences in humanities classrooms, immerses students in the complexities of general notions of ethics as they're linked to ethical decision-making as well as the sometimes-dire human consequences of our choices. We believe this is critical learning for every student going into every kind of workplace.

While studying *Beloved* and the many ethical quandaries it encourages students to consider isn't going to provide cut-and-dried answers about "here's how you come to the right ethical decision," these conversations encourage students to think about ethics as the very foundation of decisions about the human condition. We believe that when students have the experience of repeatedly considering the most fundamental question of ethics—how best to live—they're engaging in mind training.

In humanities courses, students talk about ethics in ways that give them not the answers but rather the tools to come up with their own answers. For example, we encourage students to consider context, to try to understand the various ways of seeing an ethical dilemma, to consider the future consequences of decisions and whether history can give us hints about them, and to consider how those consequences may differ depending on one's status in society.

When students regularly engage in thinking, talking, and writing about the core ethical concerns that bind us together as humans, they leave the classroom ready to think more seriously and at a deeper level about decisions they'll be asked to make in the future. No doubt, discussion of Sethe and infanticide does not correspond directly with workplace issues students may one day face. Rather, it gives students practice in considering issues of humanity and the consequences of inhumanity as it relates to issues of race in our country, lessons they can apply in myriad contexts.

Ethics for Our Lives

Daryl Koehn and Dawn Elm, editors of *Aesthetics and Business Ethics*, citing Aristotle, observe that "we do not study ethics merely for the sake of clarifying problems. We study ethics with a view to living better, fuller and wiser lives."[26] We believe that students, and their later decisions in life, are better for the deep, meaningful discussions of ethics that occur in the humanities classroom. The humanities do not necessarily make students more ethical people. Instead, they encourage students to consider the ethical dimensions of their experiences and the choices they will face as they go through their careers and their lives.

Chapter 15

Diversity, Inclusivity, and Equality

One thing is clear from the research: workplace diversity is good for business. Diverse and inclusive organizations are more innovative, smarter, more productive, and generate higher revenues. In fact, "study after study confirms that companies with a diverse workforce and inclusive policies outperform ones without."[1]

However, a healthy, productive, diverse, and inclusive workplace is difficult to achieve. Even companies like Google and Apple struggle to achieve diversity, despite concerted efforts. There are numerous obstacles to diversity and inclusiveness in many organizations.[2] That's because diversity and inclusiveness are complex systems and processes. In fact, although companies pay millions of dollars yearly for diversity programs, policies, and trainings, there is little agreement as to their effectiveness. In a study of more than seven hundred U.S. companies, for example, diversity training was shown to have no positive effect; worse, training activities may *decrease* representation of black women.[3] A *Harvard Business Review* article reports "mixed results" of diversity training programs, ranging from effective to ineffective to counterproductive.[4]

Achieving healthy diverse and inclusive workplaces also involves a more recent corporate concern with fairness and equity. For example, the mission of the CEO Action for Diversity and Inclusion, led by more than four hundred CEOs of the world's leading companies and business organizations, is explicitly aimed at collective action "to address honestly and head-on the concerns and needs of our diverse employees and increase equity for all, including Blacks, Latinos, Asians, Native Americans, LGBTQ, disabled, veterans and women."[5]

Arguably, the humanities are where this kind of education—called "critical multicultural education"—takes place, in course after course. Multicultural education aims to secure social justice and overcome group-based oppressions, usually on the basis of race, ethnicity, gender, class, nationality, disability, and sexual orientation. Multicultural education prioritizes equality, justice, and human dignity for all, not merely a tolerance or respect for diversity and difference.

Multicultural education in the humanities is nowhere close to ideal—and the notion of "ideal" is itself contested. As noted in Chapter 4, disagreement across these disciplines exists about how to strike that balance between traditional white male "masterpieces" from Western culture and diverse voices, texts, ideas, and cultures. Yet nowhere else in the curriculum do these issues get read about, written about, discussed, debated, analyzed, and assessed more than in the humanities—in our research and in our classrooms.

Through intellectual participation in issues of diversity, inclusion, and equality, students learn how to work productively with others different from themselves. They are exposed to the advantages of a multiplicity of viewpoints, learn to recognize their own and others' explicit and implicit bias, and understand the deeply entrenched inequities in society that spill over to the workplace. These are the graduates likely to become agents of change in the workplace.

Diversity, Inclusivity, and Equality in the Workplace

Advancing diversity is good business and makes financial sense.[6] Studies indicate that businesses see a 35 percent increase in return on investment for ethnically diverse companies and a 15 percent return for gender-diverse companies.[7] Based on the strong correlations between increased diversity and increased revenue, Vivian Hunt, Dennis Layton, and Sara Prince suggest that more diverse companies "are better able to win top talent and improve their customer orientation, employee satisfaction, and decision-making, and all that leads to a cycle of increasing returns."[8] Further, businesses without a diverse workforce may be less attractive to groups of customers and clients. In other words, a diverse workforce provides access to diverse markets, increasingly important in the global economy.[9]

Moreover, a diversity and multiplicity of perspectives lead to increased creativity and innovation, richer brainstorming, and better decision-making.[10] Research by organizational scientists, psychologists, sociologists, economists, and demographers overwhelmingly demonstrates that diverse groups are more creative and productive than homogenous groups in schools, the workplace, and the public realm.[11] Individuals from varied cultures, genders, races, and other categories bring different experience and knowledge. As one example, Nike's new "Pro Hijab," a lightweight, breathable headcover for female Muslim athletes, was the result of understanding the needs of a distinct demographic.[12]

In addition, professor of leadership and ethics and senior vice dean Katherine W. Phillips notes that "simply interacting with individuals who are different forces group members to prepare better, to anticipate alternative viewpoints and to expect that reaching consensus will take effort."[13] One study, for example, suggested that teams with more women outperformed teams with more men in part because they were better at understanding others' subconscious desires and needs.[14] Study after study demonstrates better productivity and creativity through diverse teams.

Increasingly, efforts to go beyond diversity and inclusiveness to equity and justice are coming to the forefront of workplace diversity through programs and policies that address structural and systemic inequities. Gender inequalities are well known—overall, women working full time earn just 80 cents for every dollar men earn. Women working full time, year-round, had median annual earnings of $41,554 in 2016, *$10,086 less per year in median earnings* than men's annual earnings of $51,640. Compared with non-Hispanic white men, white non-Hispanic women are paid 81 cents on the dollar and Asian women are paid 88 cents on the dollar. However, the wage gap is even worse for Black and Hispanic women, who earn only 65 cents and 59 cents on the *white* male dollar, respectively. In terms of the impact on women's paychecks, this means that relative to the typical white man, Black women take home $7.63 less per hour and Hispanic women take home $8.90 less per hour.[15]

American women hold nearly 52 percent of all professional-level jobs, but the evidence of the gender leadership gap is staggering, and worse for women of color. Women make up 44 percent of the overall S&P 500 labor force and a little more than one-third of first or mid-level officials and managers, but only one-quarter hold executive and senior-level positions, and only 6 percent are CEOs. Women of color comprise only 3.9 percent of executive or senior-level officials and managers and 0.4 percent of CEOs in those companies in 2015.[16]

In addition, allegations of workplace harassment constituted nearly one-third of the approximately 90,000 charges received by the Equal Employ-ment Opportunity Commission (EEOC) in 2015.[17] Sexual harassment is the most frequently reported allegation; for private sector and state and local government employers, the numbers come out to approximately 45 percent of employees alleging harassment on the basis of sex in 2015. This combined with alleged harassment on the basis of race (34 percent), disability (19 per-cent), age (15 percent), national origin (13 percent), and religion (5 percent) illustrates that far too many employees in the American workforce deal with hostile working environments.

Discrimination based on sex, gender, and sexuality is also pervasive. For example, 27 percent of transgender people who held or applied for a job in 2017 reported being fired, not hired, or denied a promotion due to their gender identity; 10 percent of lesbian, gay, bisexual, and transgender (LGBT) individuals report that an unwelcoming environment led them to leave their job; and 8 percent of LGBT employees report that discrimination negatively affected their work atmosphere.[18]

Enduring inequities based on race also exist, for example, an unemploy-ment rate for Blacks that's been approximately double the rate for whites since the 1970s.[19] Members coming from marginalized groups are often victims of what are called microinequities and microaggressions, which are subtle but powerful insults like seemingly harmless jokes, ignoring and ex-cluding, and other devaluing behaviors.[20] Mitchell Wellman puts it in starkly real terms: numerically, more minorities are attending college. However, "our country is plagued by deep and persistent inequities by race and ethnicity from classrooms to boardrooms."[21]

Therefore, much work is needed to overcome diversity, inclusivity, and equality issues. While diversity makes teams smarter, good results may not accrue from simply putting diverse people together, given the complexities of inequities and bias. Humanities education can help bridge this gap.

Diversity, Inclusivity, and Multicultural Education in Colleges and Universities

The twenty-first-century college student population is the most diverse in our nation's history, characterized by the intersection of race, gender, sexual orientation, religion, family composition, age, and economic status, among others.[22] Enrollment data from the *National Center for Education Statistics (NCES)* shows that in 2016–2017, 9.1 million college students were white, 3.2 million Hispanic, 2.2 million Black, and 1.1 million Asian out of a total of 16.9 million undergraduates.[23] In 2017 women outnumbered men by 56 percent to 44 percent.[24] LGBTQ students are "more visible" in higher education than in the past.[25] Demographic trends for the next decade predict a more ethnically diverse and more female student body; in addition, there will be fewer students who arrive straight from high school.[26]

However, it's critical to note that these general statistics vary widely across institutions. One study, for example, found that schools in the Midwest are typically less diverse, and universities in California, like Stanford, UCLA, and UC-Berkeley, are more diverse. Students will find a more diverse student body at larger universities than smaller colleges. The top 100 liberal arts colleges are less diverse than their university counterparts.[27] And within colleges and universities there is varying diversity in different majors and programs.

Furthermore, an increasingly diverse population does not translate to harmony or equity. Higher education institutions are part of the larger society, and beginning in 2015, there have been perhaps more race-related conflicts than since the 1960s Civil Rights era.[28] As multicultural educator James Banks states, "The racial, class, gender and religious divisions within U.S. society are extensive, persistent, and intractable."[29] On college and university campuses, racism and other forms of bias and discrimination abound, including a great deal of LGBTQ student harassment and victimization.[30] Microaggressions are also common, such as the assumption conveyed by some white students that Black students are on campus only due to affirmative action.[31] Many minority students report "exclusionary classroom experiences and racist encounters involving faculty members."[32]

"Critical multicultural education" is the label used for diversity education that is social justice–oriented. It's not merely about adding diverse writers, texts, histories, values, beliefs, practices, and perspectives of people from many cultural groups; it's about understanding the whole enterprise differently—about seeking new ways to understand what's valuable in literary studies or art, for example. Critical multicultural education asks what's been left out of history, why, and according to whom. Who had the authority to render "domestic arts" as low culture but oil paintings as high culture?

Critical multicultural education questions why history has long been looked at through the lenses of war, politics, and governing, spheres from which women have been excluded for most of human history, and how slavery, though abolished in 1865 by the Thirteenth Amendment, is at least partly responsible in 2018 for enduring and unequal race-based economic and educational opportunities.

Critical multicultural education focuses on justice, fairness, and respect for all human beings, aiming to close the gap between haves and have-nots by dismantling the systemic and structural inequities deeply entrenched in the social, political, and economic fabric of U.S. society. Students learn how power and authority function to retain the status quo, how stereotypes function to maintain oppressions, and how "equal opportunity" in the United States may be an ideal but has never, in fact, been reality.

Critical multicultural education exists across the humanities curriculum. As one example, teaching history with images allows students to engage more deeply with historical content, especially when learning about women or other traditionally marginalized groups. Using image analysis strategies from various disciplines (e.g., media literacy, art history, social studies education), students engage with images as an additional text to enhance (and counter) their understanding of history.[33] Students in a literature class compare and contrast working-class literature and literature of poverty by a variety of writers, including Dorothy Allison, author of *Bastard Out of Carolina*, and John Steinbeck, author of *Grapes of Wrath* and *Of Mice and Men*.

In an African American studies course, students investigate white culture's use of Black culture—by wearing certain hairstyles or twerking, for example—through the lens of history and power, questioning whether these are ethical borrowings or unethical appropriations. Linguistics students study the origins of language, questioning whether some language practices are literally "man-made"—for example, when they read Dale Spender's book documenting that eighteenth-century grammarian John Kirby created a grammatical "rule," endorsed by his fellow all-male grammarians—that the male gender is "more comprehensive" than the female gender. The grammatical rule became an Act of Parliament in 1850.[34]

Assignments like these, and the anthology of the "best rock music" described in detail below, provide students opportunities to explore, reflect on, and understand many issues related to diversity, inclusivity, and inequality.

These lessons help students to be ready to work among and with coworkers who are different from them in myriad ways, by understanding implicit biases, engaging with multiple and divergent perspectives, and respecting and admiring cultural and other differences. They graduate knowing that "diversity" and "inclusivity" are inseparable from equality and justice. Finally, these lessons prepare them to recognize and leverage the value of identity integration as it relates to creativity and innovation.

Assignment: Developing an Anthology of the "Best" Rock Music

Two decades ago, Laurie began using and modifying an assignment created by James S. Laughlin that asked students to work in small groups to create an audio anthology of the "best" 100 to 125 songs (presented on eight CDs) spanning the history of American rock and roll music.[35] Students had to make judgments about what constitutes the "best" in rock and roll, paralleling the ways that literary specialists make judgments about what literature to teach. Laurie has since used various modifications of the assignment in her literature general education courses. The assignment is an excellent example of critical multicultural education because it is both a celebration of diversity and a critique of—and window into—power. As students face the daunting task of selecting and then justifying these song selections, they confront many ways that power circulates through and constructs "winners" and "losers" in various elements of American life, including the music they love and the industry behind it.

When they first get the assignment and begin conversations in their small groups, students tend to list similar songs and artists: the Beatles' "Hey Jude"; the Rolling Stones' "(I Can't Get No) Satisfaction"; the Doors' "Light My Fire"; Aerosmith's "Walk This Way"; Pink Floyd's "Another Brick in the Wall (Part 2)"; Led Zeppelin's "Stairway to Heaven"; Jimi Hendrix's "Purple Haze"; Tina Turner's "Proud Mary"; the Beach Boys' "California Girls"; Bruce Springsteen's "Born to Run"; Neil Young's "Heart of Gold"; Chuck Berry's "Johnny B. Goode"; Elvis Presley's "Love Me Tender"; Rod Stewart's "Maggie May"; and U2's "I Still Haven't Found What I'm Looking For." This initial list, which has changed little in the two decades Laurie's taught the assignment, opens students' eyes. They ask, "Where are the women?"

"Why is there only one Black musician on the list?" "Where are musicians representing the many diverse cultures and groups in the United States?"

The assignment requires that students conduct research into the history of rock and roll as well as contemporary debates. Students are surprised and excited to learn that there is an entire body of academic research about music, and because most students love music (of various types), they become deeply engaged. They also soon find out that the research articles are like most humanities scholarship—rigorous and challenging to read and understand while opening up new ways to think about human expression in musical form. And they learn that experts have different views of what genres and musicians should be included in the category called "rock music."

Students learn about the many musical influences leading to rock and roll, from Celtic folk music in Europe to rhythm and blues, jazz, gospel, bluegrass, and more. Most students do not realize that the Beatles and the Rolling Stones credit the blues as one of their early twentieth-century influences.[36] They also learn that Black Americans and other people of color are underrepresented across the industry, for example, in awards.[37]

Students must decide on, and present to their classmates and professor, the criteria they used to make their selections. Laughlin proposes artistic merit and popularity by record sales as two important criteria. Students also came up with their own criteria, such as lyrical content and concern for representation. The assignment also asks them to discuss "any concerns, issues, hesitations, problems, or difficulties" relevant to the anthology selections they encountered along the way and how, as a group, they negotiated and resolved these issues. They also need to explain any inclusions that might be controversial.[38]

As they dig into the criteria and selection processes, students begin to see the bigger issues, for example, that artistic merit is neither universally agreed to nor—in a case like this—in the eye of the beholder. Laurie loves the moments when students debate whether male and female music differs, whether they differ based on gender or sex, whether it is biologically and/or culturally determined, and why separate Grammy awards for men and women were established and whether that should continue. These are complicated questions of diversity, difference, inclusivity, and fairness, and they are rooted in a deep and exclusionary history. Students learn that something so much a part of their lives—music—is impacted by who is in positions of power.

"Stomping on Eggshells"

Issues of race, gender, class, sexuality, and other forms of discrimination and prejudice are uncomfortable to talk about—around campus, in the classroom, and in the workplace. These conversations are also necessary both for pragmatic and humane reasons.

Multicultural education is not a cure-all. Our discussion of assignments in humanities classes in this chapter barely scratches the surface of the tensions, discomfort, and genuine learning that often takes place when, in Kyesha Jennings's words, we "stomp . . . on eggshells rather than walk . . . on eggshells."[39] In other words, at its best, multicultural education challenges students to face, confront, and acknowledge the worst facets of our nation.

At this historical moment, as business and industry realize that diversity, inclusivity, and equality are good for not only business but also humankind, graduates who leave college with critical multicultural understanding and knowledge, and not merely an appreciation of diversity, can contribute both to small- and large-scale change.

Chapter 16

Globalization, Global Understanding, and a Global Perspective

Two years after Euro Disney opened in April 1992 in Paris, the European Disney theme park had to borrow $175 million to keep operating. The company had made several mistakes: having the word "Euro" in its name, which in Europe is the nickname for their currency, not the continent; using plastic cutlery and not offering wine with meals in a country known for valuing its culinary experience; hyping Disney characters rather than characters beloved by European children; and the failure to provide product instructions in various languages appropriate to Europeans. In other words, Disney failed to "glocalize"—to understand and enact local culture in the attempt to globalize.[1] Reopening in 1994 as Disneyland Paris, the company thrived, having developed several glocalized strategies, among them renaming the theme park, reducing prices, bringing the French culture to the settings and shows, changing the food menus, and enacting different employee customs and labor policies.[2]

The success of Disneyland Paris illustrates the significance of cultural differences in the global economy.[3] And this need for understanding and navigating cultural differences is increasing. Global expansion is part of the growth plans for businesses across all economic sectors.[4] From every corner of the globe, we are all part of an interconnected network, and in the words of Erin Meyer, professor of organizational behavior, "unless we know how to decode other cultures and avoid easy-to-fall-into cultural traps, we are easy prey to misunderstanding, needless conflict, and ultimate failure."[5] Courses and programs in the humanities play a vital role in the broader questions of understanding what culture is and means, as well as insights into deep cultural differences.

Furthermore, beyond the bottom line in the global economy, understanding global cultural differences matters to the most vital human concerns, from human rights and discrimination to sustainability, world health, and poverty. Daniel Rockmore, professor of mathematics and computer science, argues that "at the end of the day, it seems that the problems of the world boil down to me not understanding others and them not understanding me, and that's a humanities problem." We must understand the human world, culture, and history to understand global threats like fundamentalism, terrorism, racism, and fascism. Technology will not solve these problems, Rockmore asserts, because "ultimately, you can't think of the human world without considering the questions that are raised in the humanities."[6]

Higher education has turned to global education to address the pragmatic and ethical needs of globalization. The number of U.S. research universities explicitly referencing internationalization in their current mission statements has doubled over the past decade. Global learning efforts include efforts to expand "intercultural competencies, opportunities for global learning, and education for global citizenship" and the move toward "reorienting policies, programs, and curricula from the national to the global."[7] The objective is for students to attain a "global perspective"—understanding that we are all shaped by culture(s); that cultural similarities and differences matter; that the world is connected economically, globally, and socially; and that as humans, we are responsible for one another.

The humanities curriculum is distinguished by its extended and extensive coverage of global humanity and all that entails. Like issues of diversity, inclusivity, and equality within the United States discussed in the previous chapter, issues related to global cultural differences are multilayered.

Globalism in the Workplace and on the Global Stage

"Difference is increasing. Borders are disappearing when it comes to trade. There are more and more players involved, countries involved," says international business professor Dennis Karney when discussing the need for global awareness across business and industry.[8] Global economic growth is projected to be 3.9 percent in 2019, according to the International Monetary Fund's World Economic Outlook.[9]

These continuing shifts mean that intercultural competence is necessary at all levels of business. Whether one sets foot in another country or not, a global mindset is necessary because "employees work virtually across borders via technology" and "interact with a globally dispersed customer base."[10] Employees must know how to cope with cultural differences and be open to others' ideas, aware that attitudes, policies, leadership styles, and communication vary from culture to culture. Leadership must think and plan strategically to be competitive in a global economy. Globalization opens up tremendous opportunities for businesses, but also presents obstacles.

In her book on global business, Meyer tells the story of American engineer Kara Williams, whose first presentation as an employee of a German firm flopped. Williams began by "getting right to the point," presenting her recommendations about reducing carbon emissions to a small group of German directors. She was surprised when just after she began her presentation, the directors asked her questions about her methodology. Williams felt her credibility was being attacked, but she later learned that Germans expect recommendations at the end of a presentation. She did not get the sale.[11]

To help workers avoid these cross-cultural pitfalls, Meyer has developed a list of eight crucial elements of global competence:

Communicating: Explicit versus Implicit;
Evaluating: Direct negative feedback versus Indirect negative feedback;
Leading: Egalitarian versus Hierarchical;
Deciding: Consensual versus Top-down;
Disagreeing: Confrontation versus Avoidance;
Persuading: Holistic versus Specific;
Scheduling: Organized time versus Flexible time;
Trusting: Task-based versus Relationship-based.[12]

For each element, Meyer identifies the extremes and then maps where various countries and cultures fall along the continuum based on how their population perceives certain actions. Her aim is to help workers prepare for cross-cultural business encounters and collaborations.[13]

For example, on the Trusting scale, the United States is placed far to the left on the scale—that is, Americans tend to build trust through business interactions. At the far right of the scale are Brazil, Russia, India, and China, indicating that for workers in these countries, trust is built on emotion and personal interactions, such as dining together. Poland, France, Italy,

Spain, and Austria fall somewhere in the middle. Meyer offers numerous suggestions regarding how one would navigate the intricacies of task-based relationships in cross-cultural exchanges.

Moreover, David Gartside, Stefano Griccioli, and Rustin Richburg identify employees' assumptions about cultural and economic superiority as a major hindrance to effective global success. As companies in the West and the East expand into each other's territories, they must "adopt . . . a genuinely neutral global perspective, without presumptions about whose role is dominant."[14] That's because the global economy is shifting. Emerging economies will begin to account for more than half of global gross domestic product (GDP) in the next ten years, and up to 65 percent by 2030. Workers at all levels may find themselves collaborating with, and supervised by, workers from countries with economies that they consider inferior—and this will cause deep, possibly irreparable damage.[15]

This attitude of superiority is often fostered in higher education, as Jennifer Trost suggests. She notes that American higher education's "deeply rooted Euro-centric understanding of the world" is decreasing, but not quickly enough. According to Trost, "American students' knowledge of the world is often sketchy at best and, as a result, many other cultural practices appear only strange to them."[16] Ethnocentrism—the assumption that one's own cultural norms are the basis by which to judge others—will cloud an individual's ability to communicate effectively and behave in respectful ways across cultures.

However, humanities courses and curricula are especially suited to facilitating cross-cultural global knowledge, communication, and understanding. Our methods of analysis and investigation promote open-mindedness, perspective taking, cultural sensitivity, understanding of power relations, and recognition that history's colonial legacies are still felt today.

Global Education, Higher Education, and the Humanities

In the academic year 2016–2017, U.S. colleges and universities hosted a record high of 1.08 million international students, the eleventh consecutive year of increase. In addition, 325,339 American students studied abroad in the academic year 2015–2016, an increase of 4 percent from the previous year.[17] American students are interacting with an increasing number of international students on and off their campuses, a good step toward a global mindset.

Global education, still in its relative infancy, is far more systematic and intentional. An indication of this intentionality is evident in the deliberate distinctions made between global learning and the more long-standing "international studies." Kevin Hovland suggests that some academics see the shift from international studies to global learning "as a political or moral imperative."[18] As Hovland notes, the vast economic, social, and political opportunities brought on by globalization for some groups of people are simultaneously vast hardships for others. As more and more of us connect to people in faraway lands through technological advances, our heightened sense of responsibility to others has also expanded.

This sense of interconnectedness as humans and our responsibility to one another are reflected in the Association of American Colleges and Universities (AAC&U) definition of global learning:

> critical analysis of and an engagement with complex, interdependent global systems and legacies (such as natural, physical, social, cultural, economic, and political) and their implications for people's lives and the earth's sustainability. Through global learning, students should 1) become informed, open-minded, and responsible people who are attentive to diversity across the spectrum of differences, 2) seek to understand how their actions affect both local and global communities, and 3) address the world's most pressing and enduring issues collaboratively and equitably.[19]

The statement emphasizes attention to difference and equality as well as a shared understanding of how actions and policies in one corner of the globe affect others. Notably, the AAC&U recognizes that global learning takes place over the entirety of a student's college career, not in a single course.[20] Moreover, global education often takes place by immersing students in local instances of global problems.

Humanities programs are an especially rich resource for global education. Culture(s) are embedded in the human experience. Literature, language, history, art, philosophy, and more are expressions of the human experience that both reflect and shape culture. Across higher education, humanities programs are global in scope—world literatures, religions, philosophies, artistic expressions, and histories, for example. The humanities have not yet found that ideal balance of Anglocentric and non-Anglocentric, but we are continuing those efforts. Moreover, nowhere else in the curriculum does a student study and explore human and cultural differences with such depth and through a critical and ethical lens.

Myriad types of courses and assignments fostering global learning exist. In a women's studies course, students might grapple with the practice of female circumcision in the context of global difference and diversity, religious freedoms, and universal human rights. In a philosophy course, students might examine the question of developed countries' responsibilities to address world hunger.[21] In a food and cultures class, students might explore cultural norms around dining, including field trips to ethnic food venues offering cultural experiences not typically found in the region.[22] The course readings and field trip introduce students to the history and cultural worldviews that underlie food selections, recipes, rituals, customs, and behaviors. In another example, Laurie recently taught Lynn Nottage's *Sweat*, winner of the 2017 Pulitzer Prize. It is a play that is set in a southeastern Pennsylvania city and that has global resonances. One cannot understand *Sweat* without examining the North American Free Trade Agreement (NAFTA), regional trade policy, and immigration. These and many other assignments immerse students in the challenges—and the wonders—of difference.

Assignment: Personal Narratives in Global Education

Jennifer Trost at Utica College has developed assignments using personal narratives to teach a global perspective in an interdisciplinary course in history, economics, and political science.[23] The course covers topics such as globalization, the emergence of international political and economic institutions, and advances in developing nations in the contexts of cultural differences, historical legacies, and differing physical geographies.

Trost pays particular attention to the role of personal narratives in helping students develop a global perspective. As she explains, it is "difficult to get [American students] to 'see' their Western identity."[24] That is Eurocentrism at play—many Americans, including students, view their cultural beliefs, values, and practices as "normal" and "the right way" and see those of other cultures as "alternative" and "inferior." Trost's students read cross-cultural personal narratives such as Jamaica Kincaid's *A Small Place* and Gelareh Asayesh's *Saffron Sky: A Life Between Iran and America*. In the context of global history, they "fit those stories into the global pattern or concept."[25] In other words, the stories draw students into another culture and then enlarge their thinking.

Trost argues that personal narratives bring students into the lives of others they would likely never meet. In so doing, students are able to momentarily "see" outside of their own point of view and "think critically about how other lives may be similar or different to theirs."[26] For example, they learn that in some cultures, having large families is about survival in places without any security net for the elderly. They learn that women have been oppressed throughout human history in nearly all cultures, and that in many countries today, women still suffer brutal treatment at the hands of men in power. They get close-up, personal views into collectivist cultures and values, and they realize that American individualism is not the only or even the "best" way to live.[27]

Trost's students also become more aware of similarities across human cultures. She says that her students learn about "other people who experience love, question the government, get drunk, fight for justice, and face the same kind of courtship anxieties they do." In other words, they see that human beings share so much from place to place, era to era, culture to culture. And yet, differences do matter as well. For example, students learn that political expression in some cultures and countries can mean prison or death. They also learn that the United States is not superior in many ways, for example, that the high crime rate that they accept as an integral part of American life does not exist everywhere, like Japan.[28]

In an essay assignment, Trost asks students to explain how Chinua Achebe, the Nigerian author of *Things Fall Apart*, and Truong Nhu Tang, the Vietnamese author of *A Viet Cong Memoir: An Inside Account of the Vietnam War and Its Aftermath*, would explain their culture and history to one another.[29] That is, students need to walk in these authors' shoes, view their cultures from within, and then articulate those views to someone from a third culture. Trost believes that this kind of exercise, embedded throughout the course in various ways, is critical to developing global mindsets. As she puts it, "If students can successfully master analysis of one person's view, they can also understand other views."[30]

In assignments that engage students with the rest of the world, humanities students move past simply knowing about others and toward an *understanding* of others. Understanding those not like us protects us from the follies of xenophobia, myths of American exceptionalism, and ethnocentrism. It fosters productive cross-cultural exchanges and collaborations and stronger human connections.

The Humanities and Global Citizenship

No doubt, the humanities' role in global education is essential to career success in an increasingly global economy. From the day-to-day hornet's nests of cross-cultural communication to the large-scale global economic decisions with worldwide impact, global education in the humanities facilitates students' capacities to work together and be open to different ways of thinking, leading to increased creativity, innovation, and success. The humanities' particular attunement with cultural difference, cultural oppression, and human rights throughout history and across the globe extends as well to education for global citizenship: that we are all in this together, and that what affects one affects all, next door, in the next state, and across the globe.

Chapter 17

Leadership

Leadership, key to organizational success, ensures that various resources such as people, capital, research, and marketing work in concert for the success of the organization. Innovation, the lifeblood of the knowledge economy, requires excellent leadership. The high-tech, fast-paced global economy demands "progressive leaders who understand what it takes to be creative and innovative" rather than staying tethered to management practices of the past.[1] Leaders who inspire innovation manage risk effectively, demonstrate curiosity, lead proactively with confidence and authority, seize opportunities, and understand important trends and their significance for the organization.[2]

Yet leadership is a hard concept to pin down, changing dramatically depending on contextual factors like diversity, industry, culture, generational tendencies, organizational history, space and place (is the organization brick and mortar or online?), and personality. But we also know that we must have leaders, and we know that some people are better at leading than others. While we may identify some people as "born leaders," others may excel in leadership because of conscious choices they've made about what they want to learn and how they want to behave. Thus, there is a great amount of complexity in the question "Can leadership be taught?" even as the continued success of our economy depends, to a good extent, on getting the answer to that question right.

Harvard University president Drew Gilpin Faust turns to the humanities as one critical answer to this question. She emphasizes "the importance of language to leadership, on the interpretive and empathetic power of words on which leaders rely, and on the necessity of the humanities and the broad liberal arts education that nurture these indispensable qualities."[3] Within specific facets of a humanities education are the kinds of skills and knowledge that help prepare students for leadership. Humanities students are especially equipped to deal with change and ambiguity, to understand how difference and diversity impact leadership at all levels, and to apply ethical decision-making to leadership challenges. Other skills fundamental to the humanities, like critical thinking and storytelling, are also important for leaders. Finally, leadership requires compassion, empathy, and a commitment to the common good over individual gains or power; these are emotions and values promoted through the study of the humanities.

Leadership in the Workplace

James Kouzes and Barry Posner's work on the most admired qualities of leaders is highly recognized in the research on leadership.[4] Spanning decades and culled from studies of more than 1,500 nonprofit and for-profit organizations all over the world, their research asks, "What values do you look for and admire in your superiors?"[5] The twenty most admirable qualities of leadership include (in alphabetical order): ambitious, broad-minded, caring, competent, cooperative, courageous, dependable, determined, fair-minded, forward-looking, honest, imaginative, independent, inspiring, intelligent, loyal, mature, self-controlled, straightforward, and supportive.

However, good leaders can be effective in some ways but perhaps not as effective in others. For example, a leader might have an exceptional sense of timing in terms of business decisions, but they might also struggle in terms of interpersonal communication and creating group cohesion. In a famous example, Apple cofounder Steve Jobs was notorious for being difficult to work for, but his attention to detail, brutal honesty, and perfectionist tendencies also changed our world in remarkable ways.

Moreover, the importance people attach to each characteristic may differ depending on many factors. For example, Valerie Sessa, Robert Kabacoff, Jennifer Deal, and Heather Brown note that all generations they studied valued honesty, knowledge about the organization's core activities, listening, and helping others achieve more than they thought they could.[6] But there are some generational differences that are important. For example, a foundational study by Ron Zemke, Claire Raines, and Bob Filipczk found that baby boomers prefer a friendly and consensual style while eschewing hierarchy; that Generation Xers lean toward egalitarianism and away from respecting

authority, also valuing honesty, impartiality, competence, and straightfor-
wardness; and that millennials prefer a "polite" relationship with authority
and expect their leaders to pull people together for collective action.[7] At the
same time, Generation Xers and millennials tend to value honesty and caring
less than other generations do, but they are more likely to value determina-
tion and ambition in their leaders.

Paul Arsenault's research suggests that baby boomers and Generation
Xers value competence more than other groups.[8] Sessa and her colleagues
also note that two behavioral themes are consistent in leadership studies:
leaders who "focus on asserting one's own power, capability, and authority to
get the job done" and leaders who "focus on creating conditions for others
to contribute and lead."[9] As globalization continues and baby boomers lose
numbers in the leadership ranks, recognizing the importance of the diverse
expectations and strengths of a new generation of leaders is paramount.

Diversity in the workplace further complicates ideas about leadership, as
more women and nonwhite males have taken on leadership positions. But in
spite of gains in these areas, 95 percent of Fortune 500 companies are still
run by white males. In addition, even when women and nonwhite workers are
promoted to leadership positions, they do not readily clear a path for other
women and nonwhite workers. In fact, women and nonwhite leaders who
do value diversity and who reflect that value in their hiring are rated more
negatively by employees than white males who behave in the same way.[10]

Leaders can expect the workplace to be more diverse in the future and
must be prepared to create an environment where people from diverse backgrounds can succeed.[11] By 2020, white members of the working-age population are expected to decrease from 82 percent in 1980 to 63 percent, while
the percentage of the workforce representing nonwhites is expected to double
from 18 percent to 37 percent, with Latinx workers projected to triple, from
6 to 17 percent.[12] Moreover, those who understand and value diversity, inclusivity, and equality—all elements of a humanities education—are more likely
to work toward greater diversity in a leadership position.

Recognizing and valuing a diversity of opinions is also the mark of a
good leader. These leaders, participating in what is referred to as representative, participative, or democratic leadership, display "behavior that influences
people in a manner consistent with and/or conducive to basic democratic
principles and processes, such as self-determination, inclusiveness, equal par-

ticipation, and deliberation."[13] A democratic style of leadership takes time and effort.

Despite the positive impacts of democratic leadership strategies and some movement toward these styles in recent years, Western organizations often still are grounded firmly in a more hierarchical/top-down structure when it comes to decision-making and taking action.[14] Sometimes, leaders must make autocratic or top-down decisions. But in terms of dealing with ambiguity, complexity, and the fluctuating contexts businesses must navigate, an organization grounded in more overall democratic processes is more likely to fare better. Warren Bennis, who many deem the pioneer of leadership studies, noted that for "rapid acceptance of a new idea," for "flexibility in dealing with novel problems, generally high morale and loyalty . . . the more egalitarian or decentralized type seems to work better."[15] The ambiguous, global, and shifting contexts of the modern and future economies are likely to require more, not less, faith in democratic leadership principles.

Another critical component of leadership relevant to the humanities is identified by Robert N. Lussier and Christopher F. Achua, who argue that leadership is "the influencing process between leaders and followers to achieve organizational objectives through change."[16] Just as leaders influence followers, followers influence formal leaders, creating a reciprocal process between the two. Too often, the focus on leadership is on the word "lead" rather than the unstated assumption in that word—that good leaders are people *others want to follow.*

Whole Foods CEO John Mackey agrees. He brings together the best minds of the company and tries to find consensus. He appreciates disagreement in these meetings because he believes that the end result is generally a better decision. And while he also comments that it takes longer to make decisions this way, implementation goes much faster because there isn't resistance and sabotage throughout the company.[17] In other words, by valuing the perspectives of others and putting the team and organization above his own preferences and power, the company makes better decisions that get more buy-in from the organization.

Lussier and Achua's interactional conception of leadership also recognizes a difference between managers and leaders, an important distinction given that many managers are not good leaders. Thus, the employee of a manager can be a leader while the manager isn't.[18] Employees should be thinking about exhibiting good leadership even if they aren't in a management position. After all, the next management position might very well go to someone who is a proven leader in the organization.

Lussier and Achua note that "contingent leaders" understand that each situation requires a response tailored to that situation and that there is no one effective leadership style. Contingent leaders develop rhetorical sensitivity. They can read the room or situation and recognize which leadership style is best suited for that particular context. They understand which "traits and behaviors will result in leadership success given the situational variables."[19] So in one situation, a leader may take a more laissez-faire approach, and in another context, they may take a very hands-on approach.

John Kotter's decades of research in leadership as both a professor at Harvard and now in a private firm is also influential. Many in the leadership field consider his "8-Step Process for Leading Change" required for any leader who wants to implement changes successfully.[20] The eight steps are to create a sense of urgency, build a guiding coalition, form a strategic vision and initiatives, enlist a volunteer army, enable action by removing barriers, generate short-term wins, sustain acceleration, and institute change. Further, balancing efforts to impact hearts and minds is critical to this eight-step model.[21] Given the significance of good, effective leadership, higher education has finally begun to take notice.

Leadership, Higher Education, and the Humanities

When leadership programs were first developed and introduced on campuses in the 1990s, they weren't taken seriously by the academic community. Leadership was often filed under "self-help" in bookstores. Many people also believed that leaders are born, not made, and thus leadership wasn't worthy of study. This tendency has shifted as business schools (most often connected to leadership training) have begun incorporating leadership education into their majors. Moreover, colleges and universities have started leadership majors, or added leadership programs to supplement degrees. Civic engagement and service learning programs are also sometimes linked to leadership development.[22] As Kerry L. Priest, Tamara Bauer, and Leigh E. Fine note, contemporary leadership education program developers understand "that our society needs more and better leaders, that leadership can be taught (and learned), and that the college environment is a strategic setting for leadership development."[23] As a result of this recognition, developing leadership in undergraduate students is now a common goal cited in the mission statements of Western universities and colleges, and almost a thousand leadership development programs have now been implemented as well.[24]

Notably, these new leadership programs highlight skills and knowledge sets emphasized in the humanities, even though they are not considered part of the humanities. Curt Brungardt, Justin Greenleaf, Christie Brungardt, and Jill Arensdorf point out that new leadership majors and programs tend to focus on the historical foundations of leadership; leadership theory; analysis of leadership in specific contexts; issues-oriented courses that focus on areas like ethics and gender; courses that offer hands-on experience, such as internships; and courses that focus on a particular skill or set of skills.[25] Among the skills courses are communication, critical inquiry/thinking, decision-making, teamwork, and persuasion, all consistent elements of the humanities classroom.

Other characteristics on Kouzes and Posner's list of the twenty most admirable qualities of leadership are honed in a humanities classroom. Broad-mindedness, fair-mindedness, and self-control are embedded in the study of wicked problems that is common in humanities courses. Concomitant discussions about ethics, equality, social justice, and diversity are bound up in the importance of being broad- and fair-minded and considering and valuing the perspectives of others. Students learn not to assume that their perception of a situation is the only perception; as a result, they learn not to launch into a conflict or communicate "the solution" without giving due consideration to other perceptions or ideas. They learn to consider the whole, not just themselves, as members of work and life communities. And when they learn about slavery, gender inequalities, Jim Crow, war, and many other significant and harmful events, policies, and laws in our national and world histories, they learn the immense costs of selfishness, greed, and the loss of self-control. By studying diverse orators, writers, social movements, and other leaders, humanities students analyze and assess qualities of courage, imagination, progressive thinking, and inspiration. Of course, they also learn about leaders who have used their skills and power in negative ways.

Kouzes and Posner also note that people prefer their leaders to be caring, cooperative, supportive, and straightforward. The many ways that students learn about effective oral communication and collaboration in the humanities classroom encourage these characteristics. Complex discussions on difficult topics help students get practice in discussing thorny problems in ways that privilege civility and care for others.

Likewise, humanities study also speaks to Kotter and Cohen's emphasis on appealing to human emotion in leadership practice. Fred Kramer outlines a number of examples of how Homer's *Odyssey* provides excellent advice to leaders. Odysseus's journey to self-awareness can be a sort of guide to discovering our own leadership potential.[26] Harvard Business School's Joseph L. Badaracco, Jr., uses various works of literature, from Arthur Miller's *Death of a Salesman* to Chinua Achebe's *Things Fall Apart*, to illuminate leaders' character traits as they face different periods and circumstances. Serious works of fiction, he says, provide "a view from the inside" and foster compassion and understanding.[27]

Students in the humanities also get practice in one of today's most important skills for business: storytelling. Linda Gehrs notes that "stories are often used by leaders to unite a group around the theme, to inspire them to action, or provide closure or an explanation for events that are unclear or difficult to understand."[28] Although numbers can make the case for a business decision, the telling of a good story "translates dry and abstract numbers into compelling pictures of a leader's goals."[29] Chris Grams, head of marketing at Tidelift, a software development company, asserts, "You can't build a community of passion without storytellers. Their stories become rallying cries, the flags people salute to, the legends they tell to the newbies, the North Star that puts you back on course when you are led astray."[30] Storytelling is one of the hottest new trends in business programs and schools, but it's been a staple of the humanities—in writing, literature, communication, and history—from the very beginning.

Humanities education and storytelling also contribute to the ability of leaders to encourage others to follow them. Students in philosophy, communication studies, and English are well trained to use persuasive and powerful language and can create a clear, succinct, and attractive vision for the future that can be shared with the organization. These students are also prepared to (re)consider the environment they're in, including asking what's important, if there are different ways that we can think about the organization, and if their results come from new ways of thinking about the situation.[31]

Lussier and Achua's identification of the need for contingent leaders is also well served by the humanities.[32] Humanities students understand

and apply past, present, and future contexts in forward-thinking decision-making. These skills become even more important as organizations change in terms of employee makeup, organizational structure, and global reach. Relatedly, history professor James Grossman argues that history students make great leaders because history is about change. Moreover, students of history learn, organize, and make sense of considerable amounts of information, and in doing so, "they learn how to infer what drives and motivates human behavior from elections to social movements to board rooms."[33] As he notes, everything has a history that must be understood before informed decisions can be made.

Finally, educators and business leaders are advocating for civic leadership education across many disciplines, including the humanities. Civic leadership is conceived as "an activity or process that energizes or mobilizes others to make progress" that stresses collective action and collaboration.[34] At their roots, the humanities promote compassion for others and active participation in social change.

Humanities Leaders on the Global Stage

Humanities courses and curricula, rather than a specific assignment, foster the skills, knowledge, and understanding of good leadership, in all its complexity and fluidity. Thus, unlike in other chapters, we're not including a discussion about one assignment that teaches leadership, because while the skills and characteristics that define good leadership can be taught, no one assignment can reasonably position all student as leaders. Humanities students, whether through their knowledge of excellent historical leaders, effective and ethical contemporary political leaders, or meaningful philosophical notions of overarching or situational ethics, leave college with the foundations for excellence in leadership. Skill sets that are fundamental to the humanities, such as creative and innovative thinking, critical thinking, communication, close textual analysis, and synthesis of information (to name only a few) are also fundamental to good leadership. Comfortable with complexity and ambiguity, recognizing multiple perspectives, and able to consider the immediate and far-reaching impact of their decisions, humanities students are well positioned to lead and to lead ethically in our quickly changing world.

Therefore, it should come as no surprise that according to a recent study by the British Council, 55 percent of world leaders have a degree in the humanities (11 percent) or social sciences (44 percent).[35] And younger leaders are more likely to have a degree in the humanities and social sciences than older leaders.[36] The world is changing quickly, and humanities students are—and must always be—among those leading the way.

Part IV

Creating and Communicating
Your Humanities Story

Chapter 18

For Prospective and Current College Students: Creating and Communicating Your Humanities Story

Two recent publications got our attention as we began writing this concluding chapter. A report from the National Academies of Sciences, Engineering, and Medicine, "The Integration of the Humanities and Arts with Sciences, Engineering, and Medicine in Higher Education: Branches from the Same Tree," stresses the crucial need for higher education to integrate the fields of the arts, humanities, and STEMM (science, technology, engineering, mathematics, and medicine):

> The outcomes associated with various approaches to integration—improved written and oral communications skills, teamwork skills, ethical decision making, critical thinking and deeper learning, content mastery, general engagement and enjoyment of learning, empathy, resilience, the ability to apply knowledge in real-world settings, and indicators of improved science literacy—are skills that will prepare students for work, life, and civic engagement in the 21st century. Higher education should strive to offer all students—regardless of degree or area of concentration—an education that exposes them to diverse forms of human knowledge and inquiry and that impresses upon them the fact that all disciplines are "branches of the same tree."[1]

In addition, the article "One College Finally Designed a Liberal Arts Education Fit for the Future of Work" describes the ways and reasons why

Clayton Spencer, president of Bates College, has embedded students' search for meaningful and purposeful work into many aspects of the college's liberal arts curriculum.[2]

Together, these articles suggest an increasing recognition of the need for the humanities in the modern and future economy and the broad core skills and knowledge—what we've identified as embedded in humanities majors— that all students need when they graduate. Further, the articles point out that acknowledging the value of the humanities major as one path to a great career is good for students, the nation, and the world. In other words, the dominant narratives that both deny the value of the humanities and promote STEM, business, and other preprofessional majors as the only credible paths forward for college students are continuing to change, though slowly.

Hopefully, by the time many of the prospective and current college students reading this book graduate from college with a humanities degree, employers will have greater awareness of the value of that degree—and the graduates who hold it. But we can't take that as a given. And even if true, you need to plan ahead—be ready for the job market by choosing your curriculum and other activities in and during college carefully and intentionally.

Humanities students need to be better at telling their stories. We undoubtedly have a personal interest in seeing students, parents, employers, politicians, academic administrators, and others better understand what the humanities are and their value not just to our economy but also to our local and national communities, the larger society, and our culture. But we also have a personal interest in seeing students study what they love, whatever that is. We believe that this book gives humanities students the tools to understand and articulate who they are, what they can do, what they know, and how they bring value to the workplace and the world.

Branding the Humanities, Branding You

We know that many in the academy will wince as we use the concept of branding to talk about graduates, and, to some extent, we agree with that perspective because we don't view college as a business transaction. But we urge people to understand that recognizing and addressing the need to market oneself as a humanities graduate takes nothing away from all that is valuable in a humanities education. Indeed, it is our hope that the greater inclusion of humanities students in organizations that may not have traditionally considered humanities graduates for employment will change those organizations for the better—that they will add humanity to these organizations that is sorely needed. So, in our view, encouraging students to brand themselves well as humanities majors in general is an important part of bringing more humanity into the worlds of business, government, and nonprofit work.

Personal branding expert Catherine Kaputa argues that the twenty-first-century job market is vastly different than before: "It used to be about, 'Can you do the job?' Now it's about 'Can you make a better impression than the other 200 people who can do the job?'"[3] The competition is greater, and as you already know, technology and globalization have vastly changed the economy and the workplace. Speed and transformation prevail.

The need to stand out among the other qualified applicants exists even in an economy that by many measures is the best in years. As of this writing, the unemployment rate of 3.9 percent is the lowest since December 2000.[4] Job openings rose in sectors including construction, retail, professional and business services, leisure, and hospitality and fell in manufacturing, finance, and insurance. Between March 2017 and March 2018, the economy created a net 2.3 million jobs, representing 65.6 million hires and 63.3 million separations. Wage increases, though, remained tepid.

Moreover, a Michigan State study refers to a "white-hot" overall hiring outlook for college graduates in 2018, up by 13 percent from 2017—the eighth consecutive year of continuing hiring expansion.[5] Among growing professions are sales development representative, customer success manager, full stack developer, and marketing content manager—with median salaries ranging from $58,000 to $82,000 (see Table 7).[6] However, stories and research findings about the "skills gap" abound. Employers say core skills such as communicating clearly, problem solving, critical thinking, and working well in teams are in short supply as they look to hire college graduates.[7]

But as *Forbes* writers Ryan Craig and Troy Markowitz suggest, too many college graduates seem unable "to make employers aware of the skills they actually have . . . developed through coursework and co-curricular activities."[8] Compounding this gap for humanities majors is often the perception that "employers don't want them," despite the strong skills and knowledge sets they have acquired through their education, given the voluminous negative

Table 7. Change in Employers' Hiring Expectations of Graduates with Baccalaureate Degrees in 2017–2018 Compared with 2016–2017

1. Information services:	60 percent
2. Administrative services:	49 percent
3. Wholesale trade:	46 percent
4. Transportation:	32 percent
5. Health care and social assistance:	32 percent
6. Professional, business, and scientific services:	30 percent
7. Construction:	29 percent
8. Nonprofits:	23 percent
9. Agriculture:	21 percent
10. Retail trade:	19 percent
11. Educational services:	17 percent
12. Accommodations and food services:	17 percent
13. Government:	7 percent
14. Finance and insurance:	7 percent
15. Real estate and leasing:	6 percent
16. Manufacturing:	-3 percent

press regarding the humanities.[9] Humanities majors are often misunderstood or even ignored because employers simply don't understand what they do and why it matters.

Fortunately, though, one of the main features of the humanities is storytelling. We tell stories to propel ideas, change beliefs, tell a more accurate picture, influence others, and make things happen. We want you to understand how to tell your stories about your humanities degree so that when you enter the job market, you boldly show your confidence in your humanities education. Employers want to hear about what makes you different and compelling, why you want to do what you want to do, what your passions are, and what your vision is for yourself and your career. They especially want to know what you can do for the company or organization. You can use your creative thinking skills to consider what your unique logo might look like and to create a succinct and crisp sentence that expresses your brand. These tools become even more useful when it comes time to design business cards to hand out in various places where you might network for your first, or even your next, job.

For prospective and current students, developing this story begins now. Doing so requires making conscious and deliberate choices about your curricular, extracurricular, work, and volunteer experiences throughout your college career. Once you are ready to enter the job market, you'll need to package and communicate these stories.

As part of our roles as faculty, Laurie and Michele advise undergraduates at all levels, first-years through seniors. We also teach courses that serve as stepping stones between the academic *study* of professional writing and communication studies, respectively, and the real-world *application* of the skills, abilities, and knowledge students acquired through their coursework in the humanities. We have experience helping students develop and communicate their humanities stories.

Creating Your Story

When the time comes for you to enter the job market as a humanities major, you will find numerous resources for the entire process.[10] You'll learn about writing effective résumés, cover letters, and digital portfolios (also called ePortfolios); preparing elevator speeches and interviews; maximizing your social media presence; how to network; and so much more.

Among the most important of these are resources about selling yourself, branding yourself, and telling your story. Career and talent management specialist Rita Allen suggests you consider the "3 Ps" of marketing yourself—preparation, packaging, and presentation.[11] Kaputa calls a student's brand their "unique selling position" and urges students to "represent something special, what you stand for and can do that sets you apart from others."[12] Jeffrey Selingo stresses the significance of creating your "career narrative."[13] As Kaputa puts it, "as the storyteller of your own life, you must create compelling narratives to empower your success."[14] We draw on these and many other resources in our capstone courses as we help students prepare to enter the job market.

In addition, we focus on the specifics of helping students tell their humanities stories. Graduating seniors must effectively and succinctly explain the value of their humanities major as it relates to specific jobs they seek. We instruct them to refer back to how their excellent humanities education trained them in the skills and knowledge most desired in the specific job they are applying for, offering clear examples of what they've learned and how they have applied these skills and knowledge sets in other areas of their lives, such as being a member of a sports team or a representative in student government, part-time work as a store clerk, volunteer work in a Meals on Wheels program, and anything and everything else. Once students understand their stories holistically, it's much easier to market themselves to employers.

When creating these important windows into who you are and what you can do, you can think about some of these questions in order to think more holistically about the story you want to tell. How did you get here? That is, were there relationships or experiences in life that led you to your major and career choices? What is the niche market you're interested in pursuing? What problems might someone already in this market need a solution for? What are your key goals and talents as a college graduate? How have you already honed the skills you think your employer is most interested in seeing in you? What makes you compelling? How will you get your message/brand out there? Will you use blogs, websites, and/or social media? A brand needs to be both multidimensional and succinct, and meeting both of these goals will take thought, time, and many attempts and edits. But this process will help you understand yourself better, and that will make it much easier to tell your humanities story in an effective way.

Talent manager and human resources brand strategist Meghan M. Biro encourages a personal inventory when thinking about marketing yourself. As she notes, an objective look at your strengths, weaknesses, personality, passions, and talents is your "career calling card."[15] Because as a new graduate you are lacking the experience of someone who's been in the field for years, you'll also need to think about how you can turn all you've learned and accomplished in college into selling points that mark you as distinct from other applicants. By carefully considering your curricular choices, volunteer and paid work, and extracurricular activities, you can figure out how to best funnel those elements of your life into a cohesive and persuasive argument to a prospective employer that highlights your experiences, skills, and knowledge. We recommend that you create a grid that allows you to visualize all you've learned and accomplished. On the Y axis (vertical) list minors, skill sets, work experience, internships, and volunteer work. On the X axis (horizontal) list key projects, roles, core skills gained (teamwork, for example), and specific skills gained (Excel spreadsheets, for instance). Crafting a personal inventory grid also helps you recognize skills and knowledge that you've gained and applied over and over again.

As one example, a student applying for an entry-level social media marketing position in the corporate headquarters of a retail giant could tell her story in a number of ways. But before thinking about the different, nuanced ways she could tell her story, she needs to have "the basics" created and organized. She'd first answer those questions from above that speak to her interests and goals. Then she can begin crafting her personal inventory, which should help her see patterns and/or a specific trajectory in her coursework in college, at part-time jobs, in her volunteer service, and so on. The foundation of her elevator speech is *who she is* as it relates to her chosen career (her brand), and then, based on her audience, she would add those patterns and trajectories carefully. She'd choose to highlight stories of her experiences and accomplishments that best suit her audience by taking account of the required skills and knowledge sets specified for that particular job and considering her activities and experiences in and out of school.

This student is very proud of her participation in the neighborhood narratives assignment (from Chapter 8) and is proud of the writing she produced for the project. In communicating her story through the various application materials, this student could use the neighborhood narratives assignment to stress her keen understanding of audience and purpose in all written communication. In addition, her primary responsibility as an intern in a local grocery store was social media. Thus, she can talk about specific successful strategies she implemented in that position. She was also a member of the Public Relations Student Society of America (PRSSA) and organized a LinkedIn workshop with outside speakers for her peers, which speaks to her event-planning and organizational skills, as well as her motivation to learn all she can about public relations through the choice to commit to working with her college's PRSSA chapter.

If this same student also applied for a community outreach position in a small nonprofit after-school program in a low-income, ethnically and racially diverse neighborhood, she could discuss the neighborhood narratives assignment in terms of communicating across cultures, having navigated the interviewing, writing, and editing phases despite language and cultural barriers. She would stress that her internship experience with social media is vital to effective community outreach work, and that organizing the LinkedIn workshop as part of her PRSSA experience helped her hone her communication and organizational skills beyond the bounds of her campus. She could also emphasize her role in both her small team and in the larger class project as a whole, stressing her ability to take on different roles in a small nonprofit. Of course, this student's story has numerous plot lines and twists, and she needs to be aware of and attentive to the context of each job application and create her stories accordingly.

Ultimately, you will need to be flexible with communicating your story in various, common job-seeking tools. For example, you'll need to prepare several "elevator speeches"—a verbal clear, brief message communicating who you are, the skills and knowledge that set you apart, and how you can benefit a company or organization—depending on the context in which you find yourself. You may run into a potential employer in an elevator (hence, the origins of the term "elevator speech") or somewhere else and take advantage of that opportunity in thirty seconds. Or you may be at a networking event where you will have a minute or two to convince the hirer that you are the right candidate. In a résumé, which you'll also need to tailor to a specific job or context, you'll want to package your story in "accomplishment statements" under the various sections of the résumé, such as work experiences. You'll write variations of a cover letter that speak specifically to how your story fits with the specific requirements of the job and to the philosophy and mission of the organization. ePortfolios enable job candidates to bring together all facets of their stories through words and images. The 2018 Hart Associates study finds that executives and hiring managers place value on seeing ePortfolios for evaluating and hiring recent graduates.[16]

Speaking of electronic sources, a social media presence is also key to a job search because most companies use social media to screen applicants. If you have no presence or your presence lacks regular posts, some will assume that you've "scrubbed" your social media presence. Your social media presence should be appropriate and persuasive. In terms of appropriateness, organizations want to see you on social media. Your posts should be both personal and professional. They want to see that you attend friends' weddings and family events. They want to see that you have an appropriate social life—that you "fit in" with others—because they need you to fit in with their organization. These posts, of course, should not include objectionable material, such as heavy drinking, inappropriate dress, or improper language or opinions. In terms of persuasiveness, recruiters look favorably on mentions of volunteerism and evidence that you're linked to professional organizations in your career field. Consider your online image a continuation of your résumé and your cover letter. A positive and substantial online presence shows that you are tech savvy and understand the technology–public communication connection.

Professional-linked sites you should be aware of are LinkedIn, Twitter, WordPress (for blogging and creating a personal website), and Visual CV, where you can plug in your résumé, portfolio materials, videos, and pictures, which can be downloaded by anyone into a PDF booklet. You should also be aware of HootSuit and Klout, sites that can track and manage your online impact. In addition, you should look into tools that help you manage your online reputation, such as Google dashboard, Branding You, Reputation. com, Who's Talkin', and Yasni. Each of these sites, in different ways, helps you see how you are seen online by others.

Planning Your Story: Suggestions for Prospective Students

Surely, we cannot promise a job for every humanities graduate. Many factors come into play when job hunting, including grades, extracurricular activities, presentation of oneself through a résumé and cover letter, interviewing skills, letters of recommendations from professors, a willingness or an aversion to relocation, and other elements involved in "marketing" oneself as a college graduate.

However, students who begin thinking early on about their college courses, applied learning projects, extracurricular activities, and paid and volunteer work in relationship to the skills and knowledge outlined in this book will be well prepared. This is what we do with the students we advise. The aim is not to lock any student into a particular four-year plan. Nor are we suggesting that all activities and choices a student makes must be on target with a job search four years later. Rather, we encourage students to be mindful of their choices knowing that this day will eventually come. And we encourage them to realize that plans may change for any number of reasons, including discovering something new, learning that your first choice really isn't a great fit, or even the creation of a job that didn't exist when you started college (as was the case for a number of our students who discovered, as they graduated, this new job called "social media director").

Curricular Choices

First, you must think carefully about your college curriculum. Most obviously, this means carefully considering the major that you choose. You can learn a lot by doing research and reaching out to faculty in areas of interest to talk with them about careers. These steps can help you avoid falling in line with the common narratives that people repeat about one major or the next without any supporting evidence to back up those claims. Choosing something that you love will likely mean a better grade point average, which may mean better chances of getting that dream job interview or being accepted to your desired graduate program. You're probably more likely to earn higher grades in courses you care about, so choose your major wisely—balance data and passion.

Also, a minor or a certificate program can add entirely new skills sets to your humanities story. You will have electives to choose from, and if you plan your courses wisely so that you don't take courses you don't need, you should have at least enough credits for a minor in your degree program. Thinking about what areas you might want to work in one day and choosing minors or certificates that speak to those areas will better prepare you to work in them. Adding a minor in business, technology, or science; a certificate in public relations; or a joint minor in communication and technology or human resources and psychology, for example, can give you an edge compared to someone who didn't use those elective credits as effectively. The possibilities are extensive and can bolster your major with a minor or a certificate that gives you an additional argument for being hired. It also shows that you have the foresight and initiative to use those electives effectively.

You should also use your general education courses carefully. The purpose of these courses is to give you a well-rounded education. Too often students complain that general education credits are "wasted" or that those credits should be linked more closely to their majors, but they are wrong. We encourage you to take advantage of those opportunities to expand your knowledge and skills with courses that add to your major, that force you to develop both sides of your brain, and that interest you, as opposed to just taking whatever fits the schedule you want—or what you've heard are the easiest or "easy A" courses. Making school the priority around which you schedule everything else makes sense because it is an investment in the rest of your life.

Finally, think about what opportunities different classes might offer you. You can talk to academic advisers, faculty, and other students and find out which courses and which faculty are engaging students in the kind of applied, project-based learning that employers want to hear about. Look for classes that will give you experience in project management, research, collaboration, service-learning, fieldwork, opportunities abroad, the ability to work with diverse groups of people, and the other kinds of high-impact experiences employers say they want to see on a résumé.[17] Pursue an undergraduate research experience that takes you beyond a particular class. You'll encounter and overcome obstacles that make for great stories about your problem-solving skills and creative thinking. You'll make the connection between theory and practice.

The high-impact experience most highly ranked by employers is the internship.[18] These experiences are opportunities for you to figure out what you love and what you don't, apply your skills and knowledge outside of the classroom, and learn about how organizations function. As important, you'll have examples of how you've applied your skills and knowledge to a job and/or specific context or problem. It is true that unpaid internships can be painful economically, and we realize that some students have a much harder time accepting those terms, but we recommend that you try to make it work. Perhaps you can take an internship as a class for your major during the semester. You could also find an internship at your current place of employment that differs from your job. For instance, we've had students who worked or volunteered at animal shelters take on social media internships with those organizations. And we've had restaurant servers take internships in marketing at their place of employment. We strongly encourage you to do what you need to do to get at least one internship under your belt before graduation.

Paid and Volunteer Work

Whether the work you've done during college has been paid, volunteer, or both, talking about those experiences can help you after graduation. As a server in a restaurant, for example, you probably developed multitasking skills, effective communication abilities, and strengths related to collaboration. In the retail world, perhaps you learned how to effectively use specific computer programs. You can also think about stories to communicate how you've applied what you've learned in school to the workplace. Working during college takes commitment and the ability to multitask, so you can point to the ways that you were able to succeed at both work and school while also fine-tuning some of the skills you used and applying what you learned in classes to contexts outside of the classroom. For example, you can tell a story about how you effectively managed a conflict in the workplace or solved a problem.

Extracurricular Activities

One of the best parts of college is finding organizations or teams that share interests with you. Whether you're talking about participating in student government, an honor society, a hobby club, or an official college sports team, you can create opportunities to apply what you've learned to those contexts. As a leader in student government, you can talk about working to increase student engagement in important issues on campus or maintaining the student government budget. As a member of an honor society, you can talk about organizing and/or promoting a donation campaign. Members of a hobby-based club can tell stories about developing the end-of-year themed event. College soccer team players can discuss what they learned about teamwork or how they led as team captain. Extracurricular activities in college give you opportunities to create persuasive stories for employers that make concrete what you've learned and applied as a humanities student.

Your Story Begins Now

Your story begins now. Look past the headlines and do your research on career opportunities and how those opportunities may shift as things like technology or globalization change the employment landscape. As you go through college, keep a running tab of your "personal inventory." That is, make sure that you write down all you've done, all of the skills you have garnered in classwork, extracurricular activities, job or volunteer opportunities you have while you are a student, and so on. Save those papers and projects to use as examples of how you have gained particular knowledge and skills in college. Pay attention to the skills and requirements listed on employment websites. Match what you've accomplished to the core skills and knowledge chapters of this book. This is how you can begin making a case for yourself as an excellent prospective employee after graduation from day one on campus. In your senior year, put all of this information together and start to construct your humanities story.

We also recommend that you explore the resources in your college or university's career services office, such as networking opportunities, interview training, and business etiquette expectations. The office may even have a job board made for and by graduates that will help you network with other former students who may hire you or help you get hired.

The story of your humanities education may be created for a job that has been a staple of our economy for decades or one that doesn't even currently exist. Regardless, your education in the humanities will go a long way in preparing you for either one of those situations, as well as the majority of the situations in between. Your humanities education will be exciting, meaning-ful, and persuasive.

Conclusion

Higher Education, Democracy, and the Humanities

In 2012 the Department of Education, the American Association of Colleges and Universities (AAC&U), and the Global Perspective Institute (GPI) published a report titled *A Crucible Moment: College Learning and Democracy's Future.*[1] *A Crucible Moment* is considered a "watershed national call to action calling on the nation to reclaim higher education's civic mission if our democracy is to thrive socially and economically."[2] AAC&U's commitment to making civic and democratic learning for all students a top national priority has only strengthened in the past six years because "the future of our democracy and our shared futures depend on a more informed, engaged, and globally responsible citizenry."[3]

Notably, *A Crucible Moment* connects democratic learning and civic participation to both the *social and economic health* of the United States. The report's authors emphasize that workplace training in higher education must acknowledge "a civic dimension to every field of study, including career and technical fields, as well as to every workplace."[4] Likewise, Hart Research Associates studies report that many employers believe that all students should graduate with knowledge of democratic institutions and values and civic skills and knowledge.[5] Employers recognize the importance of hiring workers who add value beyond the bottom line.

It is both ironic and counterproductive that at the same time colleges and universities are committing to the civic mission of higher education, they are also devaluing the humanities. All disciplines, including the humanities, must play their unique role in democratic education to ensure the long-term health of the economy and the social fabric of the United States. And all students should be given the freedom to choose how they want to contribute, whether through their college majors, career choices, or community contributions.

As Cathy N. Davidson argues, most college students "are voluntarily making sacrifices of time, money, and character—willpower—to be in college because they want something bigger, better. *It isn't just a job. They don't just want to be workforce ready.* . . . As they make their way through college, they want something more: a career, a vocation, a life path." In addition to wanting to pay back college loans and get out of their parents' homes, many college graduates seek what Davidson calls "*world* readiness."[6]

Some students will choose the humanities as the path to both work and world readiness if they are encouraged to do so. To dissuade students from humanities degrees is bad for the students, the economy, and the country. We ignore the humanities at our own peril.

The Humanities, the Global Economy, and the Common Good

A Crucible Moment affirms our argument that the "capacities needed both in the modern workplace and in diverse democratic societies" overlap.[7] As demonstrated throughout this book, the humanities are critical to the current and future economy at every level. Further, opportunities abound for humanities graduates across today's dynamic workplace, characterized by the drive for innovation; technological advances and the consequences of automation; the rapid pace of change; globalization; and the changing demographics of the workforce.

Recent studies indicate that the employment data and salaries for humanities majors are far more positive than the popular narratives of the humanities imply. Moreover, the skills and knowledge gained in a humanities major are precisely what are most desired by employers.

In addition, the humanities provide that critical connection between a "life well lived" and the general welfare of all human beings everywhere. From upholding democratic values of equality and justice to making better decisions on urgent issues before us now and in the future via an understanding of historical, political, and economic contexts of the past and present, the humanities contribute to what is called "the common good."

A Crucible Moment acknowledges the ethical and social responsibilities of business, industry, and service organizations, noting the "disastrous results when civic consequences are ignored and only economic profit is considered" and pointing to the subprime mortgage crisis from 2007 to 2010. To protect against profit over people, "workers at all levels need to anticipate the civic implications of their choices and actions."[8]

Humanities students have a working knowledge of the kinds of disciplines that protect democracy, such as history, law, government, and philosophy. They also have knowledge of foreign languages, other cultures, economics, and comparative religion, which are important for understanding our increasingly linked world. They are able to communicate about topics steeped in issues of race, age, sex/gender, region, education, and political preferences.[9] Learning "how to think," not what to think, helps students become informed and active citizens who analyze issues using evidence and reasoning.

The path to *E pluribus unum*—"Out of many, one"—is "through the rich forest of the humanities," asserts Steven Merritt Seibert, executive director of the Florida Humanities Council. "Along that path," he continues, "we become mindful of the lessons of history, the differences in culture, and the power of ideas." The humanities "tell the stories that tie us together and to the wisdom of the past," Seibert asserts, claiming that "neither tyranny nor mob rule can deceive a people who understand each other."[10] By virtue of having a broad-based education, humanities students can navigate effectively the fluctuating, complex future world and economy. This same education also protects one of the world's great democracies.

Sharing and Changing the Humanities Narrative

Major Decisions has offered a more accurate story of the humanities than those that continue to dominate. Students across all public, private, branch, and Ivy League campuses should be encouraged and enabled to make the best decisions for themselves and their futures because a college degree means so much to one's life prospects. These decisions must be informed by facts, not distorted narratives. Choosing a major in the humanities is a great investment in one's self and future in a global economy that is shifting dramatically, quickly, and in the direction of college graduates who think broadly, critically, and ethically. Moreover, the communities in which we live need humanities thinkers to help guide decisions that understand the human benefits and human costs of all that makes up the current and future economies.

The antihumanities narratives too often rely on unstated assumptions about which majors are "practical" and which are not. Bracketing the fact that what is "practical" this year may not be practical in future economies, focusing on what one might define as "practical" may lead to the opposite of the intended effect. That is, as Michael Roth argues, by concentrating on what is currently defined as "practical," we run the risk of training students for yesterday's jobs and yesterday's problems. Dissuading students from the humanities also runs the risk of dampening the creative and innovative thoughts of a generation of students. Indeed, as Roth suggests, "calls for 'practicality' are really calls for conformity, for conventional thinking that will impoverish our economic, cultural, and personal lives."[11]

It is time to take control of the humanities narrative. We are urging everyone in higher education—faculty, administrators, career counselors, academic advisers, current and future students—and employers to take the time to learn about the humanities and its vital role in the economic and social fabric of local, national, and world communities. Prospective and current students must be assured that they can make a living and have a meaningful career with a humanities degree. And caring about both salary and quality of life should be encouraged, not maligned as "selling out."

We need humanities graduates to come back into the classroom and talk about their path to success after graduation and to encourage the hiring of more humanities students, when appropriate, at their places of employment. And we need employers who already understand the value of the humanities to talk to the people in charge of hiring. As humanities graduates brand themselves through storytelling and get more opportunities to change workplaces in positive ways, the narrative should change in positive ways. If all of us tell these stories often and well enough, the narrative should become powerful and impactful. Join us and a growing chorus of voices pleading with higher education, politicians, and business and industry to recognize the absolute necessity of the humanities to the twenty-first-century economy, nation, and world.

Notes

Introduction

1. Lehrer, Jonah. 2011. "Steve Jobs: 'Technology Alone Is Not Enough.'" *New Yorker*, October 7. http://www.newyorker.com/news/news-desk/steve-jobs-technology-alone-is-not-enough.

2. Chandler, David L. 2017. "Tim Cook to MIT Grads: 'How Will You Serve Humanity?'" *MIT News*, June 9. http://news.mit.edu/2017/commencement-day-0609.

3. Jackson, Abby. 2017. "Cuban: Don't Go to School for Finance—Liberal Arts Is the Future." *Business Insider*, February 17. http://www.businessinsider.com/mark-cuban-liberal-arts-is-the-future-2017-2.

4. Bureau of Labor Statistics. 2017. "Employment Projections: 2016-26 Summary." October 24. https://www.bls.gov/news.release/ecopro.nr0.htm.

5. Koenig, Rebecca. 2018. "Healthcare Jobs Abound. Here's How to Tap into the Hot Job Market." *U.S. News and World Report*, January 10. https://money.usnews.com/careers/articles/2018-01-10/health-care-jobs-abound-heres-how-to-tap-into-the-hot-job-market.

6. American Academy of Arts and Sciences. 2017. "Bachelor's Degrees in the Humanities." Humanities Indicators. https://humanitiesindicators.org/content/indicatordoc.aspx?i=34.

7. What majors fit into which category sometimes depends on whom you reference. In addition, some careers can fall under two categories. For example, someone interested in health administration could take classes in a program housed in health sciences or in business, depending on the college or university. For our purposes, we're defining these areas broadly.

8. Bureau of Labor Statistics. 2016. "College Tuition and Fees Increase 63 Percent Since January 2006." August 30. https://www.bls.gov/opub/ted/2016/college-tuition-and-fees-increase-63-percent-since-january-2006.htm.

9. Lobosco, Katie. 2017. "College Tuition Is Still Getting More Expensive." CNN Money, October 25. http://money.cnn.com/2017/10/25/pf/college/college-tuition-price-2017-2018/index.html.

10. Experian Information Solutions, Inc. 2017. "The State of Student Loan Debt in 2017." https://www.experian.com/innovation/thought-leadership/state-of-student-lending-in-2017.jsp.

11. Dickler, Jessica. 2017. "Student Loan Balances Jump Nearly 150 Percent in a Decade." CNBC.com, August 29. https://www.cnbc.com/2017/08/29/student-loan-balances-jump-nearly-150-percent-in-a-decade.html.

12. Dickler, Jessica. 2016. "College Graduates Enjoy the Best Job Market in Years." CNBC.com, May 17. https://www.cnbc.com/2016/05/16/college-grads-enjoy-the-best-job-market-in-years.html.

13. Rugaber, Christopher S. 2017. "Pay Gap Between College Grads and Everyone Else at a Record." *USA Today*, January 12. https://www.usatoday.com/story/money/2017/01/12/pay-gap-between-college-grads-and-everyone-else-record/96493348/.

14. Carnevale, Anthony, Jayasundera, Tamara, and Cheah, Ban. 2012. "The College Advan-

tage." Georgetown University Center on Education and the Workforce. https://files.eric.ed.gov/fulltext/ED534454.pdf.

15. Rugaber, "Pay Gap."

16. Carnevale, Anthony P., Cheah, Ban, and Hanson, Andrew R. 2015. *The Economic Value of College Majors.* Georgetown University Center on Education and the Workforce. https://cew.georgetown.edu/cew-reports/valueofcollegemajors/.

17. Carnevale, Anthony P., Jayasundera, Tamara, and Gulish, Artem. 2016. *America's Divided Recovery: College Haves and Have Nots.* Georgetown University Center on Education and the Workforce. June 30. https://cew.georgetown.edu/cew-reports/americas-divided-recovery/.

18. Carnevale, Anthony P., Strohl, Jeff, and Ridley, Neil. 2017. *Good Jobs That Pay Without a BA: A State-by-State Analysis.* Georgetown University Center on Education and the Workforce. https://goodjobsdata.org/wp-content/uploads/Good-Jobs-States.pdf.

19. Lederman, Doug. 2017. "Who Changes Majors? (Not Who You Think)." Inside Higher Ed, December 8. https://www.insidehighered.com/news/2017/12/08/nearly-third-students-change-major-within-three-years-math-majors-most.

20. Strode, Timothy. 2016. "Politics and the Liberal Arts, Part II: How the Humanities Became the Liberal Arts." Nassau Community College AAUP Advocacy Chapter blog, October 16. https://aaupncc.org/2016/10/16/politics-and-the-liberal-arts-part-ii-how-the-humanities-became-the-liberal-arts/.

21. Humphreys, Debra, and Kelly, Patrick. 2014. *How Liberal Arts and Sciences Majors Fare in Employment: A Report on Earnings and Long-Term Career Paths.* Association of American Colleges and Universities, x. https://www.mass.edu/foradmin/trustees/documents/HowLiberalArtsandSciencesMajorFareinEmployment.pdf.

22. The definition is from the National Foundation on the Arts and the Humanities Act, 1965, as amended. The NEH is an independent federal agency created in 1965 from the National Foundation on the Arts and the Humanities Act. The congressional act was established "to provide for the establishment of the National Foundation on the Arts and the Humanities to promote progress and scholarship in the humanities and the arts in the United States, and for other purposes." Signed on September 29, 1965, by President Lyndon Johnson, the act established both the National Endowment for the Humanities (NEH) and the National Endowment for the Arts (NEA) as separate, independent agencies.

23. Anders, George. 2017. *You Can Do Anything: The Surprising Power of a "Useless" Liberal Arts Education.* New York: Little, Brown, 12.

Chapter 1

1. In 1939, when the Department of Labor's Bureau of Labor Statistics first published monthly data on employment by industry categories, the services to manufacturing employment ratio was 2.1:1. As of 2014, it was 9.9:1. Growth in services began accelerating in the 1960s. From Short, Doug. 2014. "The Epic Rise of America's Services Industry." *Business Insider*, September 1. http://www.businessinsider.com/growth-of-us-services-economy-2014-9.

2. Stewart, Thomas A. 1997. *Intellectual Capital: The New Wealth of Organizations.* Danvers, MA: Crown Publishing, x.

3. Bureau of Labor Statistics. 2017. "Employment Projections: Employment by Major Industry Sector." U.S. Department of Labor, October 24. https://www.bls.gov/emp/tables/employment-by-major-industry-sector.htm.

4. World Bank. 2003. *Lifelong Learning in the Global Knowledge Economy: Challenges for Developing Countries.* http://siteresources.worldbank.org/INTLL/Resources/Lifelong-Learning-in-the-Global-Knowledge-Economy/lifelonglearning_GKE.pdf.

5. Powell, Walter W., and Snellman, Kaisa. 2004. "The Knowledge Economy." *Annual Review of Sociology* 30 (1): 199–220.

6. Brandt, Deborah. 2005. "Writing for a Living: Literacy and the Knowledge Economy." *Written Communication* 22 (2): 166–197.

7. Florida, Richard. 2002. *The Rise of the Creative Class.* New York: Basic Books, 37.

8. Organisation for Economic Co-operation and Development. 2001. *Education Policy Analysis.* Paris: Organisation for Economic Co-operation and Development (OECD) Publishing, 101.

9. Hogan, Timothy. 2011. *An Overview of the Knowledge Economy, with a Focus on Arizona.* Productivity and Prosperity Project, W. P. Carey School of Business, Arizona State University, 12. https://wpcarey.asu.edu/sites/default/files/knowledgeeconomy8-11.pdf.

10. Zumbrun, Josh. 2016. "The Rise of Knowledge Workers Is Accelerating Despite the Threat of Automation." *Dow Jones Institutional News*, May 4.

11. Brinkley, Ian. 2006. *Defining the Knowledge Economy.* London: Work Foundation, 14. http://cmaptools.cicei.com:8002/rid=1200871154838_2024647570_1410/de.

12. Neef, Dale. 1998. "Rethinking Economics in the Knowledge-based Economy." In *The Economic Impact of Knowledge*, edited by Dale Neef, G. Anthony Siesfeld, and Jacquelyn Cefola. Boston: Butterworth-Heinemann, 4.

13. Gaines, Brian. 1992. "Manufacturing in the Knowledge Economy." *Proceedings of ICOOMS'92: International Conference on Object-Oriented Manufacturing.* New York: Association for Computing Machinery. 19–36.

14. Drucker, Peter F. 1994. *Managing for Results: Economic Tasks and Risk-Taking Decisions.* Boston: Butterworth-Heinemann, 5.

15. Farmakis, Epaminondas. 2014. "Fostering the Creative Economy." *Stanford Social Innovation Review*, November 24. https://ssir.org/articles/entry/fostering_the_creative_economy.

16. Nussbaum, Bruce. 2005. "How to Build Innovative Companies." *Business Week*, August 1, 61–81, quotation on 62.

17. Zakaria, Fareed. 2015. *In Defense of a Liberal Education.* New York: Norton, 83.

18. Chou, Tracy. 2017. "A Leading Silicon Valley Engineers Explains Why Every Tech Worker Needs a Humanities Education." *Quartz*, June 28. https://qz.com/1016900/tracy-chou-leading-silicon-valley-engineer-explains-why-every-tech-worker-needs-a-humanities-education/.

19. Lee, Geunbae. 2017. "Combining Humanities and Technology Is More Important than Ever for User Experience." *Muzli*, May 3. https://medium.muz.li/combining-humanities-and-technology-is-more-important-than-ever-for-user-experience-ux-f420114c22a0.

20. Farmakis, "Fostering."

21. Ibid.

22. Zakaria, *In Defense*, 86.

23. Seidman, Dov. 2014. "From the Knowledge Economy to the Human Economy." *Harvard Business Review*, November 12. https://hbr.org/2014/11/from-the-knowledge-economy-to-the-human-economy.

24. Schwab, Klaus. 2016. "Fourth Industrial Revolution." World Economic Forum, January 14. https://www.weforum.org/agenda/2016/01/the-fourth-industrial-revolution-what-it-means-and-how-to-respond/.

25. Frangos, Jean-Marc. 2017. "The Internet of Things Will Power the Fourth Industrial Revolution. Here's How." World Economic Forum, June 24. https://www.weforum.org/agenda/2017/06/internet-of-things-will-power-the-fourth-industrial-revolution/.

26. DiSanto, Bianca. 2016. "To Survive a 5G Future, Get a Liberal Arts Degree." *Hoya*, September 23. http://www.thehoya.com/to-survive-a-5g-future-get-a-liberal-arts-degree/.

27. Ibid.

28. Brandt, "Writing for a Living," 184.

29. Selingo, Jeffrey J. 2017. "Wanted: Factory Workers, Degree Required." *New York Times*, January 30. https://www.nytimes.com/2017/01/30/education/edlife/factory-workers-college-degree-apprenticeships.html?_r=0.

30. Jenkins, Aric. 2017. "Robots Could Steal 40% of U.S. Jobs by 2030." *Fortune*, March 24. http://fortune.com/2017/03/24/pwc-robots-jobs-study/.

31. Talbot, David. 2011. "'Tectonic Shifts' in Employment." *MIT Technology Review*, December 20. https://www.technologyreview.com/s/426436/tectonic-shifts-in-employment/.

32. Anders, George. 2017. *You Can Do Anything: The Surprising Power of a "Useless" Liberal Arts Education*. New York: Little, Brown, 11.

33. Patel, Eboo. 2017. "How Robots Will Save Liberal Education." *Chronicle of Higher Education*, February 5. http://www.chronicle.com/article/How-Robots-Will-Save-Liberal/239113.

34. Jerald, Craig D. 2009. "Defining a 21st Century Education: At a Glance." Center for Public Education. http://citeseerx.ist.psu.edu/viewdoc/download?doi=10.1.1.460.8011&rep=rep1&type=pdf.

35. Autor, David H. 2015. "Why Are There Still So Many Jobs? The History and Future of Workplace Automation." *Journal of Economic Perspectives* 29 (3): 3–30, quotation on 11.

36. Pearlstein, Steven. 2016. "Meet the Parents Who Won't Let Their Children Study Literature." *Washington Post*, September 2. https://www.washingtonpost.com/posteverything/wp/2016/09/02/meet-the-parents-who-wont-let-their-children-study-literature/?utm_term=.7ecf6c2d8a00.

37. Patel, "How Robots."

38. Jerald, "Defining."

39. Hartley, Scott. 2017. *The Fuzzy and the Techie: Why the Liberal Arts Will Rule the Digital World*. Boston: Houghton Mifflin Harcourt.

40. DuPraw, Marcelle E., and Axner, Marya. 1997. "Working on Common Cross-cultural Communication Challenges." PBS.org, http://www.pbs.org/ampu/crosscult.html.

41. Ibid.

Chapter 2

1. Anders, George. 2017. *You Can Do Anything: The Surprising Power of a "Useless" Liberal Arts Education*. New York: Little, Brown, 11–12.

2. Ibid.

3. Ibid., italics in original.

4. American Academy of Arts and Sciences (AAAS). 2018. *The State of the Humanities 2018: Graduates in the Workforce and Beyond*. Humanities Indicators, AAAS. 15–16. https://www.amacad.org/multimedia/pdfs/publications/researchpapersmonographs/HI_Workforce-2018.pdf.

5. Ibid.

6. National Center for Education Statistics (NCES). 2017. "Bachelor's Degrees Conferred by Postsecondary Institutions, by Field of Study: Selected Years, 1970–71 Through 2014–15." Table 322.10. https://nces.ed.gov/programs/digest/d16/tables/dt16_322.10asp?current=yes.

7. Fisher, Anne. 2016. "How to Make a Liberal Arts Degree a Career Asset." *Fortune*, May 12. http://fortune.com/2016/05/12/liberal-arts-degree-career-asset/.

8. Lafely, A. G. "A Liberal Education: Preparation for Career Success." *Huffington Post*, December 6. https://www.huffingtonpost.com/ag-lafley/a-liberal-education-prepa_b_1132511.html.

9. NCES, Table 322.10.

10. Koenig, Rebecca. 2018. "Healthcare Jobs Abound. Here's How to Tap into the Hot Job Market." *U.S. News and World Report*, January 10. https://money.usnews.com/careers/articles/2018-01-10/health-care-jobs-abound-heres-how-to-tap-into-the-hot-job-market.

11. "Failures in Communication Contribute to Medical Malpractice." CRICO Strategies, January 31. https://www.rmf.harvard.edu/About-CRICO/Media/Press-Releases/News/2016/February/Failures-in-Communication-Contribute-to-Medical-Malpractice.

12. Bailey, Melissa. 2016. "Communication Failures Linked to 1,744 Deaths in Five Years, US Malpractice Study Finds." STAT, February 1. https://www.statnews.com/2016/02/01/communication-failures-malpractice-study/.

13. Koenig, "Healthcare Jobs."

14. National Science and Technology Council. 2013. "Federal Science, Technology, Engineering, and Mathematics (STEM) Education 5-Year Strategic Plan." May 31, iv. https://www.whitehouse.gov/sites/whitehouse.gov/files/ostp/Federal_STEM_Strategic_Plan.pdf.

15. NCES. Table 318.45, 322.10.

16. Skorton, David J. 2014. "Science Alone Isn't Enough to Solve the World's Problems." *Scientific American*, January 16. https://www.scientificamerican.com/article/why-scientists-should-embrace-liberal-arts/.

17. Shubert, Charlotte. 2018. "Do I Make Myself Clear? Media Training for Scientists." *Science*, January 25. http://www.sciencemag.org/features/2018/01/do-i-make-myself-clear-media-training-scientists.

18. Jaschik, Scott. 2011. "Florida GOP vs. Social Science." Inside Higher Ed, October 12. https://www.insidehighered.com/news/2011/10/12/florida-gop-vs-social-science.

19. Beam, Adam. 2016. "Kentucky Governor Matt Bevin Wants State Colleges and Universities to Produce More Electrical Engineers and Less French Literature Scholars." *U.S. News and World Report*, January 29. https://www.usnews.com/news/us/articles/2016-01-29/in-kentucky-a-push-for-engineers-over-french-lit-scholars.

20. Teitelbaum, Michael S. 2014. "The Myth of the Science and Engineering Shortage." *Atlantic*, March 19. https://www.theatlantic.com/education/archive/2014/03/the-myth-of-the-science-and-engineering-shortage/284359/.

21. Teitelbaum, Michael S. 2014. *Falling Behind? Boom, Bust, and the Global Race for Scientific Talent*. Princeton, NJ: Princeton University Press, 2–5, esp. 3.

22. Anft, Michael. 2013. "The STEM Crisis: Reality or Myth?" *Chronicle of Higher Education*, November 11. https://www.rit.edu/news/pdfs/CHE_Hira.pdf; Costa, Daniel. 2012. "STEM Labor Shortages? Microsoft Report Distorts Reality About Computing Occupations." Economic Policy Institute, November 19. http://www.epi.org/publication/pm195-stem-labor-shortages-microsoft-report-distorts/; Camarota, Steven A., and Zeigler, Karen. 2014. "Is There a STEM Worker Shortage? A Look at Employment and Wages in Science, Technology, Engineering, and Math." Center for Immigration Studies, May 19. https://cis.org/There-STEM-Worker-Shortage.

23. Xue, Yi, and Larson, Richard. 2015. "STEM Crisis or STEM Surplus? Yes and Yes." *Monthly Labor Review*, May. U.S. Bureau of Labor Statistics. https://www.bls.gov/opub/mlr/2015/article/stem-crisis-or-stem-surplus-yes-and-yes.htm.

24. Root-Bernstein, Robert, and Root-Bernstein, Michele. 2011. "Turning STEM into STREAM: Writing as an Essential Component of Science Education." National Writing Project, March 16. https://www.nwp.org/cs/public/print/resource/3522; National Academies of Science, Engineering, and Medicine. 2017. "Effective Mentoring in STEMM: Practice, Research, and Future Directions: Proceedings of a Workshop—in Brief." National Academies Press. https://www.nap.edu/read/24815/chapter/1.

25. Eger, John M. 2015. "Arts Based Learning of STEM Works Says NSF Funded Research Firm." *Huffington Post*, December 6. https://www.huffingtonpost.com/john-m-eger/arts-based-learning-of-st_b_8724148.html.

26. Carnevale, Anthony P., and Cheah, Ban. 2015. *Hard Times: College Majors, Unemployment and Earnings*. Georgetown University Center on Education and the Workforce. https://cew.georgetown.edu/wp-content/uploads/HardTimes2015-Report.pdf.

27. Humphreys, Debra, and Kelly, Patrick. 2014. *How Liberal Arts and Sciences Majors Fare in Employment*. Association of American Colleges and Universities, 2. https://www.mass.edu/foradmin/trustees/documents/HowLiberalArtsandSciencesMajorFareinEmployment.pdf.

28. Pearlstein, Steven. 2016. "Meet the Parents Who Won't Let Their Children Study Literature." *Washington Post*, September 2. https://www.washingtonpost.com/posteverything/wp/2016/09/02/meet-the-parents-who-wont-let-their-children-study-literature/?utm_term=.e9d7220dc2f1.

29. Speed, Edward. 2016. "A CEO's Advice to a Millennial: A Liberal Arts Degree Matters." *Rivard Report*, February 8. https://therivardreport.com/a-ceo-responds-to-a-millennial/.

30. Humphreys and Kelly, *How Liberal Arts*, 9. As Humphreys and Kelly explain, the data is from the U.S. Census Bureau's 2012 American Community Survey. It "depicts median annual earnings for college graduates employed full time (35+ hours per week) by area of undergraduate major, regardless of whether or not they also attained an advanced degree in the same or a different field of

study. The American Community Survey does not identify fields of postgraduate study" (9).

31. Ibid., 10.

32. Carnevale, Anthony P., Cheah, Ban, and Hanson, Andrew R. 2015. *The Economic Value of College Majors.* Georgetown University Center on Education and the Workforce, 11–12. https://cew.georgetown.edu/cew-reports/valueofcollegemajors/.

33. Ibid., 93.

34. National Association of Colleges and Universities. 2018. *Salary Survey: Starting Salary Projections for Class of 2018 New College Graduates.* Winter 2018. http://www.naceweb.org/uploaded-files/files/2018/publication/executive-summary/2018-nace-salary-survey-winter-executive-summary.pdf.

35. Jaschik, Scott. 2015. "Humanities Majors' Salaries." Inside Higher Ed, October 15. https://www.insidehighered.com/news/2015/10/05/new-data-what-humanities-majors-earn.

36. Robinson, Wesley. 2014. "Most with STEM College Degrees Go to Work in Other Fields, Study Finds." *Washington Post*, July 10. https://www.washingtonpost.com/local/education/most-with-college-stem-degrees-go-to-other-fields-of-work/2014/07/10/9aede466-084d-11e4-bbf1-cc51275e7f8f_story.html?utm_term=.8561ef556494.

37. Taylor, Ben. 2015. "21 Wildly Successful CEOs with Liberal Arts Degrees." Business 2 Community, August 4. https://www.business2community.com/leadership/21-wildly-successful-ceos-with-liberal-arts-degrees-01293809.

38. Liu, Yujia, and Grusky, David B. 2013. "The Payoff to Skill in the Third Industrial Revolution." *American Journal of Sociology* 118 (5): 1330–1374.

39. Deming, David J. 2017. "The Growing Importance of Labor Skills in the Labor Market." National Bureau of Economics Research, 2. http://www.nber.org/papers/w21473.pdf.

40. Grothaus, Michael. 2015. "The Top Jobs in Ten Years Might Not Be What You Expect." *Fast Company*, May 18. https://www.fastcompany.com/3046277/the-top-jobs-in-10-years-might-not-be-what-you-expect.

41. Schneider, Carol Geary, and Peter Ewell. 2014. Foreword. In Humphreys and Kelly, *How Liberal Arts*, vi.

42. AAAS, *State of the Humanities 2018*, 3, 13, 20, 19.

43. Frank, Robert H. 2016. "The Incalculable Value of Finding a Job You Love." *New York Times*, July 22. https://www.nytimes.com/2016/07/24/upshot/first-rule-of-the-job-hunt-find-something-you-love-to-do.html.

44. Bryant, Adam. 2011. "Google's Quest to Build a Better Boss." *New York Times*, March 12. http://www.nytimes.com/2011/03/13/business/13hire.html.

45. Davidson, Cathy N. 2017. *The New Education: How to Revolutionize the University to Prepare Students for a World in Flux.* New York: Basic Books, 140–141.

46. Ibid.

47. Ibid.

48. Strauss, Valerie. 2017. "The Surprising Thing Google Learned About Its Employees—and What It Means for Today's Students." *Washington Post*, December 20. https://www.washingtonpost.com/news/answer-sheet/wp/2017/12/20/the-surprising-thing-google-learned-about-its-employees-and-what-it-means-for-todays-students/?utm_term=.805641011549.

49. Ibid.

50. Sadove, Steve. 2014. "Employees Who Stand Out." *Forbes*, September 5. https://www.forbes.com/sites/realspin/2014/09/05/employees-who-stand-out/#7806052769b0.

51. We discuss our methodology for this analysis in the preface to Part III.

Chapter 3

1. PayScale surveyed 2.3 million graduates of more than 2,700 colleges and universities, requesting respondents to report their pay, major, highest degree earned, and associate or baccalaureate school name. For detailed information about salaries and majors, see https://www.payscale.com/

college-salary-report/common-jobs-for-majors/humanities?page=3.

2. Bureau of Labor Statistics. 2016. "Employment by Major Occupational Group." https://www.bls.gov/emp/tables/emp-by-major-occupational-group.htm.

3. Burning Glass Technologies. 2015. *The Human Factor: The Hard Times Employers Have Finding Soft Skills*. Burning Glass Technologies. https://www.burning-glass.com/wp-content/uploads/Human_Factor_Baseline_Skills_FINAL.pdf.

4. Because "business" includes, to some extent, all of the areas we're talking about in this chapter, we aren't including a section on the very broad and almost all-encompassing category of business.

5. Litt, Michael. 2017. "Why This Tech CEO Keeps Hiring Humanities Majors." Fastcompany.com, July 15. https://www.fastcompany.com/40440952/why-this-tech-ceo-keeps-hiring-humanities-majors.

6. Anders, George. 2017. *You Can Do Anything: The Surprising Power of a "Useless" Liberal Arts Education*. New York: Little, Brown, 12–15.

7. Ibid., 13.

8. Ibid., 13.

9. Ibid., 15.

10. Litt, "Why."

11. Humphreys, Debra. 2012. "The Questions We Need to Ask *First*: Setting Priorities for Higher Education in Our Technology-Rich World." In *Game Changers: Education and Information Technologies*, edited by Diane B. Oblinger, 25–36. Louisville, KY: Educause. https://library.educause.edu/resources/2012/5/chapter-2-the-questions-we-need-to-ask-first-setting-priorities-for-higher-education-in-our-technologyrich-world.

12. Anders, *You Can*, 80, 84.

13. Ibid., 94, 93.

14. Ibid., 86.

15. Williams, Tanya. 2015. "Technically Speaking About Telephony." *Huffington Post*, August 19. https://www.huffingtonpost.com/la-tanya-williams/we-need-to-talk_1_b_7992526.html.

16. Carlson, Scott. 2017. *The Future of Work: How Colleges Can Prepare Students for the Jobs Ahead*. Washington, D.C.: *Chronicle of Higher Education*, 14–15.

17. Hipps, Bradford J. 2016. "To Write Better Code Read Virginia Woolf." *New York Times*, May 21. https://www.nytimes.com/2016/05/22/opinion/sunday/to-write-software-read-novels.html.

18. Hartley, Scott. 2017. *The Fuzzy and the Techie: Why the Liberal Arts Will Rule the Digital World*. Boston: Houghton Mifflin Harcourt.

19. Washington State Arts Commission. 2013. *Creative Vitality in Washington State in 2013*. https://www.arts.wa.gov/media/dynamic/docs/CVI%202011%20data%20report,%20lo-res.pdf.

20. National Endowment for the Arts and the U.S. Bureau of Economic Analysis. 2013. "Arts and Cultural Production Contributed $704.2 Billion to the U.S. Economy in 2013." https://www.arts.gov/news/2016/arts-and-cultural-production-contributed-7042-billion-us-economy-2013.

21. Americans for the Arts. 2017. *Creative Industries: Business and Employment in the Arts*. https://www.americansforthearts.org/by-program/reports-and-data/research-studies-publications/creative-industries/view-the-reports. Americans for the Arts focuses solely on businesses involved in the production or distribution of the arts, from nonprofit museums, symphonies, and theaters, to for-profit film, architecture, and advertising companies. They exclude industries such as computer programming and scientific research because they are not arts-focused.

22. Zakaria, Fareed. 2015. *In Defense of a Liberal Education*. New York: Norton, 86.

23. Dodd, Chris. 2015. "Creative Industries Add $698 Billion to the U.S. Economy and 4.7 Million Jobs." Motion Picture Association of America (MPAA) blog, January 14. https://www.mpaa.org/nea/#.Wh7mXdenEdU.

24. Queensland University of Technology. N.d. "Creative Industries." https://www.qut.edu.au/creative-industries/about/what-are-the-creative-industries.

25. United Nations Educational, Scientific and Cultural Organisation (UNESCO). 2015. *Cul-

tural Times—The First Global Map of Cultural and Creative Industries. http://unesdoc.unesco.org/images/0023/002357/235710E.pdf.

26. Osnos, Peter. 2011. "The Serious Business of 21st-Century Book Publishing." *Atlantic,* June 7. https://www.theatlantic.com/entertainment/archive/2011/06/the-serious-business-of-21st-century-book-publishing/240047/.

27. Kurowski, Travis, Miller, Wayne, and Prufer, Kevin. 2016. Introduction. In *Literary Publishing in the Twenty-First Century,* edited by Miller, Prufer, and Kurowski. Minneapolis: Milkweed Editions, 1–2.

28. Owens, Simon. 2015. "Self-Publishing Boom Boosts Freelance Editing Services." MediaShift, May 5. http://mediashift.org/2015/05/self-publishing-boom-boosts-freelance-editing-services/.

29. Hiltz, Allison. 2016. "Publishing in the 21st Century: The Power of Data and AI." Book Wheel, December 2. http://www.thebookwheelblog.com/publishing-in-the-21st-century-the-power-of-data-and-ai/.

30. GraphiqNewsdesk. 2016. "Who's the Largest Employer in the U.S.? Hint: It's a Government Agency." *Belleville (IL) News-Democrat,* May 24. http://www.bnd.com/living/article79507112.html.

31. Rose, Roger P. 2012. "Preferences for Careers in Public Work: Examining the Government-Nonprofit Divide Among Undergraduates Through Public Service Motivation." *American Review of Public Administration* 43 (4): 416–437.

32. Glickman, Dan. 2016. "JOBS: Don't Forget the Public Sector." *Time,* October 13. http://time.com/collection-post/4527293/2016-election-public-sector-jobs/.

33. Krasna, Heather. 2010. *Jobs That Matter: Find a Stable, Fulfilling Career in Public Service.* Indianapolis: JIST Works, 32.

34. Nonprofit HR. 2016. *Nonprofit Employment Practices Survey™ Results.* https://www.nonprofithr.com/wp-content/uploads/2016/04/2016NEPSurvey-final.pdf.

35. Bureau of Labor Statistics. 2016. "Nonprofits in America: New Research Data on Employment, Wages, and Establishments." *Monthly Review,* February 16. https://www.bls.gov/opub/mlr/2016/article/nonprofits-in-america.htm.

36. McKeever, Brice. 2015. "The Nonprofit Sector in Brief 2015: Public Charities, Giving, and Volunteering." Urban Institute, October 29. https://www.urban.org/research/publication/nonprofit-sector-brief-2015-public-charities-giving-and-volunteering.

37. Krasna, *Jobs That Matter,* 39–59.

38. Gillett, Rachel. 2015. "What Will It Take to Get a Nonprofit Job in 2020?" FastCompany, April 17. https://www.fastcompany.com/3044537/what-it-will-take-to-get-a-nonprofit-job-in-2020.

39. Gou, Chao, and Saxton, Gregory D. 2014. "Tweeting Social Change: How Social Media Are Changing Nonprofit Advocacy." *Nonprofit and Voluntary Sector Quarterly* 43 (1): 57–79; Obar, J. A., Zube, P., and Lampe, C. 2012. "Advocacy 2.0: An Analysis of How Advocacy Groups in the United States Perceive and Use Social Media as Tools for Facilitating Civic Engagement and Collective Action." *Journal of Information Policy* 2: 1–25.

40. Bureau of Labor Statistics. 2018. "Occupational Outlook Handbook: Healthcare." https://www.bls.gov/ooh/healthcare/home.htm.

41. The links between the humanities and health care also are supported by the Association of American Medical Colleges, which supports increased humanities knowledge for medical professionals such as doctors. As Mann notes, "there has been a growing recognition that studying the arts and humanities may help learners develop qualities such as professionalism, self-awareness, and communication skills that are increasingly important for physicians." Writing can help doctors "absorb and interpret what their patients are feeling," and other classes in the humanities and arts can help physicians develop empathy, better communication skills, and improved observation of patients. From Mann, Sarah. 2017. "Focusing on Arts, Humanities to Develop Well-Rounded Physicians." AAMCNews, August 15. https://news.aamc.org/medical-education/article/focusing-arts-humanities-well-rounded-physicians/.

42. Baylor University. 2018. "Medical Humanities: Frequently Asked Questions." https://www.baylor.edu/medical_humanities/index.php?id=874015.

43. Humphreys and Kelly, *How Liberal Arts*, 9.

44. Matz, Robert. 2016. "5 Myths About the Liberal Arts." *Mason Spirit*, July 19. https://spirit.gmu.edu/2016/07/5-myths-about-the-liberal-arts/.

45. Temkin, Diane Goldstein. 2014. "Letter to the Editor." *New York Times*, August 14.

46. Smith, Martha Nell. 2011. "The Humanities Are Not a Luxury: A Manifesto for the Twenty-First Century." *Liberal Education* 97 (1): 48–55, quotation on 48. See also Sadove, Steve. 2014. "Employees Who Stand Out." *Forbes*, September 5. https://www.forbes.com/sites/realspin/2014/09/05/employees-who-stand-out/#7806052769b0.

Chapter 4

1. The "common good" itself is an example of the many enduring questions and concepts addressed by the humanities. What does the common good, an ancient concept with roots in Christianity, really mean, and how has it been understood and operationalized in the political sphere? Whose general welfare is at stake?

2. Commission on the Humanities and Social Sciences. 2013. *The Heart of the Matter: Humanities and Social Sciences for a Vibrant, Competitive, and Secure Nation.* Cambridge, MA: American Academy of Arts and Sciences, 9.

3. Arnold, Matthew. 1869. *Culture and Anarchy.* London: Smith, Elder & Co. https://archive.org/stream/matthewarnoldcul021369mbp/matthewarnoldcul021369mbp_djvu.txt, xxv.

4. Plato. 381 BC. *Plato's Republic.* Edited by B. Jowett and Lewis Campbell. Oxford: Clarendon. 1894. https://books.google.com/books/about/Plato_s_Republic_The_Greek_Text.html?id=bscvAQAAMAAJ&printsec=frontcover&source=kp_read_button#v=onepage&q&f=false.

5. Chaucer, Geoffrey. 1476. *The Canterbury Tales.* New York: Macmillan. 1903. https://books.google.com/books/about/Chaucer_s_Canterbury_Tales.html?id=dfjV8a75qV4C&printsec=frontcover&source=kp_read_button#v=onepage&q&f=false.

6. Machiavelli, Niccolo. 1513. *The Prince.* Translated by George Bull. London: Penguin. 2003. Quotation on 57.

7. Harpham, Geoffrey Galt. 2005. "Beneath and Beyond the 'Crisis in the Humanities.'" *New Literary History* 36 (1): 21–36, quotation on 25.

8. Kristof, Nicholas. 2014. "Don't Dismiss the Humanities." *New York Times*, August 13. https://www.nytimes.com/2014/08/14/opinion/nicholas-kristof-dont-dismiss-the-humanities.html?_r=0.

9. Bodenner, Chris. 2017. "The Surprising Revolt at the Most Liberal College in the Country." *Atlantic*, November 2. https://www.theatlantic.com/education/archive/2017/11/the-surprising-revolt-at-reed/544682/.

10. MacDonald, Heather. 2014. "The Humanities and Us." *City Journal.* http://www.city-journal.org/html/humanities-and-us-13635.html.

11. Smith, Martha Nell. 2011. "The Humanities Are Not a Luxury: A Manifesto for the Twenty-First Century." *Liberal Education* 97 (1): 48–55, 54.

12. Corrigan, Paul T. 2017. "Want a Job with That English Degree?" *Corrigan Literary Review*, March 11. https://corriganliteraryreview.wordpress.com/2017/03/11/want-a-job-with-that-english-degree/.

13. Quigley, Charles N. N.d. "Constitutional Democracy." Center for Civic Education, Calabasas, CA. http://www.civiced.org/component/content/article/12-publications/390-constitutional-democracy.

14. Cigarroa, Francisco G. 2013. "Humanities Guides Students' Quests for the Stars." Statesman, October 4. http://www.statesman.com/news/opinion/cigarroa-humanities-guides-students-quests-for-the-stars/WK5cZVhtNpsY6ZypXzsXrO/.

15. Smith, "Humanities," 52–53.

16. Ibid.

17. Kelly, Jason M. 2013. "The Arts and Humanities Play a Critical Role in the Development of Vibrant Communities." London School of Economics, December 14. http://blogs.lse.ac.uk/us-appblog/2013/12/14/the-arts-and-humanities-play-a-critical-role-in-the-development-of-vibrant-communities/.

18. King, Martin Luther, Jr. 1964. Baccalaureate sermon at the commencement exercises for Wesleyan University in Middletown, Connecticut. https://quoteinvestigator.com/2012/11/15/arc-of-universe/.

19. Fitzgerald, Deborah K. 2014. "At MIT, the Humanities Are Just as Important as STEM." *Boston Globe*, April 30. https://www.bostonglobe.com/opinion/2014/04/30/mit-humanities-are-just-important-stem/ZOArg1PgEFy2wm4ptue56I/story.html.

20. Drakeman, Donald. 2016. *Why We Need the Humanities: Life Science, Law and the Common Good*. New York: Palgrave Macmillan, xi.

21. Ibid., 7, 37, 38.

22. Hartley, Scott. 2017. *The Fuzzy and the Techie: Why the Liberal Arts Will Rule the Digital World*. Boston: Houghton Mifflin Harcourt, 111.

23. Madsbjerg, Christian. 2017. *Sensemaking: The Power of the Humanities in the Age of the Algorithm*. New York: Hachette Books.

24. Ibid., 6, 8.

25. Ibid., 2.

26. Feloni, Richard. 2018. "Microsoft's President Says Liberal Arts Majors Are Necessary for the Future of Tech." *Business Insider*, January 21. http://www.businessinsider.com/microsoft-president-says-tech-needs-liberal-arts-majors-2018-1.

27. Microsoft. 2018. "The Future Computed: Artificial Intelligence and Its Role in Society." Amazon Digital Services. https://blogs.microsoft.com/blog/2018/01/17/future-computed-artificial-intelligence-role-society/.

28. Ibid.

29. Buxton, Madelyn. 2017. "Writing for Alexa Becomes More Complicated in the #MeToo Era." Refinery29, December 27. https://www.refinery29.com/2017/12/184496/amazo-alexa-personality-me-too-era.

30. Ibid.

31. Hume, Katherine. 2017. "The Utility of the Humanities in the 21st Century." Quam Proxime, February 20. https://quamproxime.com/2017/02/20/the-utility-of-the-humanities-in-the-21st-century/.

32. Guo, Jeffrey. 2016. "I Have Found a New Way to Watch TV, and It Changes Everything." *Washington Post*, June 22. https://www.washingtonpost.com/news/wonk/wp/2016/06/22/i-have-found-a-new-way-to-watch-tv-and-it-changes-everything/?utm_term=.02877284c45e.

33. Gilbert, Sophie. 2016. "Learning to Be Human." *Atlantic*, June 30. https://www.theatlantic.com/entertainment/archive/2016/06/learning-to-be-human/489659/.

34. Burian, Peter. 2012. "Defending the Humanities." Inside Higher Ed, June 25. https://www.insidehighered.com/views/2012/06/25/essay-how-defend-humanities.

Chapter 5

1. Cole, Jonathan R. 2016. "The Triumph of America's Research University." *Atlantic*, September 20. https://www.theatlantic.com/education/archive/2016/09/the-triumph-of-americas-research-university/500798/.

2. Kagan, Jerome. 2009. *The Three Cultures: Natural Sciences, Social Sciences, and the Humanities in the 21st Century*. Cambridge: Cambridge University Press, 5.

3. Marar, Ziyad. 2013. "Why Does Social Science Have Such a Hard Job Explaining Itself?" *Guardian*, April 8. https://www.theguardian.com/higher-education-network/blog/2013/apr/08/social-science-funding-us-senate.

4. Hult, Christine. 2006. *Researching and Writing Across the Curriculum*, 3rd ed. New York: Pearson, 149.

5. Ibid., 153–154.

6. Gilman, Charlotte Perkins. 1892. *The Yellow Wallpaper*. In *The Prentice Hall Anthology of Women's Literature*, edited by Deborah H. Holdstein, 138–151. Upper Saddle River, NJ: Prentice Hall, 2000, 139.

7. Ibid., 141.

8. Ibid., 145.

9. Smith, A. Lapthorn. 1905. "Higher Education of Women and Race Suicide." In *Men's Ideas/ Women's Realities: Popular Science, 1870–1915*, edited by Louise M. Newman, 147–152. New York: Pergamon Press, 1985, quotation on 147.

10. Gilman, *Yellow Wallpaper*, 141.

11. Nealon, Jeffrey, and Giroux, Susan Searls. 2003. *The Theory Toolbox: Critical Concepts for the Humanities, Arts and Social Sciences*. Lanham, MD: Rowman & Littlefield, 6, 8.

12. Ibid., 95.

13. Ibid., 96–99.

14. Ibid., 103.

15. Linenthal, Edward T. 2006. "Epilogue: Reflections." In *Slavery and Public History: The Tough Stuff of American Memory*, edited by James Oliver Horton and Lois E. Horton, 213–224. New York: Norton, quotation on 213.

16. Shashkevich, Alex. 2017. "Humanities Research in the Digital Age." *Stanford News*, December 14. https://news.stanford.edu/2017/12/14/humanistic-inquiry-digital-technology/.

17. Heppler, Jason, Blevings, Cameron, Hickox, Jocelyn, and Balakrishnan, Tara. 2017. "Mapping U.S. Post Offices in the Nineteenth-Century West." Center for Spatial and Textual Analysis, Stanford University. http://web.stanford.edu/group/spatialhistory/cgi-bin/site/viz.php?id=435&project_id=.

18. Shashkevich, "Humanities Research."

19. Marian, Veronica. 2015. "Stanford Historian Looks to the U.S. Postal Service to Map the Boom and Bust of 19th-Century American West." *Stanford News*, March 26. https://news.stanford.edu/2015/03/26/post-office-geography-032615/.

20. Moreau, Elise. 2017. "The Top Social Networking Sites People Are Using." Lifewire, December 9. https://www.lifewire.com/top-social-networking-sites-people-are-using-3486554.

21. Patel, Deep. 2017. "10 Social-Media Trends to Prepare for in 2017." Entrepreneur.com, September 27. https://www.entrepreneur.com/article/300813#.

22. Spiegel, Gabrielle. 2008. "The Case for History and the Humanities." *Perspectives on History: The Newsmagazine of the American Historical Association*. https://www.historians.org/publications-and-directories/perspectives-on-history/january-2008/the-case-for-history-and-the-humanities.

23. Arnold, Matthew. 1869. *Culture and Anarchy*. London: Smith, Elder & Co. https://archive.org/stream/matthewarnoldcul021369mbp/mathewarnoldcul021369mbp_djvu.txt.

24. Browne, Ray B. 2005. "Folklore to Populore." In *Popular Culture Studies Across the Curriculum: Essays for Educators*, edited by Browne, 24–27. Jefferson, NC: McFarland.

25. Nyden, Philip. 2003. "Academic Incentives for Faculty Participation in Community-Based Participatory Research." *Journal of General Internal Medicine* 18 (7): 576–585, esp. 576.

26. Fluehr-Lobban, Carolyn. 1995. "Anthropologists, Cultural Relativism, and Universal Rights." *Chronicle of Higher Education*, June 9, B1–B2. https://www-chronicle-com.ezaccess.libraries.psu.edu/article/Anthropologists-Cultural/83376.

27. Drakeman, *Why We Need*, xii.

28. "Division of Public Programs." N.d. NEH. https://www.neh.gov/divisions/public.

29. "NEH Pledges $448,100 to Create Community Reading Programs for Military Families." 2017. NEH.gov, August 3. https://www.neh.gov/news/press-release/2017-08-03-0.

30. The PHC uses the Orton Family Foundation's Community Heart and Soul® method as a

framework.

31. Founded in 1999 by the White House Millennial Council, the University of Michigan, and the Woodrow Wilson National Fellowship Foundation, Imagining America: Artists and Scholars in Public Life is a consortium of cultural and design fields in communities throughout the nation.

32. *Through the Eyes of Local African Americans: Reflections on the Civil Rights Movement in Reading and Berks County, Pennsylvania.* 2016. (Re)Writing Local Histories: Racial, Ethnic and Cultural Communities. http://sites.psu.edu/localhistories/books/african-american/. Produced through a partnership between Penn State Berks students and the Central Pennsylvania African American Museum in Reading, Pennsylvania.

33. Teagle Foundation. 2007. "Student Learning and Faculty Research: Connecting Teaching and Scholarship." American Council of Learned Societies. https://www.acls.org/uploadedFiles/Publications/Programs/ACLS-Teagle_Teacher_Scholar_White_Paper.pdf, 3, 5.

Chapter 6

1. The Universal Declaration of Human Rights (UDHR), developed in response to the Holocaust, was adopted by the United Nations General Assembly in Paris on December 10, 1948.

2. Faust, Jennifer L., and Paulson, Donald R. 1998. "Active Learning for the College Classroom." *Journal on Excellence in College Teaching* 9 (2): 3–24, quotation on 4.

3. Kuh, George. 2008. *High-Impact Educational Practices: What They Are, Who Has Access to Them, and Why They Matter.* Washington, DC: Association of American Colleges and Universities.

4. Hart Research Associates. 2015. *Falling Short? College Learning and Career Success.* Washington, DC: Association of American Colleges and Universities. https://www.aacu.org/sites/default/files/files/LEAP/2015employerstudentsurvey.pdf.

5. Enck, Suzanne M. 2015. "Planning a Gender Fair as a Semester-Long Final Project." *Communication Teacher* 29 (2): 1–8.

6. Biskind, Peter. 2001. *Seeing Is Believing: How Hollywood Taught Us to Stop Worrying and Love the Fifties.* New York: Holt; Jancovich, Mark. 2002. *Horror: The Film Reader.* Abingdon, UK: Routledge; Biskind, Peter. 2004. *Gods and Monsters: Thirty Years of Writing on Film and Culture from One of America's Most Incisive Writers.* New York: Nation; Worland, Rick. 2006. *The Horror Film: An Introduction.* Hoboken, NJ: Wiley-Blackwell.

7. Letizia, Angelo J. 2017. *Democracy and Social Justice Education in the Information Age.* Cham, Switzerland: Palgrave Macmillan, 61.

8. Eberly, Rosa A. 1999. "From Writers, Audiences, and Communities to Publics: Writing Classrooms as Protopublic Spaces." *Rhetoric Review* 18 (1): 165–178, quotation on 172.

9. Weisman, Alan. 1999. *Gaviotas.* Hartford, VT: Chelsea Green.

10. Jaschik, Scott. 2016. "Professors, Politics and New England." Inside Higher Ed, July 5. https://www.insidehighered.com/news/2016/07/05/new-analysis-new-england-colleges-responsible-left-leaning-professoriate.

11. Jaschik, Scott. 2017. "Professors and Politics: What the Research Says." Inside Higher Ed, February 27. https://www.insidehighered.com/news/2017/02/27/research-confirms-professors-lean-left-questions-assumptions-about-what-means.

12. Ibid.; Binder, Amy J., and Wood, Kate. 2012. *Becoming Right: How Campuses Shape Young Conservatives.* Princeton, NJ: Princeton University Press.

13. Burian, Peter. 2012. "Defending the Humanities." Inside Higher Ed, June 25. https://www.insidehighered.com/views/2012/06/25/essay-how-defend-humanities.

Preface to Part III

1. National Association of Colleges and Employers (NACE) Job Outlook report data are available from the following:

2018, https://www.naceweb.org/about-us/press/2017/the-key-attributes-employers-seek-on-students-resumes/.

2017, https://www.tougaloo.edu/sites/default/files/page-files/2017-nace-job-outlook-full-report.pdf.

2016, https://www.mccormick.northwestern.edu/career-development/documents/getting-started/job-search/NACE%20Job%20Outlook%202016.pdf.

2015, http://www.umuc.edu/documents/upload/nace-job-outlook-2015.pdf.

2014, https://web.iit.edu/sites/web/files/departments/career-services/pdfs/nace%20job-outlook-2014.pdf.

2013, http://career.sa.ucsb.edu/files/docs/handouts/job-outlook-2013.pdf.

2012, http://www.sjsu.edu/careercenter/docs/job-outlook-survey-NACE_2012.pdf.

2011, https://career.pages.tcnj.edu/files/2011/07/Job_Outlook_2011_Full_Report_PDF1.pdf.

2. Hart Research Associates. 2015. *Falling Short?College Learning and Career Success.* Washington, DC: Association of American Colleges and Universities. https://www.aacu.org/leap/public-opinion-research/2015-survey-falling-short.

Hart Research Associates. *2013. It Takes More Than a Major: Employer Priorities for College Learning and Student Success.* Washington, DC: Association of American Colleges and Universities. https://www.aacu.org/leap/presidentstrust/compact/2013SurveySummary; Hart Research Associates. 2010. *Raising the Bar: Employers' Views on College Learning in the Wake of the Economic Downturn.* Washington, DC: Association of American Colleges and Universities. https://www.aacu.org/sites/default/files/files/LEAP/2009_EmployerSurvey.pdf.

3. The survey also addresses specific personality traits preferred by employers, but those are outside the scope of this book.

Chapter 7

1. "Critical Thinking: Basic Questions and Answers." N.d. Foundation for Critical Thinking. http://www.criticalthinking.org/pages/critical-thinking-basic-questions-amp-answers/409. According to the foundation's website, Paul made this statement in an interview for the April 1992 issue of *Think* magazine.

2. Carlgren, Teresa. 2013. "Communication, Critical Thinking, Problem Solving: A Suggested Course for All High School Students in the 21st Century." *Interchange* 44 (1–2): 63–81, quotation on 66, emphasis in original.

3. Fisher, Christian. 2017. "How Is Critical Thinking Related to Workplace Success?" CareerTrend.com, July 5. https://careertrend.com/critical-thinking-related-workplace-success-19819.html.

4. Baldoni, John. 2010. "How Leaders Should Think Critically." *Harvard Business Review*, January 20. https://hbr.org/2010/01/how-leaders-should-think-criti.

5. Zakaria, Fareed. 2015. "Why America's Obsession with STEM Education Is Dangerous." *Washington Post*, March 26. https://www.washingtonpost.com/opinions/why-stem-wont-make-us-successful/2015/03/26/5f4604f2-d2a5-11e4-ab77-9646eea6a4c7_story.html?utm_term=.30b9cb0a0df1.

6. Neck, Christopher. 2016. *Organizational Behavior: A Critical Thinking Approach.* Thousand Oaks, CA: SAGE.

7. Neck, Christopher. 2016. "Critical Thinking Helps Managers Work Through Problems." Arizona State University, February 8. https://research.wpcarey.asu.edu/critical-thinking-helps-managers-work-through-problems/, emphasis added.

8. Korn, Melissa. 2014. "Bosses Seek 'Critical Thinking,' but What Is That?" *Wall Street Journal*, October 21. https://www.wsj.com/articles/bosses-seek-critical-thinking-but-what-is-that-1413923730.

9. Manville, Brook. 2017. "How to Hire and Develop Critical Thinkers." *Forbes*, April 23. https://www.forbes.com/sites/brookmanville/2017/04/23/how-to-hire-and-develop-critical-thinkers/#525c9c40797e.

10. Ibid.

11. Liu, Yujia, and Grusky, David B. 2013. "The Payoff to Skill in the Third Industrial Revolution." *American Journal of Sociology* 118 (5): 1330–1374.

12. Baldoni, "How Leaders."

13. Anderson, Phyllis R., and Reid, Joanne R. 2013. "The Effect of Critical Thinking Instruction on Graduates of a College of Business Administration." *Journal of Higher Education Theory and Practice* 13 (3/4): 149–167.

14. Elder, Linda, and Paul, Richard. 2010. "Critical Thinking: Competency Standards Essential for the Cultivation of Intellectual Skills, Part 1." *Journal of Developmental Education* 34 (2): 38–39.

15. Belkin, Douglas. 2017. "Exclusive Test Data: Many Colleges Fail to Improve Critical-Thinking Skills." *Wall Street Journal*, June 5. https://www.wsj.com/articles/exclusive-test-data-many-colleges-fail-to-improve-critical-thinking-skills-1496686662.

16. Arum, Richard, and Roksa, Josipa. 2011. *Academically Adrift: Limited Learning on College Campuses*. Chicago: University of Chicago Press, 36.

17. Ibid., 80–81.

18. Ibid.

19. Abrami, Philip C., Bernard, Robert M., Borokhovski, Eugene, Waddington, David I., Wade, C. Anne, and Persson, Tonje. 2015. "Strategies for Teaching Students to Think Critically: A Meta-Analysis." *Review of Educational Research* 85 (2): 275–314. https://doi.org/10.3102/0034654314551063.

20. Daud, Nuraihan Mat, and Husin, Zamnah. 2004. "Developing Critical Thinking Skills in Computer-Aided Extended Reading Classes." *British Journal of Educational Technology* 35 (4): 477–487, quotation on 478.

21. Kuh, George. 2008. *High-Impact Educational Processes: What They Are, Who Has Access to Them, and Why They Matter*. Washington, DC: Association of American Colleges and Universities.

22. Abrami et al., "Strategies," 301–302.

23. Paris, Ben. 2016. "Failing to Improve Critical Thinking." Inside Higher Ed, November 29. https://www.insidehighered.com/views/2016/11/29/roadblocks-better-critical-thinking-skills-are-embedded-college-experience-essay.

24. For detailed analyses of this assignment, see Grobman, Laurie. 2018. "'Engaging Race': Critical Race Inquiry and Community-Engaged Scholarship." *College English* 80 (2): 105–132; Grobman, Laurie, Kemmerer, Elizabeth, and Zebertavage, Meghan. 2017. "Counternarratives: Community Writing and Anti-Racist Rhetoric." *Reflections: A Journal of Public Rhetoric, Civic Writing, and Service-Learning* 17 (2): 43–68.

25. *Through the Eyes of Local African Americans*.

26. Countryman, Matthew. 2015. "Why Philadelphia?" Civil Rights in a Northern City: Philadelphia, Temple University. http://northerncity.library.temple.edu/exhibits/show/civil-rights-in-a-northern-cit/historical-perspective/why-philadelphia-.

27. Litwack, Leon F. 2009. *How Free Is Free? The Long Death of Jim Crow*. Cambridge, MA: Harvard University Press, 107.

28. Paul, Richard, and Elder, Linda. 2008. *The Miniature Guide to Critical Thinking: Concepts and Tools*. Foundation for Critical Thinking. http://web.iitd.ac.in/~nkurur/2015-16/IIsem/cml522/CriticalThinking.pdf.

29. Ibid., 4.

30. Countryman, Matthew J. 2005. *Up South: Civil Rights and Black Power in Philadelphia*. Philadelphia: University of Pennsylvania Press, 10.

31. *Through the Eyes of Local African Americans*.

32. Paul and Elder, *Miniature Guide*, 4.

33. *Through the Eyes of Local African Americans*.

34. Paul and Elder, *Miniature Guide*, 4.

35. Rogers, Kim Lacy. 1988. "Oral History and the History of the Civil Rights Movement." *Journal of American History* 75 (2): 567–576.

36. Paul and Elder, *Miniature Guide*, 4.

37. Ibid.

38. *Through the Eyes of Local African Americans.*

39. Gormley, *Critical Advantage.*

40. Arum and Roksa, *Academically Adrift.*

Chapter 8

1. Hart Research Associates, *Falling Short?*, 7.

2. Nisen, Max. 2013. "11 Reasons to Ignore the Haters and Major in the Humanities." *Business Insider*, June 27. http://www.businessinsider.com/11-reasons-to-major-in-the-humanities-2013-6.

3. Burning Glass Technologies. 2015. *The Human Factor: The Hard Times Employers Have Finding Soft Skills.* Burning Glass Technologies. https://www.burning-glass.com/wp-content/uploads/Human_Factor_Baseline_Skills_FINAL.pdf.4–5, 10–11.

4. Ibid.

5. Anders, George. 2016. "Good News Liberal-Arts Majors: Your Peers Probably Won't Outearn You Forever." *Wall Street Journal*, September 11. https://www.wsj.com/articles/good-news-liberal-arts-majors-your-peers-probably-wont-outearn-you-forever-1473645902.

6. Carnevale, Anthony P. 2008. "The Workplace Realities." *School Administrator* 2 (65). http://www.aasa.org/SchoolAdministratorIssue.aspx?id=3778.

7. Lashinsky, Adam. 2012. "Amazon's Jeff Bezos: The Ultimate Disrupter." *Fortune*, November 16. http://fortune.com/2012/11/16/amazons-jeff-bezos-the-ultimate-disrupter/.

8. Zakaria, Fareed. 2015. *In Defense of a Liberal Education.* New York: Norton, 74.

9. Corrigan, Paul T. 2017. "Want a Job with That English Degree?" *Corrigan Literary Review*, March 11. https://corriganliteraryreview.wordpress.com/2017/03/11/want-a-job-with-that-english-degree/.

10. Dishman, Lydia. 2017. "How a Degree in Scandinavian Mythology Can Land You a Job at One of the Biggest Tech Companies." Fast Company, June 2. https://www.fastcompany.com/40425362/how-a-degree-in-scandinavian-mythology-can-land-you-a-job-at-one-of-the-biggest-tech-companies.

11. Klingenborg, Verlyn. 2013. "The Decline and Fall of the English Major." *New York Times*, June 22. http://www.nytimes.com/2013/06/23/opinion/sunday/the-decline-and-fall-of-the-english-major.html.

12. Association of American Colleges and Universities. 2009. "Written Communication VALUE Rubric." https://www.aacu.org/value/rubrics/written-communication.

13. Kuh, George. 2008. *High-Impact Educational Practices: What They Are, Who Has Access to Them, and Why They Matter.* Washington, DC: Association of American Colleges and Universities.

14. Parker, Robert P., and Goodkin, Vera. 1987. *The Consequences of Writing: Enhancing Learning in the Disciplines.* Upper Montclair, NJ: Boynton/Cook; Russell, David R. 2001. "Where Do the Naturalistic Studies of WAC/WID Point? A Research Review." *WAC for the New Millennium: Strategies for Continuing Writing-Across-the-Curriculum Programs.* Urbana, IL: National Council of Teachers of English, 259–298.

15. Arum and Roksa, *Academically Adrift*, 80.

16. Selingo, Jeffrey J. 2017. "Why Can't College Graduates Write Coherent Prose?" *Washington Post*, August 11. http://blogs.workday.com/3-ways-we-can-help-college-students-find-their-way-in-the-new-economy/.

17. Walvoord, Barbara E. 2014. *Assessing and Improving Student Writing in College: A Guide for Institutions, General Education, Departments, and Classrooms.* San Francisco: Jossey-Bass, 6, emphasis added.

18. Kallgren, Dan. "JFK's Executive Orders and the New Frontier." Sample Assignments, American Historical Association. https://www.historians.org/teaching-and-learning/teaching-resources-for-historians/classroom-materials/classroom-materials-sample-assignments.

19. WIDE Research Center Collective. 2005. "Why Teach Digital Writing?" *Kairos* 10 (1).

http://kairos.technorhetoric.net/10.1/coverweb/wide/kairos5.html.

20. Sturgis, Ingrid, and Dugo, Hab. 2014. Course syllabus. https://canvas.instructure.com/courses/910884/assignments/syllabus.

21. Grobman, Laurie. 2017. "The Policy Brief Assignment: Transferable Skills in Action in a Community-Engaged Writing Project." *Prompt: A Journal of Academic Writing Assignments* 1 (1). http://thepromptjournal.com/index.php/prompt/article/view/10/17.

22. Solinger, Rickie, Fox, Madeline, and Irani, Kayhan, eds. 2008. *Telling Stories to Change the World: Global Voices on the Power of Narrative to Build Community and Make Social Justice Claims.* New York: Routledge.

23. U.S. Census Bureau. 2013. Population Estimates. https://factfinder.census.gov/faces/table-services/jsf/pages/productview.xhtml?src=CF.

24. Mallach, Alan. 2013. "Parallel Histories, Diverging Trajectories: Resilience in Small Industrial Cities." In *Revitalizing American Cities*, edited by Susan M. Wachter and Kimberly A. Zeuli, 126–145. Philadelphia: University of Pennsylvania Press, 142.

25. Klingenborg, "Decline."

Chapter 9

1. Daniels, Josephus. 1946. *The Wilson Era: Years of War and After, 1917–1923.* Chapel Hill: University of North Carolina Press, 624.

2. Williams, Tanya. 2017. "Technically Speaking About Telephony." *Huffington Post*, December 6. https://www.huffingtonpost.com/la-tanya-williams/we-need-to-talk_1_b_7992526.html.

3. Johnson, Dave. 2011. "Grow Better Managers the Google Way." CBS Money Watch, March 14. https://www.cbsnews.com/news/grow-better-managers-the-google-way/.

4. Human communication studies faculty work from both humanities and social science perspectives, depending on the field of study. But these majors are generally housed in humanities departments, as the major was formed within the humanities field of rhetoric.

5. Burning Glass Technologies, *Human Factor*, 9.

6. Bok, Derek. 2006. *Our Underachieving Colleges: A Candid Look at How Much Students Learn and Why They Should Be Learning More.* Princeton, NJ: Princeton University Press.

7. Carnevale, Anthony P., and Smith, Nicole. 2013. "Workplace Basics: The Skills Employees Need and Employers Want." *Human Resource Development International* 16 (5): 491–501, quotation on 500.

8. Watson, Wyatt. 2009. "Capitalizing on Effective Communication: How Courage, Innovation and Discipline Drive Business Results in Challenging Times." Towers Watson, December 21. https://www.towerswatson.com/en-US/Insights/IC-Types/Survey-Research-Results/2009/12/20092010-Communication-ROI-Study-Report-Capitalizing-on-Effective-Communication.

9. Grossman, David. 2011. "The Cost of Poor Communications." *Holmes Report*, July 16. https://www.holmesreport.com/latest/article/the-cost-of-poor-communications.

10. Davenport, Thomas H., Harris, Jeanne, and Shapiro, Jeremy. 2010. "Competing on Talent Analytics." *Harvard Business Review*, October. https://hbr.org/2010/10/competing-on-talent-analytics.

11. Bailey, Melissa. 2016. "Communication Failures Linked to 1,744 Deaths in Five Years, U.S. Malpractice Study Finds." STAT News, February 1. https://www.statnews.com/2016/02/01/communication-failures-malpractice-study/.

12. Thew, Jennifer. 2018. "Nurse Managers Must Model Relationship Skills." Health Leaders, January 9. http://www.healthleadersmedia.com/nurse-leaders/nurse-managers-must-model-relationship-skills?page=0%2C1.

13. Carnevale and Smith, "Workplace Basics."

14. Deming, David J. 2017. "The Growing Importance of Social Skills in the Labor Market." National Bureau of Economic Research Working Paper 21473. June 2. http://www.nber.org/papers/w21473.pdf. Deming calls them "social skills" but doesn't provide a specific definition for this term.

Instead, he references research on teamwork, collaboration, oral communication skills, emotional intelligence, and leadership skills and then notes that his paper attempts to "extend and formalize the definition of one particular dimension of 'soft skills'—the ability to work with others" (5–6). These parameters, in our view, clearly fit into the skills and knowledge learned in communication studies and communication education.

15. Rubin, Rebecca, and Morreales, Sherwyn. 2000. "What College Students Should Know and Be Able to Do." *Journal of the Association of Communication Administration* 21 (9): 53–65.

16. "Speaking in the Disciplines." N.d. Department of Communication, University of Pittsburgh. http://www.speaking.pitt.edu/about/index.html.

17. This assignment is borrowed in large part from Dr. Jill Rhea at Graceland University.

18. Broward County Public Schools. N.d. "Debate Initiative." http://www.browardschools.com/debate.

Chapter 10

1. Cook, Tim. 2013. "Apple CEO Tim Cook on Collaboration." YouTube, May 30. https://www.youtube.com/watch?v=EZPYLZ7I6gs.

2. Cragan, John F., Wright, David W., and Kasch, Chris R. 2003. *Communication in Small Groups: Theory, Process, Skills.* Belmont, CA: Thompson/Wadsworth.

3. Cross, Rob, Rebele, Reb, and Grant, Adam. 2016. "Collaborative Overload." *Harvard Business Review,* January–February. https://hbr.org/2016/01/collaborative-overload.

4. Wiart, Nikki. 2015. "Revenge of the Liberal Arts: Why a Liberal Arts Education Pays Off." *Maclean's,* July 26. http://www.macleans.ca/education/revenge-of-the-arts-why-a-liberal-arts-education-pays-off/; World Economic Forum. 2016. "The Future of Jobs: Employment, Skills, and Workforce Strategy for the Fourth Industrial Revolution." http://www3.weforum.org/docs/WEF_Future_of_Jobs.pdf.

5. Society for Human Resource Management. 2016. "SHRM Survey Findings: Entry-Level Applicant Job Skills Survey." https://www.shrm.org/hr-today/trends-and-forecasting/research-and-surveys/Documents/Entry-Level_Applicant_Job_Skills_Survey.pdf.

6. Sabine, Anne. 2016. "Why Soft Skills Are Just as Important as Academic Ability in Science Graduates." SEEK Insights and Resources. https://insightsresources.seek.com.au/soft-skills-just-important-academic-ability-science-graduates.

7. Anders, George. 2015. "That 'Useless' Liberal Arts Degree Has Become Tech's Hottest Ticket." *Forbes,* July 29. https://www.forbes.com/sites/georgeanders/2015/07/29/liberal-arts-degree-tech/2/#7249d73b40b8.

8. Turiera, Teresa, and Susanna Cros. 2013. *Co-Business: 50 Examples of Business Collaboration.* Barcelona: Co-Society. http://www.co-society.com/wp-content/uploads/CO_business_2013.pdf, 21.

9. Porath, Christine L., and Pearson, Christine M. 2010. "The Cost of Bad Behavior." *Organizational Dynamics* 39 (1): 64–71.

10. Ibid., 64–65.

11. Barkey, Elizabeth F., Cross, Patricia K., and Major, Claire Howell. 1995. *Collaborative Learning Techniques: A Handbook for College Faculty.* San Francisco: John Wiley & Sons.

12. Cabera, Alberto, Amaury, Nora, Crissman, Jennifer, Ternezini, Patrick, Bernal, Elena, and Pascarella, Ernesy. 2002. "Collaborative Learning: Its Impact on College Students' Development and Diversity." *Journal of College Student Development* 43 (1): 20–34, quotations on 30, 31.

13. Ullyot, Michael, and O'Neill, Kate E. 2016. "Collaborative Work and the Future of Humanities Teaching." *Canadian Journal for the Scholarship of Teaching and Learning* 7 (2): 12; Vanderstoep, Scott W., Pintrich, Paul R., and Fagerlin, Angela. 1996. "Disciplinary Differences in Self-Regulated Learning in College Students." *Contemporary Educational Psychology* 21 (4): 345–362.

14. Sweet, Michael, and Michaelsen, Larry K. 2012. "Critical Thinking and Engagement: Creating Cognitive Apprenticeships with Team-Based Learning." In *Team-Based Learning in the Social Sciences and Humanities: Group Work That Works to Generate Critical Thinking and Engagement,*

edited by Sweet and Michaelsen, 5–32. Sterling: Stylus Publishing.

15. Sibley, Jim. 2012. "Facilitating Application Activities." In Sweet and Michaelsen, *Team-Based Learning*, 33–50.

16. Ibid.

17. Moore Howard, R. 2001. "Collaborative Pedagogy." In *A Guide to Composition Pedagogies*, edited by G. Tate, A. Rupiper, and K. Schick, 54–70. New York: Oxford University Press, 64–65.

18. Hughes, Linda K., and Lund, Michael. 1994. "Union and Reunion: Collaborative Authorship." In *Author-ity and Textuality: Current Views of Collaborative Writing*, edited by James S. Leonard, Christina E. Wharton, Robert Murray Davis, and Jeanette Harris, 241–260. W. Cornwall, CT: Locust Hill.

19. Loss, Christopher P. 2002. "Incorporating Website Group Projects in Arts and Humanities Classes." Center for Teaching Excellence. http://cte.virginia.edu/issue/fall-2002/.

20. Zines are personally made short magazines that focus on particular topics of interest, are usually printed in black and white, and are produced with a goal of distribution by an individual or group.

21. Sweet, Michael, and Michaelsen, Larry K. 2007. "How Group Dynamics Research Can Inform the Theory and Practice of Postsecondary Small Group Learning." *Educational Psychology Review* 19 (1): 31–47.

22. Ryan, Richard M., and Deci, Edwin L. 2000. "Intrinsic and Extrinsic Motivations: Classic Definitions and New Directions." *Contemporary Educational Psychology* 25 (1): 54–67.

23. Vygotsky, Lev S. 1978. *Mind in Society: The Development of Higher Psychological Processes*. Cambridge, MA: Harvard University Press.

Chapter 11

1. Segran, Elizabeth. 2014. "Why Top Tech CEOs Want Employees with Liberal Arts Degrees." Fastcompany.com, August 8. https://www.fastcompany.com/3034947/why-top-tech-ceos-want-employees-with-liberal-arts-degrees.

2. Ibid.

3. *Merriam-Webster's Collegiate Dictionary*. 11th ed. Springfield, MA: Merriam-Webster, 2003. Continually updated at https://www.merriam-webster.com/.

4. Segran, "Why Top Tech CEOs."

5. Zwilling, Martin. 2011. "Nine Steps to Effective Business Problem Solving." *Business Insider*, July 19. http://www.businessinsider.com/nine-steps-to-effective-business-problem-solving-2011-7.

6. National Association of Colleges and Employers. Job Outlook 2018. https://www.naceweb.org/about-us/press/2017/the-key-attributes-employers-seek-on-students-resumes/.

7. Davidson, Kate. 2016. "Employers Find 'Soft Skills' Like Critical Thinking in Short Supply." *Wall Street Journal*, August 30. https://www.wsj.com/articles/employers-find-soft-skills-like-critical-thinking-in-short-supply-1472549400.

8. Manning, Becca. 2016. "What Can You Do with a Philosophy Degree?" *Wheaton News*. https://wheatoncollege.edu/news/what-can-you-do-with-a-philosophy-degree/.

9. Greiff, Samuel, Wüstenberg, Sascha, Csapó, Benő, Demetriou, Andreas, Hautamäki, Jarkko, Graesser, Arthur C., and Martin, Romain. 2014. "Domain-general Problem Solving Skills and Education in the 21st Century." *Educational Research Review* 13: 74–83, esp. 76.

10. Autor, David H., Levy, Frank, and Murname, Richard J. 2003. "The Skill Content of Recent Technological Change: An Empirical Exploration." *Quarterly Journal of Economics* 118 (4): 1279–1333. https://academic.oup.com/qje/article/118/4/1279/1925105.

11. Autor, David. 2014. "Polanyi's Paradox and the Shape of Employment Growth." National Bureau of Economic Research. http://www.nber.org/papers/w20485, 11.

12. World Economic Forum. 2016. "The Future of Jobs: Employment, Skills and Workforce Strategy for the Fourth Industrial Revolution." http://reports.weforum.org/future-of-jobs-2016/skills-stability/.

13. Quoted in Manville, Brook. 2016. "Six Leadership Practices for 'Wicked' Problem Solving." *Forbes*, May 15. https://www.forbes.com/sites/brookmanville/2016/05/15/six-leadership-practices-for-wicked-problem-solving/#2fab3b66506b.

14. Ibid.

15. Polya, George. 1945. *How to Solve It*. Princeton, NJ: Princeton University Press.

16. Bransford, John D., and Stein, Barry S. 1984. *The Ideal Problem Solver: A Guide for Improving Thinking, Learning, and Creativity*. New York: Worth Publishing; Ohno, Taiichi. 1988. *Toyota Production System: Beyond Large-Scale Production*. Philadelphia: Productivity Press.

17. Problem-based learning (PBL) also immerses students in messy problems. PBL, an instructional strategy developed in medical schools, immerses students in "authentic, ill-structured, real-world problem[s]." Hung, Woei. 2011. "Theory to Reality: A Few Issues in Implementing Problem-based Learning." *Educational Technology Research and Development* 59 (4): 529–552, quotation on 531. According to Hung, Jonassen, and Liu, PBL has been adopted across many disciplines in undergraduate education, mainly in the practical fields. Hung, W., Johassen, D. H., and Liu, R. 2008. "Problem-Based Learning." In *Handbook for Research on Educational Communications and Technology*, edited by Spector, J. M., van Merrienboer, Merrill, M.D., and Driscoll, M., 485–506. Mahweh, NJ: Erlbaum, quotation on 487.

Chapter 12

1. IBM. 2010. "IBM 2010 Global CEO Study: Creativity Selected as Most Crucial Factor for Future Success." IBM Newsroom. https://www-03.ibm.com/press/us/en/pressrelease/31670.wss.

2. World Economic Forum. 2016. "The Future of Jobs: Employment, Skills, and Workforce Strategy for the Fourth Industrial Revolution." http://www3.weforum.org/docs/WEF_Future_of_Jobs.pdf.

3. Bakhshi, Hasan, Frey, Carl, and Osborne, Michael. 2015. "Creativity vs. Robots." *Nesta*, April 17. https://www.nesta.org.uk/report/creativity-vs-robots/.

4. Florida, Richard. 2014. *The Rise of the Creative Class—Revisited*. New York: Basic Books.

5. Zhou, Jing, and Hoever, Inga J. 2014. "Research on Workplace Creativity: A Review and Redirection." *Annual Review of Organizational Psychology and Organizational Behavior* 1: 333–359.

6. Morgan, Jacob. 2015. "Five Uncommon Internal Innovation Examples." *Forbes*, April 8. https://www.forbes.com/sites/jacobmorgan/2015/04/08/five-uncommon-internal-innovation-examples/2/#4bedfa676f67.

7. Zemits, Birut Irena. 2017. "Representing Knowledge: Assessment of Creativity in the Humanities." *Arts and Humanities in Higher Education* 16 (2): 173–187.

8. Berrett, Dan. 2013. "Creativity: A Cure for the Common Curriculum." *Education Digest* 79 (2): 13–21, quotation on 18.

9. Amabile, Teresa, and Khaire, Mutki. 2008. "Creativity and the Role of the Leader." *Harvard Business Review*, October. https://hbr.org/2008/10/creativity-and-the-role-of-the-leader.

10. Creative Education Foundation. N.d. "What Is Creative Problem Solving?" http://www.creativeeducationfoundation.org/creative-problem-solving/.

11. Amabile and Khaire, "Creativity and the Role."

12. Ibid.

13. Phelps, Edmund S. 2014. "Why Teaching Humanities Improves Innovation." World Economic Forum, September 4. https://www.weforum.org/agenda/2014/09/stem-education-humanities-creativity-innovation/.

14. Ibid.

15. Amabile and Khaire, "Creativity and the Role."

16. Amabile, Teresa M., Schatzel, Elizabeth A., Moneta, Giovanni B., and Kramer, Steven J. 2004. "Leader Behaviors and the Work Environment for Creativity: Perceived Leader Support." *Leadership Quarterly* 15 (1): 5–32.

17. Cheng, Chi-Yi, Sanchez-Burks, Jeffrey, and Lee, Fiona. 2007. "Identity Integration and

Innovation." Ross School of Business Working Paper Number 1070. https://papers.ssrn.com/sol3/papers.cfm?abstract_id=973870.

18. Carlson, Tracy. 2016. "Humanities and Business Go Hand in Hand." *Boston Globe*, April 24. https://www.bostonglobe.com/opinion/2016/04/24/humanities-and-business-hand-hand/9nG9n04SSF1KoOMRJjguxK/story.html.

19. Mills, Mark, and Ottino, Julio M. 2009. "We Need More Renaissance Scientists." *Forbes*, June 3. www.forbes.com/2009/06/03/phd-engineering-science-clayton-christensen-mark-mills-innovation-research.html.

20. Edelstein, Dan. 2010. "How Is Innovation Taught? On the Humanities and the Knowledge Economy." *Liberal Education* 96 (1). https://www.aacu.org/publications-research/periodicals/how-innovation-taught-humanities-and-knowledge-economy.

21. Golsby-Smith, Tony. 2011. "Want Innovative Thinking? Hire from the Humanities." *Harvard Business Review*, March 31. https://hbr.org/2011/03/want-innovative-thinking-hire.

22. Girardi, Gherardo. 2013. "Using Cinema to Enhance the Relevance of Economics to Students' Lives." In *Creativity in the Classroom: Case Studies in Using the Arts in Teaching and Learning in Higher Education*, edited by Paul Mcintosh and Digby Warren, 43–56. Chicago: Intellect, 2013.

23. Griffiths, Dave. 2013. "Fascinatin' Rhyme: Tapping into Themes of Leadership and Management by Making Music." In Mcintosh and Warren, *Creativity in the Classroom*, 57–72.

24. Hopkinson, Clare. 2013. "Teaching and Using Poetry in Healthcare." In Mcintosh and Warren, *Creativity in the Classroom*, 101–114, esp. 105.

25. Some tactics of these organizations were linked to civil disobedience, but students in the course were neither encouraged nor allowed to engage in civil disobedience behaviors.

26. Berrett, "Creativity."

27. Siltanen, Rob. 2011. "The Real Story Behind Apple's 'Think Different' Campaign." *Forbes*, December 14. https://www.forbes.com/sites/onmarketing/2011/12/14/the-real-story-behind-apples-think-different-campaign/#5f0ba4cc62ab.

Chapter 13

1. Anders, George. 2017. *You Can Do Anything: The Surprising Power of a "Useless" Liberal Arts Education*. New York: Little, Brown, quotation on 12, emphasis in original.

2. "Technological competence" is often used synonymously with digital competency, proficiency, or skills. Technological literacy is sometimes referred to as "digital literacy."

3. Hendricks, Drew. 2013. "Benefits of Adapting to the Newest Enterprise Technology." *Forbes*, September 24. https://www.forbes.com/sites/drewhendricks/2013/09/24/benefits-of-adapting-to-the-newest-enterprise-technology/#20db439ee2b5.

4. Croft, Lucy, and Cochrane, Natasha. 2005. "Communicating Change Effectively." *Management Services* 49 (1): 18.

5. Delaney, Rob, and D'Agostino, Robert. 2015. "The Challenges of Integrating New Technology into an Organization." La Salle University Digital Commons, Mathematics and Computer Science Capstones 25. http://digitalcommons.lasalle.edu/mathcompcapstones/25.

6. Doyle, Alison. 2018. "Computer Skills That Will Help You Get Hired." Career Tool Belt, April 24. http://www.careertoolbelt.com/computer-skills-that-will-help-you-get-hired/.

7. Ibid.

8. Belshaw, Douglas A. J. 2011. "What Is 'Digital Literacy'? A Pragmatic Investigation." Ed.D. thesis, Durham University. https://clalliance.org/wp-content/uploads/files/doug-belshaw-edd-thesis-final.pdf. 207.

9. Bali, Maha. 2016. "Knowing the Difference Between Digital Skills and Digital Literacies, and Teaching Them Both." Literacy Daily (blog), February 3. https://www.literacyworldwide.org/blog/literacy-daily/2016/02/03/knowing-the-difference-between-digital-skills-and-digital-literacies-and-teaching-both.

10. Ibid.

11. Doyle, "Computer Skills."

12. McVerry, J. Gregory. 2013. "TPACK and New Literacies of Online Reading Comprehension: Preparing Today's Teachers for Tomorrow's Readers." In *Research on Technology in English Education*, edited by Carl A. Young and Sara Kajder, 87–104. Charlotte, NC: Information Age, quotation on 95.

13. Dunne, Niall. 2016. "How Technology Will Change the Future of Work." World Economic Forum, February 24. https://www.weforum.org/agenda/2016/02/the-future-of-work/.

14. Locke, Brandon T. 2017. "Digital Humanities Pedagogy as Essential Liberal Education: A Framework for Curriculum Development." *Digital Humanities Quarterly* 11 (3). http://www.digital-humanities.org/dhq/vol/11/3/000303/000303.html.

15. Jay, Paul, and Graff, Gerald. 2012. "Fear of Being Useful." Inside Higher Ed, January 5. https://www.insidehighered.com/views/2012/01/05/essay-new-approach-defend-value-humanities.

16. Cordell, Ryan. 2015. "How Not to Teach Digital Humanities." February 1. http://ryan-cordell.org/teaching/how-not-to-teach-digital-humanities/.

17. Hurst, Rachel Alpha Johnston. 2014. "A 'Journey in Feminist Theory Together': The *Doing Feminist Theory Through Digital Video* Project." *Arts and Humanities in Higher Education* 13 (4): 333–347. Hurst's analysis of the assignment is far more in depth than we have space to cover. Our focus is primarily on the intersection of the technology and the humanities.

18. Ibid., 335.

19. Ibid., 336.

20. Ibid., 337.

21. Ibid., 344.

22. The digital native narrative has been criticized for failing to acknowledge the generation's diversity and the fact that young girls are urged to learn technology at a lower rate than young boys. Locke, "Digital."

23. Christian-Lamb, Caitlin. 2017. "Starting from Scratch? Workshopping New Directions in Undergraduate Digital Humanities." *Digital Humanities Quarterly* 11 (3). http://www.digitalhumanities.org/dhq/vol/11/3/000311/000311.html.

Chapter 14

1. Hayzlett, Jeffrey. 2016. "Why Should Your Business Care About Social Responsibility?" *Entrepreneur*, October 10. https://www.entrepreneur.com/article/269665.

2. Bossman, Julia. 2016. "Top 9 Ethical Issues in Artificial Intelligence." World Economic Forum, October 21. https://www.weforum.org/agenda/2016/10/top-10-ethical-issues-in-artificial-intelligence/.

3. Weinberg, Adam. 2017. "Data Analytics and the Liberal Arts." *Huffington Post*, April 19. http://www.huffingtonpost.com/adam-weinberg/data-analytics-and-the-li_b_9721312.html.

4. Trevino, Linda K., and Katherine A. Nelson. 2017. *Managing Business Ethics: Straight Talk About How to Do It Right*. 7th ed. Hoboken, NJ: Wiley, quotation on 19.

5. Ibid., 21.

6. Ibid.

7. Ibid.

8. Ibid., 15.

9. Wissenbach, Ilona, and Cremer, Andreas. 2017. "VW Expects to Discipline More Employees in Emissions Scandal." *Automotive News*, March 7. http://www.autonews.com/article/20170307/COPY01/303079943/vw-expects-to-discipline-more-employees-in-emissions-scandal.

10. Ewing, Jack, and Bowley, Graham. 2015. "The Engineering of Volkswagen's Aggressive Ambition." *New York Times*, December 13. https://www.nytimes.com/2015/12/14/business/the-engineering-of-volkswagens-aggressive-ambition.html?_r=2&mtrref=undefined.

11. Olson, Steven D. 2013. *Shaping an Ethical Workplace*. Society for Human Resource Management Foundation. https://www.shrm.org/hr-today/trends-and-forecasting/special-reports-and-

expert-views/Documents/Ethical-Workplace-Culture.pdf. 21.

12. Ferrell, O. C., Fraedrich, John, and Ferrell, Linda. 2017. *Business Ethics: Ethical Decision-Making and Cases.* 11th ed. Boston: Cengage Learning, 3.

13. The Ethisphere Institute. 2018. "Ethisphere Institute Announces 135 Companies Honored as World's Most Ethical Companies." News release, February 12. https://ethisphere. com/2018-worlds-most-ethical-companies/.

14. Ethics Resource Center. 2014. *National Business Ethics Survey of the U.S. Workforce.* Arlington, VA. https://www.ibe.org.uk/userassets/surveys/nbes2013.pdf. The Ethics Resource Center (ERC) is an independent, nonpartisan, nonprofit organization "devoted exclusively to the advancement of high ethical standards and practices in public and private institutions." https://berkleycenter. georgetown.edu/organizations/ethics-resource-center.

15. Ibid.

16. Ibid.

17. Reiss, Robert. 2017. "Top CEOs Place High Value on Corporate Ethics and Social Responsibility to Drive Business." *Forbes,* September 11. https://www.forbes.com/sites/rober-treiss/2017/09/11/top-ceos-place-high-value-on-corporate-ethics-and-social-responsibility-to-drive-business/#3678e3a84473.

18. Schwartz, Arthur J. 2015. "The 5 Most Common Unethical Behaviors in the Workplace." *Philadelphia Business Journal,* January 26. https://www.bizjournals.com/philadelphia/blog/guest-comment/2015/01/most-common-unethical-behaviors-in-the.html.

19. De George, Richard T. 2015. "A History of Business Ethics." Markkula Center for Applied Ethics at Santa Clara University. https://www.scu.edu/ethics/focus-areas/business-ethics/resources/a-history-of-business-ethics/.

20. Haidt, Jonathan, and Trevino, Linda. 2018. "Teaching Ethics." Ethical Systems. http://www.ethicalsystems.org/content/teaching-ethics.

21. Paul, Richard, and Elder, Linda. 2014. *Critical Thinking: Tools for Taking Charge of Your Professional and Personal Life.* 2nd ed. Upper Saddle River, NJ: Pearson, 256.

22. Duska, R. 2014. "What's Literature to Ethics or Ethics to Literature? With Reflections on Business Ethics." In *Aesthetics and Business Ethics,* edited by Daryl Koehn and Dawn Elm, 67–82. Dordrecht: Springer.

23. Nussbaum, Martha C. 1997. *Cultivating Humanity: A Classical Defense of Reform in Liberal Education.* Cambridge, MA: Harvard University Press.

24. Morrison, Toni. 1987. *Beloved.* New York: Penguin. Subsequent references will be given parenthetically in the text.

25. Keinzler, Donna. 2001. "Ethics, Critical Thinking, and Professional Communication Pedagogy." *Technical Communication Quarterly* 10 (3): 319–339.

26. Koehn, Daryl, and Elm, Dawn. 2014. "Introduction." In *Aesthetics and Business Ethics,* edited by Koehn and Elm, 1–5. Dordrecht: Springer, quotation on 5.

Chapter 15

1. Mason, Meredith. 2018. "Bentley on Bloomberg: The Business Case for Diversity and Inclusion." Bentley University Newsroom, January 12. https://www.bentley.edu/prepared/bentley-on-bloomberg-business-case-diversity-and-inclusion.

2. Thakrar, Monica. 2017. "How to Lead the Push for Diversity in the Workplace." *Forbes,* June 9. https://www.forbes.com/sites/forbescoachescouncil/2017/06/09/how-to-lead-the-push-for-diversity-in-the-workplace/#16d78a1d415b.

3. Dover, Tessa L., Major, Brenda, and Kaiser, Cheryl R. 2016. "Diversity Policies Rarely Make Companies Fairer, and They Feel Threatening to White Men." *Harvard Business Review,* January 4. https://hbr.org/2016/01/diversity-policies-dont-help-women-or-minorities-and-they-make-white-men-feel-threatened.

4. Lindsey, Alex, King, Eden, Membere, Ashley, and Cheung, Ho Kwan. 2017. "Two Types of

Diversity Training That Really Work." *Harvard Business Review*, July 28. https://hbr.org/2017/07/two-types-of-diversity-training-that-really-work.

5. CEO Action for Diversity and Inclusion. 2011. "CEO Pledge." https://www.ceoaction.com/pledge/ceo-pledge/.

6. Mason, "Bentley on Bloomberg."

7. Thakrar, "How to Lead."

8. Hunt, Vivian, Layton, Dennis, and Prince, Sara. 2015. "Why Diversity Matters." McKinsey, January. https://www.mckinsey.com/business-functions/organization/our-insights/why-diversity-matters.

9. Martin, Gillian Coote. 2014. "The Effects of Cultural Diversity in the Workplace." *Journal of Diversity Management* 9 (2): 89–92.

10. Altman, Ian. 2017. "5 Reasons Why Workplace Diversity Is Good for Business." *Inc.*, March 15. https://www.inc.com/ian-altman/5-reasons-why-workplace-diversity-is-good-for-business.html.

11. Phillips, Katherine W. 2014. "How Diversity Makes Us Smarter." Scientific American, October 1. https://www.scientificamerican.com/article/how-diversity-makes-us-smarter/.

12. Altman, "5 Reasons Why."

13. Phillips, "How Diversity Makes."

14. Woolley, Anita, Malone, Thomas W., and Chabris, Christopher F. 2015. "Why Some Teams Are Smarter Than Others." *New York Times*, January 16. https://www.nytimes.com/2015/01/18/opinion/sunday/why-some-teams-are-smarter-than-others.html.

15. National Women's Law Center. 2017. *The Wage Gap: The Who, How, Why, and What to Do*. https://nwlc-ciw49tixgw5lbab.stackpathdns.com/wp-content/uploads/2016/09/The-Wage-Gap-The-Who-How-Why-and-What-to-Do-2017-2.pdf.

16. Warner, Judith, and Corley, Danielle. 2017. "The Women's Leadership Gap: Women's Leadership by the Numbers." Center for American Progress, May 21. https://www.americanprogress.org/issues/women/reports/2017/05/21/432758/womens-leadership-gap/.

17. Feldblum, Chai R., and Lipnic, Victoria A. 2016. *Select Task Force on the Study of Harassment in the Workplace*. Equal Employment Opportunity Commission. https://www.eeoc.gov/eeoc/task_force/harassment/upload/report.pdf.

18. Out and Equal: Workplace Advocates. 2017. "2017 Workplace Equality Fact Sheet." http://outandequal.org/2017-workplace-equality-fact-sheet/. This source mentions just "LGBT," not "LGBTQ."

19. Eisenberg, Richard. 2017. "How to Fix Racial Inequities in the Workplace." *Forbes*, October 27. https://www.forbes.com/sites/nextavenue/2017/10/27/how-to-fix-racial-inequities-in-the-workplace/#1108a3c954ab.

20. Out and Equal, "2017 Workplace."

21. Wellman, Mitchell. 2017. "Report: The Race Gap in Higher Education Is Very Real." *USA Today*, March 7. http://college.usatoday.com/2017/03/07/report-the-race-gap-in-higher-education-is-very-real/.

22. Higher Education Today. 2017. "Meeting the Needs of Underserved Students." https://www.higheredtoday.org/policy-research/meeting-needs-underserved-students/.

23. National Center for Education Statistics. 2018. *The Condition of Education 2018*. U.S. Department of Education. https://nces.ed.gov/pubs2018/2018144.pdf.

24. Marcus, Jon. 2017. "Why Men Are the New College Minority." *Atlantic*, August 8. https://www.theatlantic.com/education/archive/2017/08/why-men-are-the-new-college-minority/536103/.

25. Renn, Kristen. "LGBTQ Students on Campus: Issues and Opportunities for Higher Education Leaders." Higher Education Today (blog), April 10. https://www.higheredtoday.org/2017/04/10/lgbtq-students-higher-education/.

26. Wood, Maria. 2017. "The Changing Face of Today's Student: More Diverse, Older and Requiring More Personalized Learning." *Acrobatiq*, March 24. http://acrobatiq.com/the-changing-face-of-todays-student-more-diverse-older-and-requiring-more-personalized-learning/.

27. Priceonomics Data Studio. 2016. "Ranking the Most (and Least) Diverse Colleges in America." Priceonomics, July 12. https://priceonomics.com/ranking-the-most-and-least-diverse-colleges-in/.

28. Sack, Kevin, and Thee-Brenan, Megan. 2015. "Poll Finds Most in U.S. Hold Dim View of Race Relations." *New York Times*, July 23. https://www.nytimes.com/2015/07/24/us/poll-shows-most-americans-think-race-relations-are-bad.html.

29. Banks, James. 2015. "Series Foreword." In *Diversity Education: A Critical Multicultural Approach*, edited by Michael Vavrus, ix–xiii. New York: Teachers College Press, 2015, quotation on ix.

30. Renn, "LGBTQ Students on Campus."

31. Pierce, Chester M. 1995. "Stress Analogs of Racism and Sexism: Terrorism, Torture, and Disaster." In *Mental Health, Racism, and Sexism*, edited by Charles V. Willie, Patricia Perry Rieker, Bernard M. Kramer, and Bertram S. Brown, 277–293. Pittsburgh: University of Pittsburgh Press, quotation on 281.

32. Harper, Shaun R., and Davis III, Charles H. F. 2016. "Eight Actions to Reduce Racism in College Classrooms." American Association of University Professors. https://www.aaup.org/article/eight-actions-reduce-racism-college-classrooms#.WrQAmWrwaUk.

33. Schocker, Jessica B. 2014. "A Case for Using Images to Teach Women's History." *History Teacher* 47 (3): 421–450.

34. Spender, Dale. 1992. *Man Made Language*. 2nd ed. London: Pandora, 148, 150.

35. Laughlin, James S. 1997. "Beyond *Beyond the Culture Wars*: Students Teaching Themselves the Conflicts." In *Rethinking American Literature*, edited by Lil Bannon and Brenda M. Greene, 231–248. Urbana, IL: National Council of Teachers of English.

36. PBS. 2014. "History Detectives Investigations: 20th Century Music." http://www.pbs.org/opb/historydetectives/feature/20th-century-music/.

37. Smithsonian Institute. N.d. "African American Music: Achievements and Impact." https://www.si.edu/spotlight/african-american-music/recognition.

38. Laughlin, "Beyond."

39. Jennings, Kyesha. 2016. "Overcoming Racial Tension: Using Student Voices to Create Safe Spaces in the Classroom." In *Diversity and Inclusion in the College Classroom,* edited by Mary Bart, 9–10. Madison, WI: Magna. http://provost.tufts.edu/celt/files/Diversity-and-Inclusion-Report.pdf.

Chapter 16

1. Hummel, Denise Pirrotti. 2012. "Understanding the Importance of Culture in Global Business." Oracle. http://www.oracle.com/us/corporate/profit/archives/opinion/050312-dhummel-1614961.html.

2. Matusitz, Jonathan. 2010. "Disneyland Paris: A Case Analysis Demonstrating How Glocalization Works." *Journal of Strategic Marketing* 18 (3): 223–237.

3. Hummel, "Understanding."

4. Gartside, David, Griccioli, Stefano, and Richburg, Rustin. "Different Strokes: How to Manage a Global Workforce." *Outlook* 2: 1–9, 2. https://www.accenture.com/t20150522T061605Z__w__/usen/_acnmedia/Accenture/Conversion-Assets/Outlook/Documents/1/Accenture-Outlook-How-to-Manage-a-Global-Workforce.pdf.

5. Meyer, Erin. 2014. *The Culture Map: Breaking Through the Invisible Boundaries of Global Business*. New York: Public Affairs.

6. Hertog, Judith. 2017. "Why We Need the Humanities." *Dartmouth Alumni Magazine*, Mar–Apr. https://dartmouthalumnimagazine.com/articles/why-we-need-humanities.

7. Cole, Rose. 2016. "Shaping (Global) Leaders or Creating (Global) Citizens? Considering the Competing Purposes of Higher Education." *Good Society* 25 (2–3): 289–312, quotation on 294.

8. Kite, Allison. 2014. "Global Awareness Important in All Business." KU B-School Blog, March 28. http://kubschool.blogspot.com/2014/03/global-awareness-important-in-all.html.

9. World Economic Outlook. 2018. "World Economic Outlook Update, January 2018: Brighter

Prospects, Optimistic Markets, Challenges Ahead." International Monetary Fund. https://www.imf.org/en/Publications/WEO/Issues/2018/01/11/world-economic-outlook-update-january-2018.

10. HR Knowledge Center. 2015. "Understanding Workplace Cultures Globally." Society for Human Resource Management, November 30. https://www.shrm.org/resourcesandtools/tools-and-samples/toolkits/pages/understandinganddevelopingorganizationalculture.aspx.

11. Meyer, *Culture Map.*

12. Ibid.

13. Ibid.

14. Gartside et al., "Different Strokes," 2.

15. Ibid., 3.

16. Trost, Jennifer. 2009. "Using Personal Narratives to Teach a Global Perspective." *History Teacher* 42 (2): 178–189.

17. Institute of International Education. 2017. "*Open Doors Report* 2017." https://au.usembassy.gov/open-doors-report-2017-u-s-hosts-million-international-students-second-consecutive-year/.

18. Hovland, Kevin. 2014. "What Can Global Learners Do?" *Diversity and Democracy* 17 (2). https://www.aacu.org/diversitydemocracy/2014/spring/hovland.

19. Association of American Colleges and Universities. 2015. "Global Learning VALUE Rubric." https://www.aacu.org/value/rubrics/global-learning.

20. Ibid.

21. Bronstein, Marcia, Jones, Shelley, and Neuwirth, Sharyn. 2014. "Awakening Global Awareness in the Humanities." *Diversity and Democracy* 17 (2). https://www.aacu.org/diversitydemocracy/2014/spring/bronstein-jones-neuwirth.

22. This course, taught at our college by Dr. Cheryl Nicholas, was featured in our local newspaper, the *Reading Eagle.*

23. Trost, "Using Personal Narratives," 178–181.

24. Ibid., 178.

25. Ibid., 179.

26. Ibid., 179.

27. Ibid., 179–181.

28. Ibid., 179–180.

29. Ibid., 183.

30. Ibid., 179.

Chapter 17

1. Lambert, Sonia, Bassell, Myles, and Friedman, Hershey. 2017. "Leadership in a Knowledge Economy: Building an Innovative Marketing and Branding Association." *Atlantic Marketing Journal* 7 (1): 33–46. https://digitalcommons.kennesaw.edu/cgi/viewcontent.cgi?article=1237&context=amj.

2. Graham-Leviss, Katherine. 2016. "The 5 Skills That Innovative Leaders Have in Common." *Harvard Business Review*, December 20. https://hbr.org/2016/12/the-5-skills-that-innovative-leaders-have-in-common.

3. Faust, Drew Gilpin. 2016. "To Be a 'Speaker of Words and Doer of Deeds': Literature and Leadership." Commencement address, U.S. Military Academy, West Point, NY, March 24. https://www.harvard.edu/president/speech/2016/to-be-speaker-words-and-doer-deeds-literature-and-leadership.

4. Kouzes, James M., and Posner, Barry Z. 1987. *The Leadership Challenge: How to Make Extraordinary Things Happen in Organizations.* San Francisco: Jossey-Bass.

5. Ibid.

6. Sessa, Valerie I., Kabacoff, Robert, Deal, Jennifer, and Brown, Heather. 2007. "Generational Differences in Leadership Values and Behavior." *Psychologist-Manager Journal* 10 (1): 47–74.

7. Zemke, Ron, Raines, Claire, and Filipczak, Bob. 1999. *Generations at Work: Managing the Clash of Veterans, Boomers, Xers, and Nexters in Your Workplace.* New York: AMACOM.

8. Arsenault, Paul M. 2004. "Validating Generational Differences: A Legitimate Diversity and

Leadership Issue." *Leadership and Organization Development Journal* 25 (1/2): 124–141.

9. Sessa et al., "Generational Differences," 69.

10. Heckman, David R., Johnson, Stefanie K., Foo, Maw-Der, and Yang, Wei. 2016. "Does Diversity-Valuing Behavior Result in Diminished Performance Ratings for Non-White and Female Leaders?" *Academy of Management Journal* 60 (2). https://doi.org/10.5465/amj.2014.0538. Findings abbreviated at http://gap.hks.harvard.edu/does-diversity-valuing-behavior-result-diminished-performance-ratings-nonwhite-and-female-leaders.

11. Lussier, Robert N., and Achua, Christopher F. 2016. *Leadership: Theory, Application, and Skill Development.* Boston: Cengage, 376.

12. National Center for Public Policy and Higher Education. 2005. "Fact #1: The U.S. Workforce Is Becoming More Diverse." Policy Alert, November. http://www.highereducation.org/reports/pa_decline/decline-f1.shtml.

13. Gastil, John. 1994. "A Definition and Illustration of Democratic Leadership." *Human Relations* 47 (8): 953–975, quotation on 3.

14. Ibid., 956.

15. Bennis, Warren G. 1962. "Towards a 'Truly' Scientific Management: The Concept of Organization Health." *General Systems Yearbook*, December, 273.

16. Lussier and Achua, *Leadership*, 5.

17. Big Think Edge. 2017. "4 Decision-Making and Problem Solving Examples in the Workplace." http://www.bigthinkedge.com/blog/4-decision-making-and-problem-solving-examples-in-the-workplace.

18. Lussier and Achua, *Leadership*, 6.

19. Ibid., 110, 17.

20. Kotter, John. N.d. "8-Step Process for Leading Change." Kotter Inc. https://www.kotterinc.com/8-steps-process-for-leading-change/; Tanner, Robert. 2018. "Kotter's Eight Step Leading Change Model." Management Is a Journey. https://managementisajourney.com/summary-of-kotters-eight-step-leading-change-model/.

21. Kotter, John, and Cohen, Dan S. 2002. *The Heart of Change: Real-Life Stories of How People Change Their Organizations.* Boston: Harvard Business Review Press.

22. Greenwald, Richard. 2010. "Today's Students Need Leadership Training Like Never Before." *Chronicle of Higher Education*, December 5. https://www.chronicle.com/article/Todays-Students-Need/125604.

23. Priest, Kerry L., Bauer, Tamara, and Fine, Leigh E. 2015. "The Hunger Project: Exercising Civic Leadership with the Community for the Common Good in an Introductory Leadership Course." *Journal of Leadership Education* 14 (2): 218–228, quotation on 219.

24. Buckner, Kirk J., and Williams, Lee M. 1995. "Applying the Competing Values Model of Leadership: Reconceptualising a University Student Leadership Development Program." *Journal of Leadership Studies* 2 (4): 19–34; Zimmerman-Oster, Kathleen, and Burkhardt, John C. 1999. "Leadership in the Making: A Comprehensive Examination of the Impact of Leadership Development Programs on Students." *Journal of Leadership Studies* 6 (3/4): 51–66; Eich, Darin. 2008. "A Grounded Theory of High-Quality Leadership Programs." *Journal of Leadership and Organizational Studies* 15 (2): 176–187.

25. Brungardt, Curt, Greenleaf, Justin, Brungardt, Christie, and Arensdorf, Jill. 2006. "Majoring in Leadership: A Review of Undergraduate Leadership Degree Programs." *Journal of Leadership Education* 5 (1): 4–25.

26. Kramer, Fred A. 2006. "Perspectives on Leadership from Homer's *Odyssey*." In *Leaders and the Leadership Process: Readings, Self-assessments, and Applications*, 4th ed., edited by John L. Pierce and John W. Newstrom, xx–xxiii. Boston: McGraw-Hill/Irwin, 2006.

27. Badaracco, Joseph L., Jr. 2006. *Questions of Character: Illuminating the Heart Through Literature.* Boston: Harvard Business School Press. This book focuses on male authors, but serious fiction by women also "illuminates the heart of leadership."

28. Gehrs, Linda M. 1994. "The Relationship Between Literature and Leadership: A Hu-

manities-Based Approach for Studying Leadership." *Journal of Leadership Studies* 1 (4): 145–158, quotation on 154.

29. Denning, Steve. 2011. "Why Leadership Storytelling Is Important." *Forbes*, June 8. https://www.forbes.com/sites/stevedenning/2011/06/08/why-leadership-storytelling-is-important/#602d12e9780f.

30. Grams, Chris. 2010. "Why Storytelling Is Essential for Business Leaders." *Fortune*, November 9. http://fortune.com/2010/11/09/why-storytelling-is-essential-for-business-leaders-2/.

31. Cunliffe, Anne L. 2009. "The Philosopher Leader: On Relationalism, Ethics and Reflexivity—A Critical Perspective to Teaching Leadership." *Management Learning* 40 (1): 87–101.

32. Lussier and Achua, *Leadership*, 110.

33. Grossman, James. 2016. "History Isn't a Useless Major. It Teaches Critical Thinking, Something America Needs Plenty More Of." *LA Times*, May 30. http://www.latimes.com/opinion/op-ed/la-oe-grossman-history-major-in-decline-20160525-snap-story.html.

34. Chrislip, David D., and O'Malley, Edward J. 2013. "Thinking About Civic Leadership." *National Civic Review*, Summer, 3–12.

35. A number of degrees listed as social science, such as political science, also have humanities scholars in those disciplines. In addition, law is listed as a social science when there is an extensive humanities component to the study of law.

36. British Council. 2015. *The Educational Pathways of Leaders: An International Comparison.* https://www.britishcouncil.org/sites/default/files/edupathwaysofleadersreport_final.pdf.

Chapter 18

1. National Academies of Sciences, Engineering, and Medicine. 2018. *The Integration of the Humanities and Arts with Sciences, Engineering, and Medicine in Higher Education: Branches from the Same Tree.* National Academies Press. https://www.nap.edu/resource/24988/Branches%20from%20the%20Same%20Tree-Report%20Highlights.pdf.

2. Anderson, Jenny. 2018. "One College Finally Designed a Liberal Arts Education Fit for the Future of Work." Qz.com, April 29. https://qz.com/1260478/this-college-is-moving-beyond-what-color-is-your-parachute-and-designing-for-students-to-find-purposeful-work/.

3. Kaputa, Catherine. 2016. *Graduate to a Great Career: How Smart Students, New Graduates, and Young Professionals Can Launch Brand You.* Boston: Nicholas Brealey, 4.

4. Sho, Chandra. 2018. "U.S. Job Openings at Record, Almost Matching Unemployed Workers." Bloomberg, May 8. https://www.bloomberg.com/news/articles/2018-05-08/job-openings-in-u-s-jumped-in-march-to-record-6-55-million.

5. Kauflin, Jeff. 2017. "The Industries Hiring the Most College Grads in 2018." *Forbes*, October 24. https://www.forbes.com/sites/jeffkauflin/2017/10/24/the-industries-hiring-the-most-college-grads-in-2018/#74438cc236db.

6. Segarra, Lisa Marie. 2018. "This Is the Fastest Growing Job in America. Here's How Much It Pays." *Fortune*, April 5. http://fortune.com/2018/04/05/fastest-growing-jobs-us/.

7. Davidson, Kate. 2016. "Employers Find Soft Skills Like Critical Thinking in Short Supply." *Wall Street Journal*, August 30. https://www.wsj.com/articles/employers-find-soft-skills-like-critical-thinking-in-short-supply-1472549400.

8. Craig, Ryan, and Markowitz, Troy. 2017. "The Skills Gap Is Actually an Awareness Gap—and It's Easier to Fix." *Forbes*, March 17. https://www.forbes.com/sites/ryancraig/2017/03/17/the-skills-gap-is-actually-an-awareness-gap-and-its-easier-to-fix/#b925ce93ff4a.

9. Fisher, Anne. 2016. "How to Make a Liberal Arts Degree a Career Asset." *Fortune*, May 12. http://fortune.com/2016/05/12/liberal-arts-degree-career-asset/.

10. See, for example, Coplin, Bill. 2012. *10 Things Employers Want You to Learn in College.* Rev. ed. Berkeley, CA: Ten Speed Press; Kaputa, *Great Career*; Selingo, Jeffrey J. 2016. *There Is Life After College: What Parents and Students Should Know About Navigating School to Prepare for the Jobs of Tomorrow.* New York: William Morrow.

11. Allen, Rita B. 2012. "Personal Branding and Marketing Yourself." Boston.com, February 16. http://archive.boston.com/business/blogs/global-business-hub/2012/02/personal_brandi.html.

12. Kaputa, *Great Career*, vii.

13. Selingo, *Life After College*, 237.

14. Kaputa, *Great Career*, 11.

15. Biro, Meghan M. 2013. "Five Steps to Empowering the Brand You." *Forbes*, February 24. https://www.forbes.com/sites/meghanbiro/2013/02/24/5-steps-to-empowering-the-brand-you/#5106978132d6.

16. Hart Research Associates. 2018. *Fulfilling the American Dream: Liberal Education and the Future of Work*. Association of American Colleges and Universities. https://www.aacu.org/sites/default/files/files/LEAP/2018EmployerResearchReport.pdf.

17. Hart Research Associates. 2015. *Falling Short? College Learning and Career Success*. Association of American Colleges and Universities. https://www.aacu.org/sites/default/files/files/LEAP/2015employerstudentsurvey.pdf.

18. Ibid.

Conclusion

1. The National Task Force on Teaching and Learning. 2012. *A Crucible Moment: College Learning and Democracy's Future*. Association of American Colleges and Universities. https://www.aacu.org/sites/default/files/files/crucible/Crucible_508F.pdf.

2. Association of American Colleges and Universities. "Civic Learning and Democratic Engagement (CLDE)." https://www.aacu.org/clde.

3. Ibid.

4. National Task Force, *Crucible Moment*, 10.

5. Hart Associates, *Falling Short*; *It Takes More*; *Raising the Bar*. We discuss democracy and civic skills and knowledge here rather than in a separate chapter in Part III because so much of what constitutes democratic institutions and values and civic skills and knowledge is infused throughout the other chapters, from understanding diversity, inclusivity, and equality to ethics to critical thinking and more.

6. Davidson, Cathy N. 2016. "Educating Higher." *Liberal Education* 102 (3). https://www.aacu.org/liberaleducation/2016/summer/davidson, emphasis in original.

7. National Task Force, *Crucible Moment*, 10–11. The report lists "effective listening and oral communication, creative/critical thinking and problem solving, the ability to work effectively in diverse groups, agency and collaborative decision making, ethical analyses of complex issues, and intercultural understanding and perspective taking" (11).

8. Ibid., 10.

9. Seibert, Steven Merritt. 2017. "In Praise of the Humanities." *Tampa Bay Times*, February 18. http://www.tampabay.com/news/perspective/column-in-praise-of-the-humanities/2313555.

10. Ibid.

11. Roth, Michael. 2012. "Creative, Humanistic, and Pragmatic: Liberal Education in America." *Diversity and Democracy* 15 (2). https://www.aacu.org/publications-research/periodicals/creative-humanistic-and-pragmatic-liberal-education-america.

Index

Figures and tables are indicated by page numbers followed by *fig.* and *tab.*, respectively.

Acknowledgments

Laurie Grobman

My thanks go to Damon Linker, consulting editor at the University of Pennsylvania Press, who has supported and guided us from prospectus through publication, and to all the members of the marketing and editorial and production teams as well as the Faculty Editorial Board. I also appreciate the hard work of the peer reviewers and Susannah Clark.

I express my appreciation to the many CEOs, journalists, and scholars who have begun to speak publicly and positively about the value of the humanities in this complex, challenging global society and economy. Perhaps we are on the cusp of a movement.

My colleagues at Penn State Berks and around the country and world have inspired me to fight for the humanities. Your work is brilliant and significant. Working with students year after year reminds me of the great joy and meaning I obtain by teaching, studying, and learning in the humanities.

Finally, I thank my family for helping brainstorm titles for this book.

E. Michele Ramsey

At the University of Pennsylvania Press, I am grateful to our consulting editor, Damon Linker, who managed the publication process efficiently and with good humor. I am also grateful to the marketing and editorial and production teams and the Faculty Editorial Board at Penn Press, along with the peer reviewers for their suggestions and support, and for the help of Susannah Clark.

I am grateful for research support from Penn State Berks. I am very grateful for my college's librarians—no one has better librarians than we do. Colleagues I'm privileged to call friends helped make this path much easier. I thank Holly Ryan, Jessica Schocker, Jeanne Rose, Sandy Feinstein, Colleen English, Valerie Cholet, Lauren Martin, Lolita Paff, Cesar Martinez Garza, and Ben Infantolino for their continuous encouragement. I especially thank my work wife, Cheryl Nicholas, and her wife, Heidi Mau, for their years of friendship, support, and advice.

I was fortunate to be mentored by remarkable people. I thank the late John S. Gossett, the late Mark Deloach, Jay Allison, Ralph Hamlett, Jill Rhea, Jim Meernik, Bonnie Dow, and Celeste Condit for showing me excellent examples of teaching, mentoring, and scholarship. I use many of Jill Rhea's assignments in my conflict management course, but her Conflict Management Personal Inventory assignment is a staple and the assignment discussed in Chapter 9.

I am grateful to the people who helped start this conversation for us. George Anders and Randall Stross were very supportive of our project and kind enough to respond to our questions.

I am grateful to my discipline of communication studies and its faculty who excel in teaching many of the core skills and knowledge fundamental to the humanities and to society. One of those faculty members, Holly Hutchins, generously lent her expertise to the chapter on leadership. Donnie Pollard, Kendall Phillips, Suzanne Enck, and Dave Tell were patient listeners and helpful friends as I rattled on about this project with them. And with their balance of intellectual curiosity and great compassion for others, my students regularly remind me why it is so important to stand up for the humanities.

Finally, I want to thank my family. My grandmother, Jean Eaton, was offered a debate scholarship to Baylor University at the beginning of the Great Depression but couldn't afford to go. I'm proud to teach and research in the discipline she would have most likely studied in college. My aunt, Evelyn McKee, has always taken me seriously and probably taught me my first humanities lesson when, in response to my question about why people couldn't just walk into the grocery store and get what they needed without paying, she replied by explaining socialism to an eight-year-old. My husband, Michael, tolerated many nights of sharing me with a computer and has always generously supported me as a teacher, mentor, and scholar, including weekend trips with students, graduation parties in our home, and hosting the occasional student in need of a temporary place to live.

Most important, I thank my parents, Elizabeth and Jack Ramsey. It took a while for me to find my calling, but even before I found it, they were always, and continue to be, my biggest cheerleaders. I especially thank my mom for teaching me to stand up for myself, to be strong, and to fight for what I believe is right.

I stand on the shoulders of a very big group of inspiring and brilliant people—many more than I have the space to mention here. Thank you all.